RAF
COASTAL
COMMAND
-1936-1969-

Other books by the same author:

Action Stations 5
Military airfields of the South West

Action Stations 9
Military airfields of the Central South & South East

Encyclopaedia of Modern Royal Air Force Squadrons

Avro's Maritime Heavyweight: The Shackleton

Patrick Stephens Limited, a member of the Haynes Publishing Group, has published authoritative, quality books for enthusiasts for a quarter of a century. During that time the company has established a reputation as one of the world's leading publishers of books on aviation, maritime, military, model-making, motor cycling, motoring, motor racing, railway and railway modelling subjects. Readers or authors with suggestions for books they would like to see published are invited to write to: The Editorial Director, Patrick Stephens Limited, Sparkford, Nr Yeovil, Somerset, BA22 7JJ.

RAF
COASTAL
COMMAND
1936-1969

CHRIS ASHWORTH

Patrick Stephens Limited

First published in 1992

British Library Cataloguing in Publication Data
A catalogue record for this book is available from
the British Library

Library of Congress catalog card no. 92-85348

ISBN 1 85260 345 3

Patrick Stephens Limited is part of the Haynes
Publishing Group P.L.C., Sparkford, Nr Yeovil,
Somerset BA22 7JJ.

Typeset by BPCC Techset, Exeter.
Printed by Redwood Press, Melksham, Wilts.

Contents

Maps and Diagrams

Introduction

STARVED OF RESOURCES throughout the 1930s RAF Coastal Command entered the Second World War with a small and largely obsolescent force of flying boats and landplanes almost completely devoted to 'reconnaissance' for the Royal Navy. Five and a half years later it had increased four-fold in size and immeasurably in effectiveness, and was certainly no longer 'coastal' in attitude or action, being capable of seeking out and destroying U-Boats in vast areas of ocean, and of taking on well-armed German convoys. Additionally the Command was responsible for the Air-Sea Rescue organization, for meteorological reconnaissance and photographic reconnaissance.

The change was not achieved painlessly, it being a long time before the Command had the equipment and expertise to be effective in its major anti-submarine and anti-shipping roles, or for the Admiralty to accept the RAF as an equal partner in the war at sea.

This book outlines the struggle to reach that equality, gained in the face of conflicting priorities, ignorance and occasional downright obstruction at the highest level. It takes the reader from the formation of the Command in 1936 through to eventual absorption by Strike Command in 1969. Its successor, No.18 Group, has different and much more potent aircraft and equipment but the basic operational roles are the same, for the United Kingdom is still just as dependent on shipborne supplies as it has ever been, and they would be a prime target for any aggressor.

My personal involvement with Coastal Command, albeit post-war, was confined to anti-submarine work, in which an individual crew is almost invariably pitted against the enemy alone, and the action, if there is to be any, can come at any time during the patrol. I hope I have not allowed this experience to weight the book at the expense of the anti-shipping arm of the Command, for I have the greatest admiration for the crews of what are now called 'strike' aircraft. U-Boats sometimes fired back and it required courage to continue an attack, but German shipping invariably put up a formidable flak barrage, and aircrew knew what they would have to face long before they reached the target. The task required commitment of the highest order as well as courage, and I salute them.

It would be impossible to write on such a subject without consulting many books, publications and records, and I acknowledge with gratitude the assistance of the Air Historical Branch (RAF) and the Public Records Office, Kew. I am also very grateful for the help provided by a number of individuals who have searched their personal records and their memories, and have generously allowed me to use both information and photographs. In alphabetical order they are: Chaz Bowyer, P.H.T. Green, R. Hayward, J.D. Oughton, J.D.R. Rawlings, B. Robertson, R.C. Sturtivant and A.S. Thomas. The interpretation of the information is, of course, my responsibility alone.

In 1942 Doenitz, the talented and much respected German naval commander said: 'the aircraft can no more eliminate the U-Boat than a crow can fight a mole,' and in Volume II of his monumental treatise *The Second World War*, Winston Churchill wrote: 'The only thing that ever really frightened me during the war was the U-Boat peril. . . . The Admiralty, with whom I lived in the closest amity and contact, shared these fears. . . .' Very fortunately Doenitz had to eat his words and by a level of co-operation between air and surface forces rarely achieved before or since, Churchill's fears were assuaged, though at terrible cost. It is a story worth telling. I hope that I have done justice to it and to everyone concerned.

R.C.B. Ashworth
Padstow, 1992

CHAPTER 1

In the Beginning

WHEN THE ROYAL Flying Corps and the Royal Naval Air Service were formally amalgamated on 1 April 1918 to form the Royal Air Force, the Admiralty reluctantly handed over 2,949 aircraft (including seaplanes and flying boats), and transferred 5,378 officers and 49,688 men. The transfer of personnel was automatic, but the Air Council did allow them the option of returning to the Royal Navy, providing application was made within the first three months of the new Service's existence. Few took advantage of this dispensation, but the Admiralty's determination to regain control of any RAF unit involved in so-called 'naval areas of interest' remained, a situation which was to undermine the maritime units of the RAF for the next two decades, and which led to many unsatisfactory compromises.

The re-organization which followed the formation of the RAF was complicated. In the United Kingdom, *Areas* were formed on 1 May 1918, initially numbered but soon becoming geographical (i.e. No.2 became South Western Area). Within the geographical *Area* functional *Groups* were in immediate command of bases and units, ten maritime *Groups* having been formed within the five *Areas* by the end of November 1918. Almost immediately, however, the rapid contraction which followed the Armistice had its effect, and by May 1919 only Nos.10, 28 and 29 Groups remained. On 21 August 1919 the Air Council proposed a reduction in the number of *Areas* to four, two to remain geographical as *Northern* and *Southern* and two to become functional as *Naval* (or *Coastal*) and *Army* (or *Inland*). The proposal was adopted and *Coastal Area* was formed on 15 September 1919 with its headquarters at 4 Thurloe Place, London SW7, and Air Commodore A.V. Vyvyan, CB, DSO, in command. No.28 Group was absorbed by No.29 (Fleet) Group at Leuchars, the latter controlling the

handful of seagoing aircraft allotted to the Fleet, while No.10 Group at Warsash, Southampton, continued to administer the remaining land-based aircraft, seaplanes and flying boats—a top heavy organization largely retained to placate the Admiralty.

By the end of 1919 Coastal Area was little more than a framework on which to build. For its role of 'fleet co-operation' it had one recce/spotting squadron and a 'fighting' Flight at Leuchars, half a torpedo squadron at Gosport, No.230 (Flying Boat) Squadron at Flight strength at Felixstowe, and the Naval Co-operation Flight of seaplanes at Calshot. In July 1920 Coastal Area moved to the Russell Court Hotel, Tavistock Place, London WC1, and No.10 Group moved to Lee-on-Solent. The units were also re-organized, the Fighter Flight at Leuchars becoming No.203 Squadron (Camels) and the Fleet Reconnaissance Unit reforming as No.205 Squadron (Panthers). No.186 Squadron at Gosport was disbanded and re-appeared as No.210 Squadron with Cuckoo torpedo carriers, while No.230 soldiered on at Felixstowe with F.3 flying boats and Fairey IIIC seaplanes. Little real progress was made because it had become clear that the Admiralty was actively promoting the return of the air assets allocated for maritime work, and with the War Office claiming army co-operation units the continued existence of the RAF was in jeopardy. However, the Chief of Air Staff, Sir Hugh Trenchard, fought back, and after two years of often bitter recriminations, the Air Ministry won the day.

With the situation at least temporarily resolved rationalization at unit level was undertaken in 1923. The 'shipboard' squadrons were disbanded and re-formed as independent Flights, each of six aircraft, while the Naval Co-operation Flight and No.230 Squadron at Calshot were amalgamated to form No.480 Flight, a more realistic indication of the unit

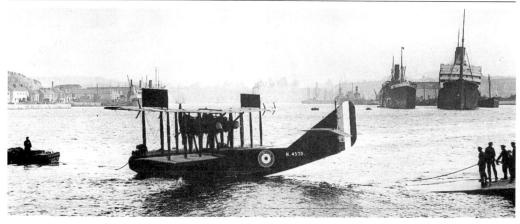

Above: *Porte F.5 N4570 being launched on the Cattewater 1921—a time when Coastal Area's fortunes were at a very low ebb. (Fleet Air Arm Museum)*

Below: *Mainstay of the flying boats during the latter half of the 1920s and early 1930s—The Southampton. S1645 a Mk.II of No.201 Squadron seen alighting after passing under the Forth Bridge. (Author's collection)*

Above right: *On land the torpedo element was initially provided by Horsleys at Donibristle. (RP/MAP)*

strength! Procurement of new aircraft also went ahead, and a year later, on 1 April 1924, the Fleet Fighter, Fleet Spotter, Fleet Reconnaissance and Fleet Torpedo Flights came under the umbrella of the Fleet Air Arm of the Royal Air Force, administratively under command of HQ Coastal Area, but when on board ship operationally controlled by the Admiralty. The Fleet Fighter units were soon re-equipped with the excellent Flycatcher, and the Fleet Reconnaissance units were also fortunate in receiving the Fairey IIID, but from Coastal Area's point of view the most important aircraft was the Supermarine Southampton. This elegant machine, ordered straight off the drawing board of R.J. Mitchell (of Schneider and Spitfire fame), quite literally saved the day for the flying boat—the authorities being on the point of abandoning the development of such aircraft completely after a number of expensive failures. Entering service with No.480 Flight in the summer of 1925, the Southampton had few crew comforts but this was nothing new for the fiercely independent 'flying boat union'. What was new was the seaworthiness of the craft which, combined with an excellent performance in the air, resulted in the flying boat component being much more effective during the remainder of the 1920s, even though numbers hardly altered.

In 1927 Coastal Area comprised all the units at Calshot, Cattewater, Donibristle, Felixstowe, Gosport, Lee-on-Solent and Leuchars, HQ units in aircraft carriers in home waters, Flights embarked in such carriers and all recruiting depots. As more aircraft carriers were commissioned the number of shipborne Flights was increased to a peak of 27 in 1932, 20 of the Flights being disbanded during the following year and reformed as 12 Squadrons.

Meanwhile No.482 Flight had been formed at Cattewater (later renamed Mount Batten) on 15 September 1928, and the following month the Horsley-equipped Coastal Defence Torpedo Flight at Donibristle was upgraded as No.36 Squadron. On 1 January 1929 No.480 Flight became No.201 Squadron at Calshot and No.482 Flight became 203 Squadron, both still flying the stalwart Southampton. A little over a month later No.203 Squadron left for Iraq but was immediately replaced by a reformed No.204 Squadron. Further increases in strength came during 1930-31 with the formation of No.209 Squadron with the Blackburn Iris and No.210 Squadron with Southamptons, the latter soon moving into the new flying boat base at Pembroke Dock. Both No.36 Squadron and its replacement, No.100, went to Singapore but, equipped with the new Vickers Vildebeest, No.22 Squadron was reformed on 1 May 1934 to fill the gap.

Headquarters Coastal Area moved from London to Lee-on-Solent on 18 January 1932 and took over direct control of all the units under command, No.10 Group being disbanded. The move coincided with an upsurge in annual armament practice camps, fleet exercises and extended 'cruises', the latter providing much needed experience of operating from temporary bases in Europe and the Mediterranean areas. The obsolescence of both the Southampton and the Iris was becoming very apparent, but the economic crisis which hit the country at the end of 1929, and the Disarmament Conference which started in 1931, had given politicians the excuse to procrastinate over the defence budget, and for a period even the modest expansion achieved in the late 1920s was halted. Replacement 'boats' were ordered, but in disturbingly small numbers, the Blackburn Perth, Saro London and Short Singapore all entering service with Coastal Area by the mid 1930s, while behind the scenes the British Government became increasingly concerned about reports of German rearmament. Following a powerful speech in the House of Commons by Mr Winston Churchill in July 1934, the mood in both Parliament and the country at large began to change, an increase

Above: *Vildebeests replaced Horsleys, the Torpedo Flight at Gosport employing Mk.IIIs, amongst them K2813 seen here over the Isle of Wight in the 1930s. (J. Curtiss via P.H.T. Green)*

Below: *One of the most successful of the various flying boats which went into Coastal service in small numbers was the Singapore III. K8567/M of No.210 Squadron took part in Anglo-French operations from Arzeu in 1937 to protect shipping during the Spanish Civil War. (No.210 Sqn records via P.H.T. Green)*

Above right: *Swordfish of A Flight, Gosport—part of the training organization controlled by No.17 Group following the formation of Coastal Command in 1936. (RAF Museum)*

in defence expenditure becoming acceptable to the majority. A series of RAF 'Expansion Schemes' were proposed, and Scheme 'C', which aimed at doubling the existing strength of the Metropolitan Air Force was approved in May 1935. It was soon clear that the current organization of the home-based RAF would be unable to cope, and on 13 July 1936 Air Defence Great Britain and the Areas were abolished and the following day Commands were formed, all based on function rather than location.

Coastal Area became Coastal Command, but apart from the name there was little immediate change. The headquarters remained at Lee-on-Solent, all the units were retained and Air Marshal A.M. Longmore and his staff continued in post. In practice they had very little under immediate command because Nos.204, 210 and 230 Squadrons had been deployed to the Mediterranean area in September 1935 to bolster RAF forces in response to Italy's Abyssinian adventure, and did not return until August 1936. The fruits of the Expansion Schemes were now evident with the Anson, the first coastal reconnaissance landplane since World War I, already coming off the production lines in quantity. The first squadron, No.48, was temporarily seconded to the School of Air Navigation at Manston to provide air training for the rapidly increasing number of aircrew needed, and four months after the formation of No.206 Squadron in 1936, its Ansons started training pilots destined for multi-engined Coastal and Bomber aircraft, a task not completed until June 1937. Three more squadrons had been formed by the end of the year however, and with additional units planned for 1937 Air Marshal P.B. Joubert de la Ferte, who had taken over Coastal Command in August 1936, was ready to delegate some of his responsibilities. On 1 December 1936 No.16 (Reconnaissance) Group and No.17 (Training) Group were formed at Lee-on-Solent, each taking over a number of stations and their based units a month later. Also during December the torpedo-bomber component at Donibristle was nominally doubled by the formation of No.42 Squadron, and at Pembroke Dock No.228 Squadron was established. The latter unit received a mixed collection of Scapas, Londons and Singapores, highlighting the poor supply position of flying boats. Indeed the last of the classic biplanes, the Supermarine Stranraer, was still awaited and the famous Sunderland did not reach an operational Coastal Command squadron until June 1938. The situation regarding landplanes was nearly as bad, for the Bristol Beaufort and Blackburn Botha, intended as replacements for the Anson and Vildebeest in the general reconnaissance/torpedo bomber role, had not been ordered until 1936, and were not expected in service until March 1939. Planning was going ahead

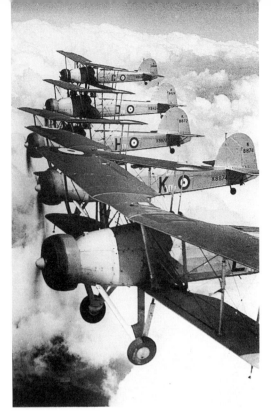

for their introduction though, and for that of the second-string flying boat, the Saro Lerwick.

Expansion Scheme 'F', approved in February 1936, aimed to double the size of the home-based RAF by March 1939 but left the shore-based and flying boat elements of Coastal Area/Command virtually unaltered at seven general reconnaissance landplane squadrons (126 aircraft), a torpedo bomber wing (30 aircraft) and six 'boat' squadrons (36 aircraft). However, it allowed for a considerable expansion in the establishment of fleet aircraft, reflecting the increased number of aircraft carriers expected in commission, and the Royal Navy's continued confidence in their ability to keep the sea lanes open virtually unaided. Indeed the role of the RAF in maritime tasking was again in question, the Admiralty mounting another strong campaign in 1936 aimed at the complete take-over of the FAA, the transfer of all shore-based maritime establishments and Coastal Command assets. The Government was divided on the issue and the Attorney General, Sir Thomas Inskip, Minister for the Co-ordination of Defence, found that one of his first tasks was an inquiry into the controversy. His report backing the Admiralty case for the control of the FAA but not the take-over of Coastal Command was accepted by the Government, the Prime Minister announcing on 30 July 1937 that the responsibility for the organization and administration of the FAA was to pass to the Admiralty. It sounded like the classic compromise which would end up pleasing no one and

Coastal Command was responsible for the School of Naval Co-operation at Lee-on-Solent, Blackburn Sharks being amongst the aircraft types employed by the unit during 1937. (RAF Museum)

prove unworkable, but the decision was generally considered the correct one and it certainly came as a considerable relief to the new C-in-C, Air Marshal Sir Frederick W. Bowhill and the staff of Coastal Command. It signalled the effective end of the inter-departmental friction which had endured since 1918, and greatly assisted implementation of plans already being made to re-organize the Groups so that their areas of responsibility coincided with those of the Naval C-in-Cs.

In the same month came the first detection of ships at sea from an aircraft carrying location equipment, later known as radar. The value of such an aid was immediately recognized but in 1937 the United Kingdom early warning system was top priority and it was to be a long time before practical airborne

Amongst the early Anson coastal reconnaissance squadrons was No.220, based at Bircham Newton. Three of the unit's aircraft are seen here in their attractive pre-war silver paint and colourful markings.

In March 1938 the Torpedo Bomber Wing, consisting of Nos.22 and 42 Squadrons, moved to Thorney Island. Vildebeest K8080 of No.42 Squadron on exercises with 'Blue' forces against a 'Red' fleet, 30 March 1938. (British Official)

radar sets were available to operational Coastal Command crews.

Meanwhile four more Anson squadrons had been formed and No.240 reappeared at Calshot in February 1937 'temporarily' equipped with Scapas instead of the intended Stranraers. Another 'out of area' detachment occurred later in the year when Nos.209 and 210 deployed their Singapores to the Mediterranean to join a Franco-British naval force protecting shipping from submarine attack during the attempted blockade of Spanish Mediterranean ports by fascist forces supported by Italy. The ten flying boats returned to the United Kingdom in December, just as five Londons of No.204 Squadron left for Australia to take part in the celebrations surrounding the 150th anniversary of the founding of Sydney.

Such deployments were welcome and valuable training but did little to resolve the AOC-in-C's continuing problem—imprecise tasking and priorities which made forward planning difficult, but at the end of the year he at last received an Air Ministry directive on the subject. It tentatively laid down his strategic tasks and provided estimates of the number of aircraft required to fulfil them, viz:

(a) Protection of trade (213 aircraft)
(b) Reconnaissance in support of Fleet operations (84 aircraft)
(c) Co-operation with the Royal Navy (42 aircraft)

In March 1938 the Torpedo Bomber Wing (Nos.22 &

42 Squadrons) moved from Donibristle to newly-opened Thorney Island where they were joined the following month by the School of General Reconnaissance. No.18 Group formed on 25 August at Lee-on-Solent in readiness for a major re-organization of Coastal Command, and No.48 Squadron, relieved of its training duties, arrived at Eastchurch in September as an operational GR Anson unit just in time for the deployment of the whole Command to war stations during the Munich Crisis which lasted until 6 October.

During November 1938 the operational Groups moved out of their temporary home at Lee and set up joint operations rooms with the appropriate naval staffs. No.16 went to Chatham and No.18 to Donibristle, the two Groups taking responsibility for stations and sea areas either side of a dividing line drawn from Flamborough Head to the Horn Reef off the Danish coast in the east, and north-west from the Mull of Kintyre in the west.* The public at large may have accepted the Prime Minister's assertions of 'peace in our time' on his return from Munich at the end of September 1938, but the military certainly did not, and war plans were urgently updated. The paper strength of Coastal Command was increased by the transfer of three Auxiliary Air Force squadrons, Nos.500, 502 and 612, though Anson replacements for their Hawker biplanes did not reach them until the early months of 1939, when they were joined by No.608 Squadron.

*See map—Group Boundaries.

By the end of 1938 operational squadrons had received unit codes, but retained in their silver paint. Saro London K5261 of No.201 Squadron on detachment at Falmouth and coded VQ-U. (Osborne Studios)

Exercises became more frequent and realistic, units of No.16 Group supporting the Home Fleet in the south-west approaches in January 1939, for operations against an 'enemy' force of two raiding cruisers, a number of destroyers and several submarines. Despite poor weather, useful reconnaissance information was provided for the Admiral, and good training for the crews.

No.17(T) Group moved to Fort Grange, Gosport, on 24 February, and the following month its quarters at Lee were used to accommodate the reformed No.15 Group which was almost immediately involved in a major exercise, six GR squadrons and a FAA squadron co-operating in a test of the organization set up to protect seaborne trade in the western approaches.

In May two significant events occurred. The final stage of the take-over of the Fleet Air Arm by the

Stranraer K7296 of No.228 Squadron coded TO-V—probably at Calshot. (via A.S. Thomas)

Empire Air Day, Pembroke Dock, May 1939. Modernity at last in the form of Sunderland L5799 carrying the codes of No.210 Squadron, VG-D. This aircraft was lost off Norway on 7 April 1940. (Gp Capt G.A. Bolland via J. Evans)

Admiralty was completed, No.17(T) Group relinquishing control of Donibristle, Ford, Lee-on-Solent and Worthy Down on the 24th, and the first Lockheed Hudson was delivered to No.224 Squadron at Leuchars, thus beating the Beaufort and the Botha into squadron service by a considerable margin. That the aircraft was available to plug the general reconnaissance gap left by the continuing delays suffered by the two British aircraft was fortuitous indeed, for the Lockheed 14 airliner from which it was developed had originally been looked at by the British Purchasing Commission (BPC) as a navigation trainer. Lockheeds had also prepared a mock up of a bomber version, and when the BPC criticized several features the Company impressed the team by making all the suggested changes and having it ready for another inspection within 24 hours! It was recognized that the revised aircraft would make a useful reconnaissance bomber for maritime work, and on 23 June a contract for 200 was signed, a storm of protest being caused in Britain when it was publicly announced in July that 400 aircraft (the other 200 were Harvard trainers) were being purchased from the USA. Fortunately this was ignored, and in fact a commitment was made to take any additional Hudsons up to a maximum of 250 that could be delivered by December 1939. This figure was actually achieved in October of that year, but by then such restrictions had been rescinded!

Meanwhile the functions of Coastal Command had been firmly laid down, the priority order becoming:

(a) Reconnaissance in home waters
(b) Co-operation with the Royal Navy in convoy protection
(c) Counter offensive action in defence of seaborne trade

Offensive operations were still clearly subsidiary to the reconnaissance role—the Admiralty being confident in the ability of *Asdic* as a submarine location device, and the capability of the Royal Navy's capital ships, assisted by carrier borne aircraft, to deal with the German surface navy at sea—while the destruction of enemy shipping in port was the task of Bomber Command. This was the reason for the continued parsimonious provisioning of aircraft for Coastal Command, and for the appalling neglect of suitable offensive armament.

The only bombs available for immediate use by Coastal Command were standard 100 and 250-lb General Purpose for use against surface vessels, and 'special' 100-lb ordnance for attacks on submarines, the latter still in production even though it had been demonstrated as early as 1917 that it was useless. Another problem was the complete lack of a suitable low level bomb sight, pilots being expected to 'eyeball' the forward throw of a weapon they had not practised with, for all training was with 8-lb break-up bombs. The situation regarding torpedoes was better, although nothing had been done to prepare for the greater dropping speeds required with the new generation of aircraft, and much the same applied to aerial mines, development of the magnetic 'A' Mk. 1 having been started pre-war though it was not ready for production until February 1940.

International tension, which had again started to rise in April 1939 as Hitler continued on the rampage, reached fever pitch in the summer with an attack on Poland plainly imminent, and preliminary mobilization was started on 24 July with units moving to their war stations in August. To complicate matters, Coastal Command headquarters was also on the move, transferring on 7 August to Eastbury Park, Northwood, Middlesex, where a hotel and the surrounding grounds had been purchased late in 1938. Amongst numerous wooden huts erected on the site was an inconspicuous building protected by earthworks and camouflaged by trees. This was the Command Operations Room used by successive C-in-Cs to conduct day-to-day maritime air operations until a large underground complex became available.

During August Hitler at last accepted that Britain and France really meant to stand by their guarantees to Poland, and on the 19th 14 U-Boats slipped out into the Atlantic, followed a few days later by the battle cruisers *Graf Spee* and *Deutschland*. Organized patrols by Coastal Command were not underway until the 24th, so none of these movements was detected,

and nor were another 16 U-Boats which transitted in thick North Sea fog on the 25th. Due to a mixture of mismanagement and misfortune the British had unwittingly made a bad start. From the German viewpoint the deployment was a brilliant success and it was indeed fortunate that they were not able to sustain it, many of the smaller submarines having returned to port by early September.

The Coastal Command 'Order of Battle' at the outbreak of war is shown at Appendix II. Nominally Anson squadrons each had 24 aircraft, the Vildebeest squadrons 15 and the flying boat units six each. The actual strength totalled 298 aircraft, of which 171 were available for operations, a ratio which was to hold good for most of the war. The practical, as opposed to theoretical, operational performance of the aircraft was as follows:

Type	Radius of Action(nm)	Endurance (hrs)	Bomb Load (lb)
Anson	255	$4\frac{1}{2}$	2 × 100
Hudson	490	6	10 × 100 or 4 × 250
Sunderland	850	$12\frac{1}{2}$	8 × 250
London	225	$5\frac{1}{4}$	8 × 250
Stranraer	330	$7\frac{1}{4}$	4 × 250
Vildebeest	185	$4\frac{1}{4}$	4 × 250 or one 18″ torpedo.

Camouflaged and with 'low visibility' national markings, Anson K8822 of No.269 Squadron surprisingly has its pre-war code letters painted in distinctive light grey. (A. Simpson via A.S. Thomas)

A foretaste of things to come—the Consolidated Model 28 P9630 on test at the MAEE Felixstowe during 1939. This aircraft was the forerunner of the Catalina. (via P.H.T. Green)

It can be seen that Coastal Command entered the Second World War with just two aircraft types, the Sunderland and Hudson, capable of carrying a reasonable bomb load over a useful radius of action, but neither were available in sufficient quantity, nor could they be equipped with offensive weapons which could cause real damage. The General Purpose (GP) bomb was likely to bounce off surface vessels, and the uselessness of the anti-submarine bomb was soon to be amply demonstrated. The prospect was daunting for both crews and commanders but fortunately young men are resilient!

CHAPTER 2

Against the Capital Ships–Anti-Shipping Operations 1939-41

THROUGHOUT THE 1930s the Admiralty held firm to their philosophy that the surface raider, not the submarine, was the greatest danger to the seaborne trade on which the United Kingdom depended for its

HM King George VI on a visit to Coastal Command Headquarters at Northwood in 1939 accompanied by Air Chief Marshal Sir Frederick Bowhill and Sir Kingsley Wood, Under Secretary of State for Air. NAAFI girls are prominent in the welcoming party! (via C. Bowyer)

very survival. It was certainly true that the most likely enemy, Germany, had been engaged in building some impressive ships during this period—as well as many U-Boats! In August 1939 the battleships *Bismarck* and *Tirpitz* were still on the stocks but the battle cruisers *Scharnhorst* and *Gneisenau* were complete, as were three heavy cruisers, the *Graf Spee*, *Admiral Scheer* and *Deutschland*, and three *Hipper* class cruisers. The conventional threat posed by such a force ensured that a considerable British naval force had to be kept in United Kingdom waters, but it was the possibility of their undetected passage into the North Atlantic to operate independently against merchant shipping which really worried the Admiralty.

The most likely route from North Germany into the Atlantic was through the Norwegian Sea, so plans had long been laid for Coastal Command to maintain a standing patrol between Scotland and the south-west tip of Norway. The 'endless chain' patrol was to be carried out by Ansons, but unfortunately the aircraft's range was insufficient, and until Hudsons were available a gap of some 50 miles had to be covered by British submarines. The air patrol which started on 24 August, over a week before the outbreak of war, could only be maintained during daylight and so was supplemented by a dusk patrol to the south of the main barrier by Hudsons of No.224 Squadron from Leuchars, and to the north with dawn sorties by London and Stranraer flying boats from Sullom Voe (Shetlands) and Invergordon. These patrols also had as subsidiary roles the detection of merchant ships attempting to slip through the blockade and of U-Boats on passage, for which purpose the aircraft were armed with AS bombs. Special photographic reconnaissance patrols were also flown for a few weeks by the Extended Reconnaissance Flight of No.224 Squadron to check on ships in anchorages, 24

Blenheims from Bomber Command being held on 'short notice' standby to attack naval units which did venture out, it being policy during the first months of the war not to allow bombing of ships in port for fear of civilian casualties!

With visual lookout still the only detection aid and frequent bad weather hampering the search, most crews had little to report from their long hours on the barrier patrol, for as recorded in Chapter 1 the main quarry had already escaped, but for a few there was almost immediate action. On 5 September, just two days after the war started, Plt Off Yorke of No.233 Squadron sighted a submarine on the surface and attacked with two 100-lb AS bombs and eight 20-lb Coopers. The bombs went off on impact with the sea surface and shrapnel riddled the underside of the Anson puncturing the fuel tanks. As Yorke approached Leuchars he ran out of fuel and was forced to 'ditch' in St Andrews Bay. The crew survived, and were relaxing in the mess when called to Operations and informed that they had attacked HMS *Seahorse* and that the Admiralty was not pleased! It was the sort of situation which was almost bound to occur until the position of both submarines (which were supposed to operate in prescribed areas) and aircraft could be more accurately plotted, but extremely embarrassing none

the less. Off the Dutch coast on the same day, Flg Off Kean and his 206 Squadron crew also sighted a submarine and attacked it. This time it was a U-Boat, but the damage claim they submitted—Coastal Command's first—was not accepted. The 5th also saw the first aerial combat involving the North Sea patrols, an Anson of 206 Squadron being intercepted and shot down by two Bv138 flying boats.

Nos.220 and 233 Squadrons both began re-equipment with Hudsons during September 1939, and by the end of the month 'A' Flight of 220 was operational, their Ansons being relegated to escort work, convoying having been hastily introduced following the sinking of the SS *Athenia*. All the sightings made by the standing patrols during September had been of U-Boats, but on 8 October the crew of a 224 Squadron Hudson sighted a battleship, a cruiser and four destroyers off the south-west coast of Norway. Bomber Command Wellingtons were despatched as soon as possible but heavy rain and low cloud prevented the bombers gaining contact, a situation anticipated by the C-in-C Coastal Command for he had little faith in the ability of Bomber Command to find and successfully attack ships at sea. He had already determined that as soon as sufficient Hudsons were available he would go on the offensive with

Ready for war! A Vildebeest of No.42 Squadron at its 'war station', Bircham Newton, late August 1939. These ancient torpedo bombers were used for reconnaissance patrols during the first months of the war. (RAF Bircham Newton records)

Amongst the most successful reconnaissance aircraft was the Hudson—a Mk.I of No.233 Squadron on patrol low down over the sea. (*RAF Museum*)

'Battle Flights', and by coincidence such a three-aircraft formation from No.224 Squadron had been despatched on a roving commission that same day. The crews did not find any shipping, but they did sight a Dornier Do18 low down over the water. The leader, Flt Lt A. Womersey, attacked with his front gun, forcing the flying boat down, and the Germans took to their dinghy. The Hudson crews then destroyed the Do18, the first enemy aircraft claimed by the RAF in the Second World War.

On 2 November the *City of Flint*, which had been captured during the *Deutschland*'s foray into the Atlantic, was sighted in Norwegian territorial waters by the crew of a No.228 Squadron Sunderland. Rather than face the Royal Navy the German prize crew took the ship into Bergen and surrendered to the Norwegians. This was something of a success but despite Coastal's best efforts the cruiser itself managed to slip back into the Baltic later in the month undetected. Even more frustrating was the Germans' clever use of the weather to evade patrols and get both the *Scharnhorst* and the *Gneisenau* out on a raiding mission without the knowledge of the Admiralty. Complete success was only foiled because they were seen by the British armed merchant cruiser *Rawalpindi* which managed to send a sighting report before being blown out of the water by the *Scharnhorst*. Their position known, the ships turned for home, impossible

weather so hampering a wide ranging search by Sunderlands of No.228 Squadron and the Consolidated 28–5 (a forerunner of the Catalina which was undergoing service trials at Invergordon) that they also reached their base undetected.

Both Flights of No.220 Squadron had converted to the Hudson by the end of November and were engaged on convoy patrols and anti-shipping/submarine sweeps, the latter resulting in very few sightings until 13 December when four enemy destroyers were sighted off the west coast of Denmark. Permission to attack was given, the crew dropping two 250-lb AS bombs from 2,000 ft before coming under fire from four He115 floatplanes. It is extremely doubtful whether any damage was done, but the attack was noteworthy as the first by a Coastal Command aircraft on an enemy ship.

Over 9,000 hours had been flown on North Sea patrols by the end of 1939, but other tasks increasingly complicated the work of both Nos.16 and 18 Groups. The Skagerrak, Heligoland Bight, the Dutch and Belgian coasts all had to be kept under surveillance, and assistance given to Fighter Command in looking after East Coast convoys, North Sea fishing fleets and British minelayers engaged in laying a barrage from Dover to the north of Scotland. Much of this additional work fell to the Ansons, Hudsons, and in the early days to Vildebeests, of No.16 Group,

A rare photograph of two DWI Wellingtons of No.1 GRU at Manston, with degaussing rings fitted for triggering magnetic mines—probably in February 1940. (S. Challen)

and it was obvious that more aircraft were needed. Four 'trade protection' squadrons of Blenheim fighters were therefore transferred from Fighter to Coastal Command, the first, No.254, beginning convoy protection work on February 1940. Nos.235, 236 and 248 Squadrons joined in as they became operational.

Meanwhile the arrival of the German magnetic mine in British waters in the autumn of 1939 achieved complete tactical surprise despite the work being done in Britain on a similar device. De-gaussing of ships helped but the approaches to ports still had to be cleared and this proved extremely dangerous for minesweepers. The solution, a somewhat desperate one, was the speedy development of a variant of the Wellington fitted with means of producing a magnetic field powerful enough to explode the mines by flying over them. No.1 General Reconnaissance Unit was formed at Manston on 15 December 1939 within No.16 Group and the first DWI (Directional Wireless Installation)* Wellington arrived on 4 January 1940. Four days later the first sortie over the Thames

*A cover name.

A fully-armed Anson of No.321 Squadron—a unit manned largely by Dutch aircrew. (via P.H.T. Green)

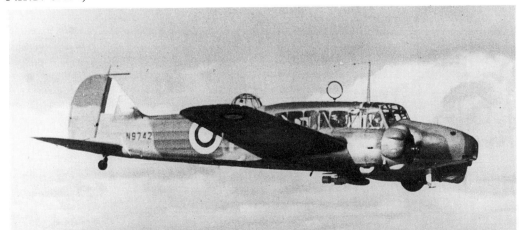

Not all losses were from enemy action. Anson N9673 of No.269 Squadron after a take-off accident at Wick on 21 March 1940. (via J.D. Oughton)

Estuary was flown, and proved a success—a mine being detonated without damage to the aircraft, and by 31 March the unit had accounted for 13 more mines. A second unit was formed at Bircham Newton in March and No.1 GRU left for the Middle East in June, the remaining DWI aircraft at Manston being formed into No.3 GRU, which operated for a further two months before disbandment; other less dangerous ways of destroying the mines having been devised.

In January 1940 the first Hudsons fitted with IFF and ASV Mk.1 radar reached the squadrons and, as soon as sufficient aircraft had been fitted, 220 Squadron also formed a 'Battle Flight' maintained on permanent standby ready for immediate despatch to attack enemy shipping on receipt of a sighting report. The weather in the North Sea was terrible during the winter of 1939-40 and it proved impossible to make

the barrier patrol secure even with the help of radar. Most sightings were of minesweepers off the Belgian and Dutch coasts. They were heavily armed and proved formidable opponents for both Ansons and Hudsons, the latter catching fire very easily, both in combat and following crash landings. On the few occasions when larger German naval vessels were located the reports were rarely followed up quickly enough, poor return for the many hours spent on patrol during the early months of the war.

It was a disappointing time but spirits were lifted by the *Altmark* affair. Two months after the *Graf Spee* was scuttled off Montevideo her supply ship, the *Altmark*, arrived off the coast of Norway with 299 British Merchant Navy seamen on board, the crews of the five ships sunk during the surface raider's Atlantic foray. Information on the *Altmark's* whereabouts

Blenheim IVF fighters were much in evidence on shipping reconnaisance work in 1940. From North Coates Nos.235 and 254 Squadrons were responsible for many such operations. (No.235 Squadron records)

reached the Admiralty, and on 16 February 1940 No.220 Squadron sent out three Hudsons to search the Norwegian coast. One of the crews located the vessel and a naval force was sent to the reported position, but meanwhile the German vessel had slipped into Jossing Fjord where she was spotted by the crew of a 233 Squadron Hudson. HMS *Cossack* followed her into Norwegian waters, returning in triumph, a boarding party having released the prisoners after a short fight.

The *Altmark* affair apparently convinced the German High Command that the Norwegians favoured the Allied cause, though that was certainly not the British view. Hitler decided to invade the country to protect his Swedish iron ore imports shipped through Narvik. The disappearance of a large German force, which included the *Scharnhorst* and *Gneisenau*, from the Wilhemshaven anchorages on 6 April was initially assessed as a North Sea force build-up, possibly to test British reaction. The ships were sighted by Hudson crews the following morning and 12 Blenheims of No.107 Squadron, Bomber Command, led by Wg Cdr B.E. Embry DSO, AFC, attacked the force, giving its composition as one battleship, a 'pocket' battleship, two or three cruisers and a large destroyer escort, and its position 70 miles NNW of the Horns Reef. Though not quite accurate the sighting report was invaluable and the British Admiralty concentrated their attention on this force, still thought to be on manoeuvres, though in fact it was the German task force on its way to seize Trondheim and Narvik. Poor visibility in the area of the Heligoland Bight and the Skagerrak resulted in other German invasion forces escaping detection com-

pletely, and unfortunately reports from the Naval Attaché in Copenhagen and sightings by British submarines were considered merely indications of a strengthening of the exercise force in the North Sea.

On 8 April the crew of a No.204 Squadron Sunderland sent to search the Norwegian coast, sighted a battleship of the *Scharnhorst* class, accompanied by two *Leipzig* type cruisers and two destroyers. At last it was becoming clear that the reported German forces were directly involved in an invasion of Norway, a fact confirmed when reports of landings started pouring in to the Admiralty. Coastal Command immediately laid on a sustained reconnaissance effort to locate vessels in port or at sea, and on the 9th the crew of a London reported a German cruiser in Bergen harbour, a Sunderland crew found a *Hipper* class cruiser in Trondheim Fjord and Bomber Command Wellingtons sighted enemy warships and transports at Kristiansund. The *Konisberg* (at Bergen) was attacked by Wellingtons which dropped 30 500-lb armour-piercing bombs, scoring one hit, and the next day 16 Skuas of 800 and 803 Squadrons, FAA, flying from Hatston, carried out a brilliant attack which sank the ship. Interception and shadowing patrols successfully located warships returning home from Norway but attacks by both land-based and carrier aircraft unfortunately all failed.

On 17 April the crew of a No.233 Squadron Hudson were given another new task, that of gun spotting for the heavy cruiser *Suffolk* engaged in bombarding Stavanger airfield. Due to communications difficulties and inexperience the co-operation was a dismal failure, though the ship's Walrus spotter amphibians did not do much better, and most of the

A fully-loaded Blenheim IVF/LA-R of No.235 Squadron climbs away with undercarriage still retracting. Note the twin gun dorsal turret, the ventral gun pack and the bombs mounted on under fuselage carriers. (MAP)

202 eight-inch shells expended undoubtedly missed the target. To compound a catalogue of errors the ship was then ordered to intercept a number of German destroyers as she withdrew and was therefore not where her planned escort of Blenheim fighters expected her to be at rendezvous time. Unescorted, the *Suffolk* was subjected to fierce attack by the Luftwaffe and was so badly damaged that she had to be beached the following day after struggling into Scapa Flow.

Meanwhile it had been found that by fitting a parachute to the 'A' Mk.1 magnetic mine it could be successfully launched from the Beaufort, and during March/April No.22 Squadron completed their work-up with the weapon in readiness for the moonlight period, laying their first batch on 15 April in the Schillig Roads, north of Wilhelmshaven. The Beauforts were few in number, however, and following representations by the AOC-in-C Coastal Command, 815 Squadron, FAA, was moved to Bircham Newton to help out with magnetic mine laying—their first mission on 22/23 April when six Swordfish laid mines off Schiermonnikoog, a Danish island west of Borkum.

No.206 Squadron carried out its first Hudson operation during April, and on the 20th No.233 Squadron's 'Battle Flight' was credited with Coastal's first successful bombing attack on a ship when the 1,940 ton *Theodor* was damaged in Grimstad Fjord. The situation in Norway was still very fluid and the Allies belatedly started landings in the north of the country on 14 April. They were soon forced to evacuate Andalsnes and Namsos, but the situation around Narvik appeared more favourable and Coastal Command worked hard to provide the necessary reconnaissance cover. During May they even managed to take part in the regular nightly attacks on Stavanger airfield, using Hudsons of Nos.224, 233 and 269 Squadrons, the latter still undergoing conversion from Ansons. Beauforts were also becoming more plentiful, allowing No.42 Squadron to start training on the aircraft, while on 7 May six Beauforts of No.22 were sent on their first bombing sortie, attacking a vessel off the Frisian Islands reported as a cruiser but actually a destroyer. One aircraft was lost to 'flak' and none of the three crews that dropped bombs could claim any success—an inauspicious start.

The German attack on France and the Low Countries on 10 May put paid to plans to hold northern Norway, and all that could be done was to capture Narvik and destroy its facilities before evacuating the country. Alerted by radio intercepts and air reconnaissance that sea traffic between Norway and Scotland was exceptionally heavy, the German High Command sent the *Scharnhorst* and *Gneisenau* to the area on 8 June, and during the afternoon their crews sighted HMS *Glorious* and her destroyer escort sailing

alone. Salvoes of heavy shells soon found their target and the carrier was sunk. So were the escorts, but one managed to fire a salvo of torpedoes one of which struck the *Scharnhorst* putting two of her engines out of action. She limped into Trondheim Fjord where the ship was discovered two days later, accompanied by the *Gneisenau* and the *Hipper*. It was decided to mount an attack using 12 Hudsons of No.269 Squadron, operating from Sumburgh. Led by the CO, Wg Cdr F.L. Pearce DSO, DFC, each aircraft dropped three 250-lb SAP bombs while flying in formation at 15,000 ft—a form of pattern bombing! The cruiser and a supply ship were hit, for the loss of two Hudsons, but the battle cruisers escaped damage. Two nights later *Ark Royal* launched 15 Skuas for an attack on the same target, long range Blenheim fighters providing an escort, while Beauforts of No.22 Squadron created a diversion by bombing nearby Vaernes airfield. The *Scharnhorst* was hit twice, but eight Skuas were lost, and the vessel was obviously not badly damaged because she sailed for Kiel on the 20th in company with the *Gneisenau*. The *Gneisenau* was torpedoed by the submarine HMS *Clyde* and had to return to Trondheim, but the *Scharnhorst* pressed on and was sighted by the crew of a No.233 Squadron Hudson 50 miles north of Bergen. A 'maximum effort' operation was mounted against this dangerous and elusive quarry, six Swordfish from Hatston being followed by Hudsons of Nos.224 and 233 Squadrons which attacked in the face of intense 'flak'. Sqn Ldr Feeny's aircraft disappeared in a ball of flame, the remaining four crews, harried by Bf109s from Stavanger, overshooting the target. Problems with the aircraft, engines and equipment had delayed torpedo training, so the next attackers, nine Beauforts of No.42 Squadron from Wick, were each loaded with two 500-lb SAP bombs. They attacked from 6,000 ft in a steep dive and claimed hits on the *Scharnhorst* but in fact they were all near misses, and though they survived the 'flak' four Beauforts were shot down by Bf109s as they attempted their escape at low level. Twenty minutes later, at 16.45 hrs, came the last attack of the day—by six Hudsons of No.269 Squadron. They tried a precision bombing run at 14,500 ft but heavy 'flak' resulted in every aircraft being damaged and all the bombs fell wide. The *Scharnhorst* had escaped yet again, and it was becoming patently clear that a capital ship at sea was a difficult adversary and unlikely to be sunk by bombing; certainly not until better sights and bombs with better penetration had been devised.

Further south, meanwhile, most activity still concerned hostile aircraft and submarines in the vicinity of British coastal convoys. Their care had become the main task of the Anson crews of Nos.48, 206 and 500

Squadrons operating from No.16 Group bases, and of Nos.217 and 502 Squadrons in No.15 Groups's area where cover was provided over ships in St Georges Channel, the Irish Sea and off the north coast of Ireland. When sufficient Hudsons became available, a detachment of 206 Squadron commenced training at the Coastal Command Pool, Silloth, and A Flight started operations from Bircham Newton on 12 April. Anti-shipping work off the Dutch coast now became a practical proposition but the crew's work-up period, and that of No.235 Squadron (Blenheim IV fighters), was painfully short, for the German attack on the Low Countries and the invasion of France changed the whole tempo in the southern part of the North Sea. On 11 May No.235 Squadron was used to cover the landing of troops at the Hague in a forlorn attempt to help the Dutch, and shortly after its capture by German paratroops five Beauforts of No.22 Squadron dropped ten 500-lb bombs on Waalhaven Airport, Rotterdam. No.206 commenced intensive armed reconnaissance along the German and Dutch coasts, and after permission was received for German cities and ports to be attacked, joined 220 (which had moved down to Bircham Newton) and 233 Squadrons in bombing raids on oil storage tanks at Hamburg and Bremen on the 18th. Similar attacks by five Beauforts at Rotterdam caused extensive fires, and on the 29th No.22 Squadron made the unit's first daylight ship-ping attack—on motor torpedo boats in Ijmuiden harbour. These were merely pin pricks, as were attacks by 'Battle Flights' of Nos.48 and 500 Squadron Ansons on 'E' Boats off the Dutch coast, and had no effect on the situation in Northern France which rapidly became untenable. Operation *Dynamo*, the evacuation of the British Expeditionary Force from the beaches of Dunkirk started during the evening of 26 May. To combat the threat of interference by German warships, Hudsons of Nos. 206 and 220 Squadrons commenced crossover patrols off the Dutch coast between Ijmuiden and Texel on the 28th, and also kept up more direct shipping protection duties by providing continuous daytime cover over a triangle joining North Foreland, Calais and Dunkirk. No.235 Squadron, and even the Ansons of Nos.48 and 500 Squadrons flew standing patrols over the flotillas of ships off Dunkirk, ready to take on all comers and risking being shot down by trigger-happy Royal Navy gunners whose aircraft recognition was abysmal. So desperate was the situation that during the night of 30/31 May Ansons bombed enemy-held harbours in France and the following day Plt Off P. Peters flying an aircraft of No.500 Squadron tackled a couple of Bf109s, shooting down one with his front gun while his gunner, LAC Pepper disposed of another using the turret—an extraordinary achievement!

A Hudson off Dunkirk during early June 1940 at the time of Operation Dynamo, the evacuation of the British Expeditionary Force. The sky is blackened by the smoke from burning oil tanks. (via J.D. Oughton)

No.220's *Battle Flight* intercepted 40 Ju87s dive bombing rescue launches off Dunkirk on 1 June and managed to shoot down four before Spitfires arrived. These 'fighter' activities by Hudsons were continued during the evening of 3 June, Flt Lt Biddell of No.206 Squadron leading his two wing men into an attack on six Bf109s which were engaged in a fight with FAA Skuas. The German fighters were forced to break off after losing two of their number! Meanwhile the mining task had increased considerably, No.22 Squadron having to cover not only the approaches to German ports but also those in Denmark, Holland and Belgium, a mammoth task in which they were ably assisted by 812 and 815 Squadrons, the former having joined Coastal Command on attachment early in May.

The Dunkirk evacuation was completed on 4 June, No.16 Group units having flown 327 sorties in direct support and many others indirectly. Within days the whole of Norway was in German hands, and the collapse of the French had taken place. The maritime, as well as the military situation, was immediately transformed, the Kriegsmarine now having access to port facilities stretching from Northern Norway to the Spanish frontier. The task of the British Admiralty, trying to cover convoys from surface raiders and U-Boats alike was made infinitely more difficult, while Coastal Command now had to try to keep the coasts of Holland, Belgium and France under surveillance, lay on special anti-invasion patrols in the Channel

Blenheim IVs attacking a merchant ship—a photograph taken through a 'mirror' camera. (No.82 Squadron records)

area and provide long range fighter protection for Sunderlands in the Atlantic approaches in addition to its other duties. Slender resources were stretched to the utmost.

There was just one crumb of comfort in the face of this potentially disastrous situation. Any shipping found off the coast of Northern Europe was now virtually certain to belong to the enemy, or to be working for them, making identification much less of a problem. Armed reconnaissance and *Battle Flight* activity was intensified, and offensive action was taken whenever possible; though attacks on land targets proved more profitable, the crews of six Hudsons sent to attack De Kooy on the 24th June claiming considerable damage.

Further north in No.18 Group's area, similar work was being carried out, a 6,000 ton freighter being attacked and set on fire off Kristiansund on 22 June by a No.220 Squadron crew on an armed reconnaissance. Three Bf110 twin-engined fighters appeared but the Hudson escaped in cloud—such interceptions becoming more frequent as both fighters and radar stations were deployed further north. In the southwest approaches the story was much the same, No.236 Squadron's Blenheims being detached to St Eval for day/night patrols along the Le Havre/Cherbourg section of the French coastline and to escort Sunderlands. All four Blenheim fighter squadrons were highly mobile, detachments moving around the country as dictated by the main plot at Northwood.

Anti-invasion reconnaissance was naturally a priority, two ex-Army Co-operation Blenheim squadrons, Nos.53 and 59 transferring to Coastal in July 1940 specifically for this task. Flying from Detling and Thorney Island respectively they formed the backbone of Coastal's coverage of the 'invasion' ports, though they also took part in anti-shipping attacks when the opportunity arose. It was also feared that the Germans might mount an invasion of Scotland from Norway, so Nos.21 and 57 Squadrons of No.2 Group, Bomber Command, were sent to Lossiemouth as an anti-shipping strike force, and were soon sending six-aircraft formations on daily sweeps to within 100 miles of the Norwegian coast in co-operation with No.254 Squadron.

With their Ansons now operating over the Channel within a few minutes flying time of German fighter bases, No.500 Squadron crews got their armourers to mount extra side guns. They were also likely to stumble over very well armed 'E' Boats, and with the panache so typical of the 'auxiliaries', some of their aircraft were fitted with a free-mounted 20mm cannon firing through the floor of the cabin. The vibration caused when the cannon was fired loosened the mounting, but the directors of the British Cannon

Catalinas entered RAF service early in 1941 and soon made their mark, grabbing the headlines when Flg Off D.A. Briggs and crew of the newly-equipped No.209 Squadron re-located the Bismarck in May far out in the Atlantic. The aircraft involved, AH545, is seen alighting after a sortie. (SAAF)

Manufacturing Company were so impressed by the unit's ingenuity that they designed and presented to the Squadron a properly manufactured mount. There is no record of any success with the weapon but it made the crews feel less naked. Barge concentrations had spread all along the coast from Den Helder to Brest by September, totalling some 2,500, plus 240 ships. Attacks on them started immediately and continued for the remainder of the year. Harbours, docks, shipyards, airfields, oil installations, canals, factories and marshalling yards were also subject to bombing raids by No.16 Group squadrons, assisted by the Fairey Battles of Nos.12 and 142 Squadrons operating from Eastchurch on attachment to Coastal from Bomber Command.

In August the Blackburn Botha had started to replace the Anson with No.608 Squadron at Thornaby, and a few also reached No.502 Squadron at Aldergrove. The first operational patrol was made on 10 August, but the aircraft's poor performance when loaded, and vehement complaints by crews about the abysmal view from the cockpit, resulted in its use being confined to convoy patrol, and its withdrawal after three months and 298 operational flights. No.608 Squadron had to revert to Ansons while No.502 received Whitleys in October 1940, a bitter disappointment for crews and commanders alike.

Meanwhile No.217 Squadron had started a very lengthy conversion to Beauforts in May 1940, but was still using Ansons in September to bomb enemy shipping in Brest harbour at night, already a hazardous occupation, for the defences of the port were

daily becoming more formidable. Beaufort units were still restricted to mine-laying or bombing sorties, the latter almost suicidal against capital ships. Their use as torpedo bombers was continually delayed because the weapons were proving unpredictable at the higher dropping speeds necessary with the Beaufort, and suitable tactics had still to be evolved. On 17 July the aircraft was grounded for other problems and the opportunity was taken to send Beaufort crews of No.22 Squadron to Gosport to help in trials work on modified torpedoes. Operations restarted on 31 August and, after taking part in attacks on barge concentrations, the Squadron at last got the chance to use their primary weapon on 11 September when Flt Lt R. Beauman led a formation of five Beauforts on a convoy strike off Ostend. Three torpedoes failed to release and another exploded on a sandbank, but Beauman's hit a 6,000 ton freighter, and despite heavy flak from the escorts all the Beauforts returned safely. Six days later a set piece night torpedo strike against shipping in Cherbourg's outer harbour was planned. Six Beauforts were to be accompanied by eight Blenheims of 59 Squadron to drop bombs and light up the area with flares, with 53 Squadron backing up with more bombs and incendiaries, all aimed at creating the maximum confusion to divert attention from the Beauforts. Despite a last minute rush following a sudden change in the weather the plan worked well, 12 Blenheims and five Beauforts reaching the target. One Beaufort was shot down over the harbour but the other four dropped their torpedoes, a 1,600 ton freighter being sunk and a torpedo boat so badly damaged that it had to be scrapped. Oil tanks in the area burned uncontrollably for several days and part of the dock area was badly damaged.

No.42 Squadron resumed flying in September, and on the 26th carried out a night mining operation off Lorient, followed by recce patrols off Cherbourg, Le Havre and Dieppe. Their first foray with torpedoes came on 10 October when two aircraft flown by Flt Lt Hibberd and Flg Off G. Rooney penetrated Boulogne harbour. Unfortunately Hibberd's torpedo exploded before reaching the target and Rooney was attacked by four Bf109s immediately after releasing his weapon and saw nothing more of it. The whole Squadron was back at Wick by mid-October and on the 26th Sqn Ldr G. Smith led three Beauforts on a *Rover*: an offensive recce. He torpedoed and sank a 2,500 ton transport in Aspd Fjord, and Flg Off K. Trigance ran in on a 1,000 ton vessel, but his torpedo missed. He was then intercepted by Bf109s, one of which was shot down by his gunner, Plt Off Gow. Trigance was able to shake off the remaining fighters and his aircraft was the only one to return—a 66% loss rate not unusual against shipping heavily defended by flak and fighters.

Further south No.206 Squadron started taking the war to the enemy with attacks on German airfields in occupied France, 'Race' single aircraft sorties pioneering the 'Intruder' operations so popular in succeeding years. No.217 was at last able to despatch some Beauforts on operational mining sorties, choosing the approaches to the Atlantic ports of Brest and Lorient as their first targets. Impact Magnesium Percussion Mines (IMPS) and Time Impact Mines (TIMS) were the Beaufort's main weapons, No.217 finally with-

drawing their Ansons from night attacks on the Biscay ports in December.

The need to role specialize as the squadrons moved over to the offensive was recognized but it was for the future, for currently the squadrons still took on all sorts of tasks, such as the assault on the Bergen-Oslo railway line which was started on 19 December by 15 Hudsons from Nos.224 and 269 Squadrons, accompanied by six No.42 Squadron Beauforts, and continued for several days in a determined attempt to disrupt German lines of communication to northern Norway.

The Admiralty's long term concern over the use of the French Atlantic ports was certainly justified, for in December the *Hipper* sought sanctuary in Brest after damage sustained in an engagement with the heavy escorts of a troop convoy 700 miles west of Cape Finisterre. The ship then used the port as a base for a 14-day commerce raid in February 1941, during which seven ships of Convoy SLS-64 were sunk in a single day—which did not auger well for the future. Coincidently, major organizational moves on the British side were taking place, No.19 Group forming at the Area Combined HQ, Plymouth, to take over the south-west approaches from No.15 Group on 5 February 1941, the latter going to Liverpool to work alongside the Commander-in-Chief Western Approaches. No.15 Group was then primarily concerned with the provision of escorts for Atlantic convoys while No.19 concentrated on coastal convoys in the western part of the English Channel and southern part of the Irish Sea, and attacks on enemy shipping in French ports.

Increasingly worried by mounting shipping losses

Following a difficult work-up, Beauforts were fully operational by mid-1941, including No.217 Squadron based at St Eval. Here one of the unit's aircraft is flown by Flt Lt Percival over the Camel Estuary near Padstow. (M.C.B. Anderson)

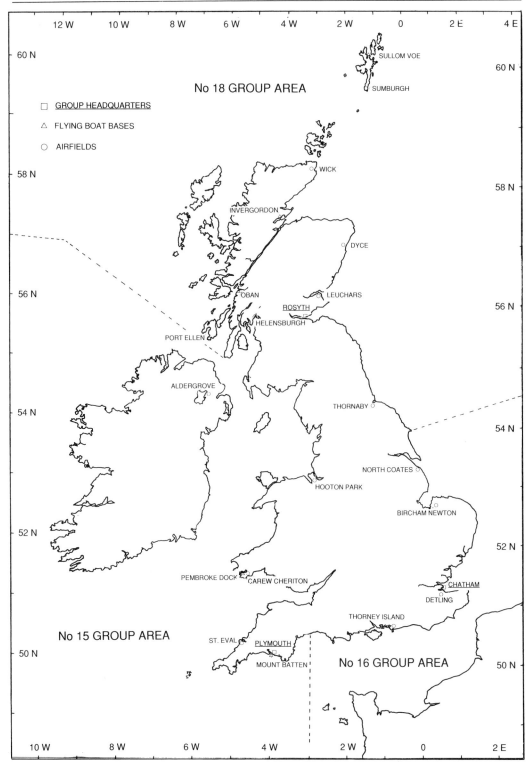

12 W   10 W   8 W   6 W   4 W   2 W   0   2 E   4 E

60 N

SULLOM VOE

No 18 GROUP AREA

SUMBURGH

☐ GROUP HEADQUARTERS

△ FLYING BOAT BASES

○ AIRFIELDS

58 N

WICK

INVERGORDON

DYCE

56 N

OBAN   LEUCHARS

ROSYTH

HELENSBURGH

PORT ELLEN

ALDERGROVE

54 N

THORNABY

NORTH COATES

HOOTON PARK

BIRCHAM NEWTON

52 N

PEMBROKE DOCK   CAREW CHERITON   CHATHAM

DETLING

THORNEY ISLAND

No 15 GROUP AREA

ST. EVAL   PLYMOUTH

50 N

MOUNT BATTEN   No 16 GROUP AREA

10 W   8 W   6 W   4 W   2 W   0   2 E

COASTAL COMMAND GROUPS (PRE FEBRUARY 1941) AND BASES (SEPTEMBER 1940)   RCBA

No.269 Squadron's detachment at Kaldadarnes, Iceland, was upgraded to full unit strength in May 1941, and one of the aircraft used was Hudson III, T9465, the famous 'Spirit of Lockheed-Vega Employees', paid for by the American company's workforce. (No.269 Sqn records via P.H.T. Green)

from U-Boat attacks, and apprehensive lest the other German capital ships should emulate the *Hipper*, the Admiralty now pressed for Bomber Command to concentrate on the war at sea, not only by bombing ports and surface ships, but also U-boat lairs and even the submarines themselves. The Prime Minister, Mr Winston Churchill, agreed and on 6 March 1941 issued one of his famous directives, giving the 'Battle of the Atlantic' full priority and requiring Bomber Command to concentrate on naval targets. No.114 Squadron had already been detached to Coastal on 2 March for reconnaissance work over the North Sea, but Nos.18, 21, 107 and 139 Squadrons of No.2 Group now joined in attacks on enemy ships carrying Swedish iron ore from Norway to Germany, and on coastal convoys transporting material for the occupation forces in Holland, Belgium and France, while heavy bombers stepped up their raids on the ports, notably Brest. On 24 April No.101 Squadron was transferred to Manston for 'Channel Stop', an operation designed to close the Dover Straits to enemy shipping using aircraft during the day and MTBs at night.

Longer term, the decision had been made earlier in the year to establish a dedicated 'strike' force within Coastal Command consisting of 12 squadrons equally split between long range fighter, bomber and torpedo bomber units. Four Blenheim fighter squadrons already in service were to be rearmed with Beaufighters, the three Beaufort torpedo bomber units

brought up to strength and another formed, and four Blenheim bomber squadrons transferred to the force. In fact Nos.235 and 252 Squadrons already had some Beaufighters on strength, the latter unit making the aircraft's first operational 'coastal' sorties on 6 April 1941, by which time No.272 Squadron was undergoing conversion. Unfortunately this promising start was not maintained, for later in April the requirements of Middle East Command took precedence, and on the 25th No.252 squadron was ordered to send 15 aircraft and crews to Malta. Not surprisingly they did not return, and nor did No.272 Squadron sent abroad at the end of May. It was the start of a steady haemorrhage which put the 'strike' concept in abeyance for many months, a situation mirrored for a shorter period by 'Channel Stop' which had to be temporarily halted on 9 May following appalling losses which made No.2 Group's earlier daylight operations over France and the Low Countries seem a 'picnic' in comparison.

Meanwhile, the dreaded *Scharnhorst* and *Gneisenau* again slipped out into the Atlantic and, avoiding convoys, sank 22 ships totalling 115,600 tons. There was little that could be done to catch them at sea, but the extensive patrols maintained in the northern approaches and off the west coast of France finally paid off on 21 March when the crew of a Hudson on station off Ushant located the ships on ASV radar and shadowed them until bad weather caused contact to be lost. They were relocated in Brest and during the night of 30/31 March were attacked by a force of 50 Wellingtons, 24 Whitleys, 16 Blenheims, 15 Hampdens and four Manchesters—without success. It was the start of a four month diversion for Bomber Command, one which was bitterly opposed by the C-in-C but one which he had to accept. Frequent mining of the approaches to Brest was also undertaken, but until the *Gneisenau* was unexpectedly moved out of dry dock into the inner harbour on 5 April there was no opportunity for Coastal Command to attack with torpedoes. A strike by No.22 Squadron, on detachment to St Eval, was immediately ordered and the CO, Wg Cdr F.J. St-G. Braithwaite, decided to use all his six available aircraft, three carrying torpedoes and the others 'TIM' mines which he hoped would blow holes in the torpedo net assumed to be protecting the ship. The attack did not go to plan. For various reasons none of the mine carriers reached Brest and neither did one of the torpedo Beauforts. However, Flg Off K. Campbell and his crew found their way through poor weather to the narrow harbour approaches almost on schedule and, after waiting briefly for the others, went in alone. The full story has been told in detail many times* and as an example of raw courage it is unsurpassed. Campbell positioned his aircraft perfectly for the very difficult drop, the *Gneisenau* receiving a direct hit which blew a 40 ft hole in the starboard side. Immediately after release the Beaufort was hit by murderous anti-aircraft fire and crashed into the harbour killing the crew. Half an hour later a second Beaufort found Brest and started a run, but in the intense flak the pilot lost sight

of the target and the crew were lucky to escape into cloud. Campbell posthumously received the Victoria Cross, but his crew, Sergeants J.P. Scott, R.W. Hillman and W.C. Mulliss got no recognition. Only the VC can be awarded posthumously.

Continuous patrols off Brest codenamed *Stopper* were instigated by No.19 Group, designed to prevent either ship putting to sea. In the case of the *Gneisenau*, which received further damage on 10/11 April from Bomber Command attacks, operations were unlikely for some time, but the *Scharnhorst* continued her run of luck. However, her refitting was delayed by damage to port facilities and the German High Command's plan for a co-ordinated attack by the ships at Brest, and the *Bismarck*, now ready for sea, was frustrated. The *Bismarck*'s mere presence was, however, a reason for constant concern and the Royal Navy was put on full alert following reports on 22 April of a strong naval force at Narvik which might include the ship. It was a false alarm, but not so a month later when the Naval Attaché in Stockholm sent reports of two capital ships passing through the Kattegat on 20 May, and photographs obtained by a PRU Spitfire† off Bergen confirmed that the *Bismarck* and the cruiser *Prinz Eugen* were at sea. They went into Bergen, and attempts to bomb them at their moorings were made during the night of 21/22 May by six Whitleys of No.612 Squadron and Hudsons from Wick. It was

*For a full dramatized account see *Torpedo Airmen* by Roy Conyers Nesbit.
†See Chapter 11.

Cleared to carry torpedoes at last, three Beauforts of No.22 Squadron set off on a Rover. The nearest aircraft, coded OA-L is X8934. (via J.D. Oughton)

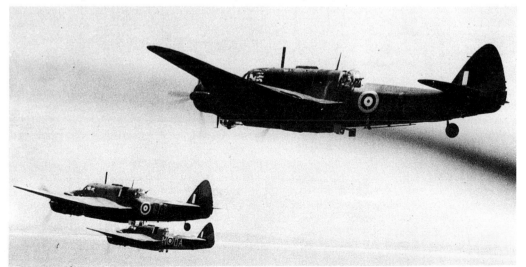

foiled because the ships had sailed at 20.00 hours on the 21st and they were not relocated until spotted on radar by HMS *Suffolk* in the Denmark Straits (between Iceland and Greenland) having avoided extensive air patrols by sailing north of Iceland.

On the 24th a Sunderland of No.201 Squadron, captained by Flt Lt Vaughan, arrived just in time to witness the action on 24 May 1941 between German and British capital ships, in which the *Hood* was sunk. He shadowed the *Bismarck* and *Prinz Eugen* as they went south with *Norfolk* and *Suffolk* in contact, and at midnight on 24/25 May eight Swordfish flying off HMS *Victorious* (825 Squadron led by Lt Cdr E.K. Esmonde RN, attacked with torpedoes, one of which struck the *Bismarck* amidships and ruptured some fuel tanks. Shortly afterwards the shadowers lost contact and a frantic air and sea search ensued. Three Catalinas of No.210 Squadron flew a parallel track search between 20 and 30 degrees west which just missed the *Bismarck*, and it was the ordering by the AOC-in-C Coastal of cross over barriers by two Catalinas further south than the Admiralty assessment suggested which saved the day. Plt Off D.A. Briggs of the newly equipped No.209 Squadron sighted the ship tracking south-east at 10.30 hours on the 26th, any doubt being dispelled when very accurate AA fire forced the crew to withdraw. Fortunately a Catalina of No.240 Squadron was on hand and took over until aircraft from *Ark Royal* gained contact. The fate of *Bismarck* was sealed when an attack by 15 Swordfish 810, 818 and 820 Squadrons resulted in two torpedoes striking the ship and wrecking the steering gear, and the ship was finally despatched the following morning by torpedoes from the cruiser *Dorsetshire* after a battering by the guns of Force H and Home Fleet ships. Meanwhile the search for the *Prinz Eugen* was on, Sunderlands of No.10 Squadron, RAAF, and Wellingtons of the newly operational No.221 Squadron being joined by Hudsons of No.206 Squadron and even Blenheims of No.236 Squadron, the latter flying cross-over patrols. All were unsuccessful, the heavy cruiser having gone far to the south to meet oilers before returning to Brest on 1 June undetected.

There was no respite for hard-pressed anti-shipping aircraft, for on 11 June reports reached the Admiralty of another German naval force in the Baltic getting ready for sea and it was later confirmed that the *Lutzow* (the *Deutschland* renamed) and a four destroyer escort had passed through the Kattegat and was thought to be repositioning for a breakout into the Atlantic. Bowhill had 14 torpedo bombers at his immediate disposal in Scotland, five Beauforts of No.22 Squadron at Wick and nine of No.42 at Leuchars. It was axiomatic never to commit a strike

force without an up-to-date sighting report, but the AOC-in-C was in a dilemma, for an attack in daylight left the Beauforts vulnerable to fighters and the night during June in northern latitudes was short. If he waited for a reconnaissance sighting it might be too late to despatch his force and 24 hours later the ships would be out of range, while on the other hand if he 'launched' them in the hope of a position report he might be faced with the Beauforts on their way back and short of fuel before it came through. He decided to break the rules and send the Wick aircraft to a position off Stavanger (the estimated maximum distance the *Lutzow* could have travelled) and the 42 Squadron Beauforts to Lister from where they would turn north to meet 22 Squadron coming south in a classic pincer movement. No.42 Squadron left Leuchars at 23.15 hours in three 'vics' of three and the gamble came off, for on the way a positive sighting report was received from the crew of a 114 Squadron Blenheim. They were well placed, but flying at low level in bad light was tricky and Sgt R. Loviett, flying on the port side of the CO was caught in his leader's slipstream and nearly flew into the sea. Finding that he had lost touch with the rest of the formation, he continued alone to Lister and then made for Egersund on the assumption that the ships would make 26 knots since the reported position. Nothing was seen and, disappointed, the crew turned for home. Almost immediately they flew over a vessel's wake and then in the moonlight saw a capital ship, unmistakably the *Lutzow*. Loviett turned to position for an attack in another patch of light and still unchallenged, found himself perfectly positioned. The torpedo ran well and apparently hit the target amidships. His attack report brought other Beauforts to the scene but they were unable to attack through the smoke screen put up by the destroyers. Four days later the *Lutzow* was in dry dock at Kiel, out of action for six months at a crucial stage of the Atlantic war.

A few days later, on 14 June 1941, Air Chief Marshal Bowhill relinquished his command of Coastal after nearly four years at the helm. The anti-shipping element of the Command had not had an easy time and many mistakes had been made, but he left an effective reconnaissance force largely composed of aircraft equipped with radar, an aid starting to show its worth though still temperamental. Mining and torpedo attack capability was also slowly improving, but bombing results were disappointing against anything other than the most thin skinned of targets. All anti-shipping operations had proved extremely dangerous in the face of increasingly powerful flak, but it was confidently expected that the strike force concept would be the answer—when it could be introduced.

CHAPTER 3

Defence to Offence–
Anti-Submarine
Operations 1939-41

AS ALREADY OUTLINED* the Germans succeeded in getting 39 of their 58 U-Boats out into the Atlantic undetected during August 1939, and they made very sure the Allies knew they meant business by sinking the SS *Athenia*, a passenger ship, on the very first day of the war, 3 September. The attack was in contravention of international agreements, and the British thought that the destruction of the vessel was the start of unrestricted submarine warfare, and took measures accordingly. In fact, Admiral Karl Doenitz, Flag Officer U-Boats, had imposed strict controls, and it was a mistake, the captain of the U-30 being under the impression that the ship was an auxiliary cruiser!

Convoying started almost immediately, first along the east coast of the United Kingdom and then, from 7 September, across the Atlantic, the ships being escorted by destroyers out as far as $12\frac{1}{2}$ degrees west (300 nm). Ansons provided the bulk of East Coast convoy cover and these aircraft also attended shipping in the Irish Sea. Atlantic cover was the province of flying boats, each convoy being escorted by one aircraft during daylight out to about 100 nm west of the Scillies, any further cover being dependent upon the availability of the only long-range aircraft, the Sunderland. To try to stretch the cover, detachments of flying boats were sent to Brest and Falmouth, but both bases were considered unsatisfactory and were relinquished after a few weeks.

Initial problems with convoying and the many dispersed home-coming ships meant easy targets for U-boats on station in the approaches to the British Isles, and the results were grim—41 ships totalling some 153,800 tons going to the bottom of the sea during the first month of the war. It was obvious that the losses would continue too, for neither the few fast ships nor the many very slow ones could be sensibly integrated with the convoy system. They continued to

sail independently and, with the inevitable stragglers from convoys, provided the majority of U-boat successes for the remainder of 1939.

The flying boat units were also expected to carry out reconnaissance sorties intended to locate German surface raiders, and to co-operate with naval anti-submarine groups operating around the British Isles. It was immediately obvious that the Command was seriously overstretched and in an attempt to fill gaps in their cover in the south-west approaches the Admiralty tried using carrier-borne FAA aircraft. The result was almost inevitable, a narrow escape on 14 September for HMS *Ark Royal* being followed three days later by the loss of *Courageous* when she was torpedoed by the U-29. This mis-employment of the carrier force ended rapidly, and much of the operational effort of two Sunderland units, Nos.204 and 228 Squadrons (the latter brought home hastily from the Mediterranean) was diverted onto anti-submarine work.

The AOC-in-C Coastal asked for further assistance, and Bomber Command detached No.58 Squadron to No.15 Group at the end of September to fly convoy escort and anti-submarine patrols over the western part of the English Channel. The Squadron, flying ancient Whitley IIIs, operated from Boscombe Down, usefully if uneventfully until mid-February 1940, when it returned to Linton-on-Ouse and resumed bomber operations. Similar detachments from a reluctant Bomber Command followed at intervals.

Up north in No.18 Group's area No.201 Squadron had moved its Londons to the Shetlands in August 1939, mooring in Sullom Voe and using the SS *Manela* as accommodation, while No.209 Squadron took its Stranraers to the slightly more attractive

*See Chapter 1.

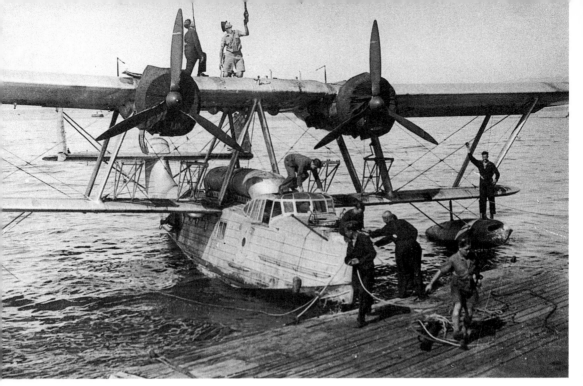

London II K6932/TQ-B of No.202 Squadron being moored at New Camp, Gibraltar. (No.202 Sqn records via P.H.T. Green)

surroundings of Invergordon. Both units were used on patrols between Scotland and Norway, and by the end of October, with the convoy routine settling down and a reduction in the number of U-Boats on patrol, sinkings by submarines showed a perceptible decline. In November losses decreased still further which at the time was put down to a reshuffle of No.18 Group patrols, aimed at getting the most effective aircraft in the best locations. In fact, the apparent lack of U-Boat activity was due to German determination to exploit their newly introduced magnetic mine which was being laid in numbers along the east coast of Britain by surface vessels, aircraft—and U-Boats. When this new threat was recognized the initial counter was an increase in North Sea and Channel area patrols by diverting resources from other areas, and to maintain some inshore anti-U-Boat cover Tiger Moth and Hornet Moth biplanes were hastily distributed around the coast in 'Flights', each attached to a squadron at the same base. Thus No.217 Squadron parented No.5 Coastal Patrol Flight at Carew Cheriton and No.3 CPF was attached to No.502 Squadron at Hooton Park. The other CPF's were No.1 at Dyce (Aberdeen), No.2 at Abbotsinch (Glasgow), No.4 at Aldergrove (Belfast) and No.6 at St Eval (Newquay). Operating in pairs the aircraft were flown as single-seaters on 'Scarecrow' patrols throughout the harsh winter of 1939-40—usually without seeing a thing of interest. Pilots of No.1 CPF appear to have experienced the

most excitement, a periscope being seen on 17 December, and on 25 January 1940 an oil slick, the head of which was moving steadily forward. Flg Off P.C. Hoyle signalled nearby destroyers by firing a green Very light, and under his direction one of them released a pattern of depth charges over the slick, but no positive claim could be made even though oil continued to bubble up from the position for several weeks.

Meanwhile, on 13 November, the location of and attacks on U-Boats had been officially declared of equal importance to the search for surface ships, a significant shift of attitude by the Admiralty who had previously considered the destruction of submarines strictly their business! Coastal Command, whose crews had already been taking every opportunity to attack U-Boats, became steadily more 'U-Boat minded' though they could report no definite success during 1939. This was not surprising, for crews lacked training in the difficult art of submarine attack, and worse, their weapons were virtually useless. This had been suspected pre-war* such doubts being supported by the results of accidental attacks on British submarines during the first few days of the war. A potentially more serious incident occurred on 3 December when HMS *Snapper* was hit at the base of her conning tower by a 100-lb AS bomb, but the

*Outlined in Chapter 1.

damage only amounted to four light bulbs and some crockery! The 250-lb AS bomb was more capable, but it needed to explode within six feet of the pressure hull to cause serious damage. Any real chance of success required a 'stick' of bombs and only the Hudson had a distributor capable of accurate spacing. It was also the only aircraft with a bomb sight, the Mk.IX, but this was useless at low level so all Coastal crews were reduced to visual judgement for bombing. This needed practice which they had not had because they were trained for reconnaissance work—'Catch 22'. The weapon situation bordered on the ludicrous, and further vacillation was out of the question, but the answer, the airborne depth charge, did not become available for general operational use for months, and the low level sight took even longer.

In December 1939 No.209 Squadron started receiving Saro Lerwicks at Oban, the first operational patrol with the aircraft being flown on Christmas Day. The Lerwick had actually first entered squadron service with No.240 Squadron at Calshot in July 1939 but had so many faults that it was withdrawn in September. Production was cancelled in October, but with no immediate hope of accelerated production of Sunderlands and a desperate shortage of maritime aircraft it was re-instated on 1 November as a temporary measure, the longer term solution being to order the Consolidated PBY-5, named Catalina by the RAF.

Air-to-Surface (ASV) Mk.1 radar made its operational appearance during January 1940 in Hudsons and proved useful in finding convoys. In ideal conditions it could detect a fully surfaced submarine at ranges up to three miles, though it was quite incapable of 'painting' a periscope or conning tower, and 'clutter' prevented the target being held to an 'on top'. Fortunately the increasingly efficient convoy system resulted in shipping losses continuing to decline. At the same time U-Boat losses were steadily mounting, and in January 1940 Doenitz still only had 32 operational 'boats', which meant a maximum of eight on patrol at any one time, though of course a larger force could be concentrated after a lull in operations. Forty ships totalling 111,200 tons were sunk by U-Boats during the month but at last a definite 'kill' could be claimed by Coastal Command—with the help of both surface forces and the enemy! On 30 January 1940 the crew of a No.228 Squadron Sunderland, captained by Flg Off E.J. Brooks, sighted and attacked a surfaced U-Boat which had earlier been depth-charged by convoy escorts. Unable to submerge and with aircraft and surface vessels in the area, Kapitän-leutnant Heidel scuttled the U-55 (Type VIIB) and it was officially part credited to the Squadron.

In October 1939 it had been agreed by the Australian government that No.10 Squadron, RAAF, in the United Kingdom at the beginning of the war to work up on Sunderlands, should be retained for operations with Coastal Command. The unit was declared operational at Pembroke Dock early in February 1940 bringing the number of Sunderland

Declared operational in February 1940, No.10 Squadron RAAF moved to Mount Batten in April, where N9048/RB-B is drawn up on the hardstanding in front of the old First World War hangars. (RAF Museum)

No.240 Squadron flew Stranraers such as K7295/BN-L on anti U-Boat patrols until April 1941, carrying a single AS bomb under each wing. (MAP)

squadrons in the Command to four—and was a welcome fillip for No.15 Group.

U-Boats sank 45 ships totalling 169,500 tons in February, about half of them in the North Sea, but relief was on its way with the decision by the Germans to invade Norway. This resulted in the temporary withdrawal of U-Boats from the Atlantic and a reduction in shipping losses to 23 during March, a month which saw the destruction of three U-Boats, one by an aircraft—but of Bomber Command!

No.10 Squadron, RAAF, moved to Mount Batten on 1 April, releasing No.204 for operations from Sullom Voe, while at Invergordon No.201 completed conversion to the Sunderland. The number of really useful flying boats in service was slowly increasing and, with the Norwegian campaign in full swing, shipping losses attributable to U-Boats fell further during April, just seven out of the total of 58 sunk during the month. This was a tribute to the effectiveness of British anti-submarine forces when they could be concentrated, for the Allied landings in northern Norway meant that there were many troopships and supply vessels in the area, but U-Boats were unable to take advantage of such tempting targets.

Side issues, but ones with important repercussions on the Atlantic anti-submarine war, were the British occupation of the Faeroe Islands on 13 April, and the invasion of Iceland on 10 May. The latter was to prevent the Germans using the island to support their U-Boat campaign and, almost as vital, to set up a destroyer and aircraft base for British anti-submarine forces. No.98 Squadron was transferred to Coastal

Command and on 31 July its Fairey Battles, the only aircraft which could be spared, arrived in Iceland and started operations from Kaldadarnes.

Operations covering the supply route to Norway continued into May, the decision to withdraw the Allied forces only serving to increase the pressure on Coastal Command. During the April/May period a total of 182 merchant ship convoys and 176 'special' convoys were supported, and May losses to U-Boats were again small, 13 ships (55,000 tons), though mining and air attack raised the total to 101 ships (288,400 tons). The traumatic events in France at the end of May maintained the strain on the anti-submarine forces, particularly those of No.16 Group. They were responsible for preventing U-Boats interfering with the evacuation ships during Operation *Dynamo*, and in this they were extraordinarily successful, though little appreciated by sailors and soldiers at the time. Longer term, the sudden French collapse naturally had a profound effect on British strategy, and like all arms of the Services, Coastal Command was faced with new tasks not envisaged in the War Plan.* It was to be expected that U-Boats would soon be based in western France, which would allow them more time on patrol, or greater penetration of the Atlantic thus forcing an extension of British air escorts and anti-submarine patrols with consequent dilution of Coastal's resources. A grim scenario soon to be turned into fact.

In June the U-Boats returned to the Atlantic, and

*See Chapter 2.

shipping losses increased dramatically, 58 vessels totalling 284,100 tons being sunk by submarines during the month. For Coastal Command the lack of suitable bases in the south-west of the British Isles was only too apparent, the shipping toll continuing to increase as U-Boats were redeployed to the Biscay ports. In July the Air Ministry was advised, in no uncertain terms, that immediate reinforcement by three flying boat, one general reconnaissance and two long-range fighter squadrons was essential, though where the flying boats were to come from was problematical. Sunderland production was only just keeping pace with losses and there were only 34 available to the Command, No.228 Squadron having returned to the Mediterranean following the entry of Italy into the war on the German side. This move was partially off-set by the transfer of Gibraltar-based No.200 Group to Coastal, energetic efforts being made to enlarge the flying boat base in the harbour currently occupied by six Londons of No.202 Squadron. Work was also pressed forward on the airfield at North Front, but of other 'new' resources there was no immediate prospect.

On 1 July Flt Lt W.N. Gibson and crew of No.10 Squadron, RAAF, although briefed for an anti-submarine patrol, were diverted to convoy escort and then to search for the attacker of a torpedoed ship some 250 miles WSW of the Scillies. The submarine was spotted a couple of miles away from the stricken ship and Gibson attacked with four 250-lb AS bombs as it submerged. A few minutes later it re-appeared and Gibson attacked again. Despite gunfire from a fast

approaching destroyer the U-Boat remained on the surface, for the captain, already shaken by earlier depth charging by HMS *Gladiolus*, had had enough. He ordered his crew to abandon ship before scuttling her. The U-26 (Type IA) was shared between the *Gladiolus* and the Sunderland crew, the second such incident and, as it turned out, the last 'kill' of 1940 in which an aircraft had a direct hand. Other attacks were made, one by Flg Off E.R. Baker and his No.210 Squadron crew while on convoy escort on 16 August being noteworthy because it is believed to have been the first using airborne depth charges.

In August 1940 Admiral Doenitz ordered a change in U-Boat tactics and they started concentrating night attacks on individual ships and poorly escorted convoys. Even in bright moonlight the crew of an aircraft stood little chance of locating a U-boat by visual means while ASV radar, fitted to about a sixth of Coastal aircraft at this time was still very temperamental. It had been expected that the much improved ASV Mk.II would be in service in August, but fighter Airborne Interception (AI) sets had been given priority and the ASV was delayed. In any case aircraft had no means of illuminating the target at night, and because it was feared that switching on ASV would alert U-Boat crews to the presence of a convoy its use was not allowed when on escort duty until a convoy was under attack. Under these circumstances it was still considered pointless to further overstretch resources by giving air cover at night, but it meant that U-Boats were virtually immune from attack at night if they remained on the

Hornet and Tiger Moths of No.5 Coastal Patrol Flight attached to No.217 Squadron at Carew Cheriton. (via D.J. Smith/A.S. Thomas)

surface for *Asdic* was only effective against submerged targets.

On 17 August Hitler declared a total blockade of the British Isles, stating that neutral ships would be sunk on sight, and during the month U-boats sank 56 ships of 267,000 tons out of a total of Allied and neutral losses of 397,200 tons. Worse was to follow in September when Fw200 Condors operating from Bordeaux started long range attacks on shipping. Their targets were single ships or stragglers as far out as 18 degrees west, but just as dangerous was their reconnaissance capability. Out of range of the defenders they could shadow groups of ships and report position, course and speed, enabling several U-Boats to intercept the same convoy, follow it by day and attack at night. It was the start of the 'pack' system, a serious development, difficult to combat.

During October 1940 Coastal Command aircraft started to be fitted with ASV Mk.II, the first sets going to No.502 Squadron re-equipping at Aldergrove with Whitley Vs. The range of the equipment, already better than the Mk.1, was further improved by rearrangement of the aerials—to look sideways rather than forwards! Other changes were the steady improvement in depth charges, and the installation of short range R/T in both ships and aircraft enabling them to communicate without having to rely on the Aldis lamp. There was also the prospect of another new aircraft from the same stable as the Catalina, the Consolidated Model 32 four-engined bomber which

had been ordered by both the French and British early in 1940. The aircraft's long-range characteristics were seen as the answer to two problems, that of a long haul transport for trans-Atlantic operation, and provision of an anti-submarine landplane capable of sorties into mid-Atlantic where U-Boats were already starting to lurk undisturbed by air cover. After the first six had been produced as transports, 20 were completed as LB-30Bs (later named Liberators) for Coastal Command, but they were not due for delivery until the spring of 1941, shortly after the first Catalinas.

In the meantime, frantic efforts were made to intercept the Condors. Their frequent W/T messages made them comparatively easy to plot, but interception was much more difficult. No.236 Squadron Blenheim crews based at St Eval tried catching them as they returned to base, and detachments of Nos.235, 236 and 254 Squadrons operated out of Aldergrove during late 1940, all with singular lack of success. One was intercepted by three Blenheims on 30 November but they couldn't close on it—it was going too fast! Suggested solutions were the fitment of light flight decks and catapults on oil tankers and grain ships so that fighters could accompany convoys—and that Beaufighters should replace Blenheims. Both schemes were adopted, No.252 Squadron being formed late in November to introduce the Beaufighter to Coastal Command, while the 'catafighter' and the MAC ships also appeared in due course.

Lerwick L7255/WQ-A of No.209 Squadron on patrol from Oban, early 1940. (F.E. Thomas via J. Evans)

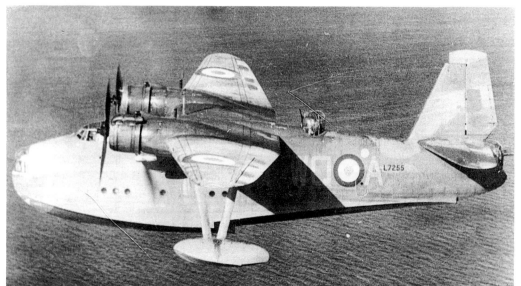

Although convoys were now being escorted as far as 30 degrees west (about 300 nm west of Ireland) and the Canadians were giving similar cover from their coastline, losses made grim reading during the autumn of 1940. U-Boats sank 352,400 tons of shipping in October out of a total of 443,000 tons (103 ships), a figure almost matched in November when 385,700 tons (97 ships) were lost. This was way above anything the shipbuilding industry could replace and the level of imports fell alarmingly. The First Lord of the Admiralty, A.V. Alexander, requested immediate and long-term increases in the strength of Coastal Command, stating the need for a minimum of 826 shore-based 'naval co-operation' aircraft in the eastern Atlantic/North Sea areas (an addition of at least 300 aircraft). He also criticized the training of crews and standard of equipment. The next day, at a meeting of the Defence Committee, Lord Beaverbrook, Minister of Aircraft Production, suggested that the solution was for Coastal Command to be handed over to the Royal Navy to operate as part of an expanded Fleet Air Arm, stating that he anticipated no difficulty in supplying the aircraft needed! As a panacea it sounded depressingly familiar, but fortunately the First Sea Lord, Admiral of the Fleet Sir Dudley Pound, was more interested in safeguarding shipping during the next few crucial months than attempting to absorb Coastal Command. An inquiry was held but no action, precipitate or otherwise, was taken. At the next meeting of the Committee, the Prime Minister, Mr

Winston Churchill, merely added the proviso that operational control of the U-Boat war must rest with the sailors—a re-statement of a situation which had pertained for some time.

The furore did have one useful result, bringing the desperate equipment situation to the attention of those at the top, and they authorized the formation of 15 additional squadrons by June 1941. In practice, supply of aircraft and crews was insufficient to allow such an increase, but in the short term Coastal Command received immediate anti-submarine re-inforcement in the form of sufficient ASV Mk.II-fitted Wellingtons to equip a squadron, and the prospect of four more squadrons of various types during 1941, subject only to the timely delivery of Catalinas. In addition seven anti-shipping squadrons were to be formed during the year.

Bad weather hampered Atlantic operations by U-Boats and aircraft alike during December, resulting in only one convoy being attacked, though there was much activity off Portugal and West Africa, and a total of 37 ships were sunk by German submarines. The spreading of the submarine war down the coast of Africa was very worrying, and on 15 January 1941 No.95 Squadron was formed from a Flight of No.210 Squadron and began the long transit flight to Freetown, Sierra Leone, two weeks later.

The need to bolster the understandably amateurish efforts at naval reconnaissance by No.98 Squadron from Kaldadarnes was also recognized, and on

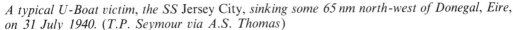
A typical U-Boat victim, the SS Jersey City, *sinking some 65 nm north-west of Donegal, Eire, on 31 July 1940. (T.P. Seymour via A.S. Thomas)*

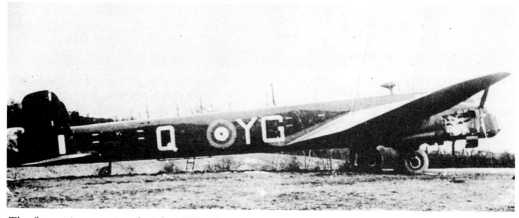

The first unit operational with ASV radar was No.502 Squadron. The extra aerials can be seen mounted on the top of the fuselage of Whitley V, YG-Q, at Limavady early in 1941. (via A.S. Thomas)

1 January 1941 the formation of an Iceland Area Force was approved. No.269 Squadron was to be deployed there as soon as possible, as was No.204 Squadron, the latter using moorings at Reykjavik reconnoitred unofficially in September 1939 by the crew of Consolidated Model 28–5.

The weather in the Atlantic remained bad throughout January resulting in a dip in Allied shipping losses to 21 vessels totalling 126,800 tons, most U-Boat 'successes' being in mid-Atlantic after convoys had dispersed and there was no air cover. The terrible weather was naturally also a problem for Coastal crews, but despite this Flt Lt E.R. Baker DFC, of

No.210 Squadron, managed to attack the Italian submarine *Marcello* some 750 miles west of Cape Wrath on the 6th. At the time this was thought to be the first unassisted 'kill' by Coastal Command but the vessel had escaped—only to be sunk by an escort on 22 February.

On 7 February 1941 the Western Approaches Naval Command was established, and No.15 Group was moved to Liverpool, to operate alongside the naval staff in a combined operations room, being replaced at Plymouth by No.19 Group. This new Group worked with the reorganized Plymouth Naval Command, which was concerned primarily

Short 'G' Class boats at Queens Island, Belfast, March 1941, prior to delivery to No.119 Squadron as ASV radar-equipped and turreted operational aircraft. (Shorts)

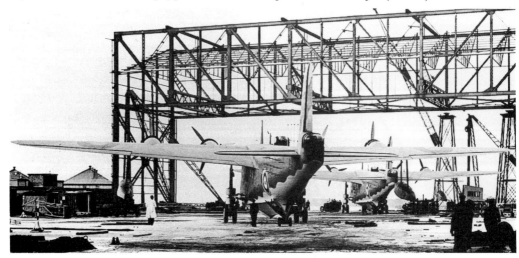

with the south-west approaches and the Bay of Biscay area.

The comparatively poor results achieved by the U-Boats during January was doubly misleading, for not only were they affected by the weather but also by a temporary trough in the number of operational submarines, at 22 the lowest since the beginning of the war. There were another 67 on trials or in training, however, and they soon made an impact, 39 ships totalling 196,800 tons being sunk in February, when the only comfort for Coastal chiefs was a damaging attack on U-93 by the crew of a 502 Squadron Whitley—of special note because the initial detection was made on the aircraft's ASV Mk.II.

Catalinas started to arrive in Britain early in 1941 and on 5 March the first operational delivery was made to No.240 Squadron at Stranraer, the unit's Supermarine Stranraers being completely replaced the following month, when Nos.209 and 210 Squadrons also re-equipped. This welcome increase in the long range capabilities of the Command was not a moment too soon, for in March the Germans launched a major campaign in the Atlantic aimed at defeating Britain by, as Hitler had prophesied on 24 February, 'ending the struggle within 60 days'. New ocean-going U-Boats, aircraft and surface raiders were all to play their part. The threat was immediately recognized by the War Cabinet, including Churchill, who issued his 'Battle of the Atlantic' directive on 6 March calling for immediate measures to strengthen British forces and the setting up of a high level Battle of the Atlantic Committee to regularly monitor the situation. Convoys were directed further north to reduce the effectiveness of the U-Boats based in Biscay ports, and Blenheims of No.2 Group, Bomber Command, were attached to Coastal, partially taking over North Sea operations so that experienced Coastal units could be moved into the north-west of the British Isles for operations with No.15 Group.

Most of the aircraft were Blenheim fighters which were of limited use, but Hudsons of No.224 Squadron and Wellingtons of No.221 were valuable additions to the anti-submarine forces in the area. A strong plea for Halifax aircraft, just entering Bomber Command service, was made but rejected, it being considered better to earmark more Liberators, and to place an immediate order for another 150 Catalinas—a figure later amended and supplemented by later acquisitions.

Operations by No.95 Squadron from West Africa started on 24 March but it was soon obvious that reinforcements were necessary, and plans were made for the establishment of a Hudson squadron and the provision of more Sunderlands. Nearer home Catalinas were at last replacing the venerable Londons with No.202 Squadron at Gibraltar, though the last of the biplanes did not leave until June. Five U-Boats had been sunk by surface forces during March and this was undoubtedly the turning point, though not immediately apparent for the loss rate amongst merchant vessels from submarine attack rose again in April to 43, totalling 249,000 tons. Most of the losses occurred amongst unescorted ships in mid-Atlantic, this ploy being countered to some extent by escorts using refuelling facilities in Iceland. This enabled them to provide convoy protection out to 35 degrees west— more than halfway across. Since mid-March a detachment of No.269 Squadron Hudsons had been operating from Kaldadarnes, and with No.30 Wing set up in Iceland, working under No.15 Group, No.204 Squadron moved from Sullom Voe to Reykjavik on 5 April, and on the 25th No.330 Squadron was formed in Iceland to operate Northrop N3P-B floatplanes purchased by the Norwegian government in exile and flown by Norwegian personnel.

Operational control of Coastal Command was formally taken over by the Admiralty on 15 April, it having been agreed that the Royal Navy would be responsible for the strategic direction of the war at sea regardless of whether sea or air forces were involved. The Royal Navy laid down the tasks and detailed their priority, the AOC-in-C Coastal, through his Group AOC's, being responsible for carrying them out. Aircraft were controlled from the Area Combined HQ except when carrying out close support work, and even then they could be diverted onto other tasks or recalled by the Group HQ. The co-ordination of operations was achieved by the use of a secure

The main plotting board in the Operations Room of the Area Combined Headquarters, Liverpool, 1941. (British Official)

One of the Sunderlands of No.95 Squadron, N9050, undergoing maintenance at Fourah Bay, Freetown, in April 1941 after the long journey from the United Kingdom to West Africa. (Wg Cdr S.G. Baggott via A.S. Thomas)

telephone network connecting the Operations Room at Northwood with the Admiralty submarine tracking room in Whitehall and the four Combined Area HQs where RN and RAF staffs worked side by side. After a briefing on the overall situation by Admiralty staff, convoys and independent ships thought liable to threat would be listed as priority tasks for air cover. When the number and disposition of aircraft for convoy patrol had been agreed, Group Commanders were free to allocate remaining available aircraft to other tasks, both anti-submarine and anti-shipping, their staffs turning the instructions into operations orders transmitted to stations on Form Green signals.* It was a simple but effective system.

The night attack problem remained—but a sol-

*One of a series of coloured forms, each having a particular function and a standard format.

Catalina deliveries began in earnest in April 1941, amongst the first being AH550/DA-L of No.210 Squadron (RP/MAP).

Sunderlands went to Iceland during 1941, including T9072/KG-F of No.204 Squadron, an aircraft which crashed on 5 December 1941 when on No.10 Squadron RAAF strength. (MAP)

ution was at last in sight, for in response to a letter from Air Chief Marshal Bowhill requesting 'bright ideas', circulated around the Command during September 1940, an administrative officer at Northwood, Sqn Ldr H. de Verde Leigh, had suggested the use of a searchlight fitted in the nose or under the belly of the aircraft. The scheme was enthusiastically endorsed by Command staff and it subsequently appeared as the Leigh Light* but despite steady improvement in radar

and in the numbers and quality of available aircraft Coastal Command had still, after 18 months of war, to make a contribution to the defeat of the U-Boat which would finally silence the critics. Valuable lives and ships were undoubtedly being saved as the result of the deterrent effect of aircraft on convoy escort duties, but operations had been largely defensive and

*See Chapter 13.

Wellingtons were early recipients of ASV radar, amongst them the aircraft of No.221 Squadron including W5674/DF-D. (Bristol Aeroplane Co. via J.D. Oughton)

were not destroying U-Boats. Those that had been attacked had rarely been damaged, never mind 'killed', but the specially developed Mk.VIII depth charge was available in quantity at last, and it had also not gone unnoticed that most sightings of U-Boats had been from aircraft engaged on barrier patrols designed to locate surface vessels and not, as might have been expected, whilst on close support to convoys. U-Boats still had to pass through fairly well defined areas on passage to and from the Atlantic, and it was well known that although a submerged submarine could in 1941 travel at about eight knots it quickly exhausted its batteries at this speed, and a more average rate of progress was two to three knots. Even at the lower speed the U-Boat had to surface several times in every 24 hours to recharge the batteries and to ventilate the interior. This information formed the basis of a study which concluded that if a continuous search in an area lying across the transit route and wide enough to cover the distance travelled submerged in 24 hours could be maintained, several detection opportunities would be presented every time a submarine passed through. Indeed, in theory, detection could be made certain if no part of the patrol area was left unobserved for longer than the minimum time required for battery recharging.

In practice, however, visual ranges on surfaced submarines was quite low, and in poor visibility very low, and radar ranges were still not much better, especially in rough weather. The number of aircraft required to maintain a secure search was therefore

high and, of course, there remained for the present the night time difficulties. In May 1941 there were certainly insufficient aircraft for a secure search in the Bay of Biscay or the Iceland/Faeroes gap, but nevertheless it was decided that the plan should be tried. Aircraft allocation for convoy escort was accordingly reduced to a minimum, and the bulk used on patrols in the two main transit areas and for offensive sweeps along the convoy lanes. Concurrently a Newfoundland Escort Force, largely provided by the Canadian Navy, was established and continuous surface escort was henceforth provided for eastbound convoys all the way across the Atlantic, destroyers operating from Iceland and Britain rendezvousing with the convoys in mid-ocean.

The Allies lost 58 ships (325,500 tons) to U-Boats in May which didn't indicate much of an improvement, but half of them were sunk by a small force of six submarines operating off Freetown. Here the Royal Navy and the RAF were weak, only the three Sunderlands of No.95 Squadron being available to cover the whole area until June when No.200 Squadron arrived in the Gambia with Hudsons. A month later two Sunderlands of No.228 Squadron arrived to supplement No.95, their eventful flight from Aboukir, Egypt, having taken over a month.

On 2 June 1941 No.120 Squadron formed at Nutts Corner, near Belfast, with a specific purpose, that of closing the mid-Atlantic gap in air cover using Liberators. It would be several months before the squadron was operational, but at least the conquering

This Catalina, AH567/WQ-P of No.209 Squadron can be seen to be carrying weapons, probably large depth charges, under the wings. AH567 survived until 19 May 1944 when it crashed on take-off whilst being operated by No.413 Squadron. (G.K. Bayly via A.S. Thomas)

A closer view of depth charges under the wing of a Catalina—being loaded at Oban from a bomb scow (a specialist barge) by an exceptionally smart team of armourers. (via B. Robertson)

of the 'gap' was in prospect, and not before time, for the operational strength of the U-Boat force had recently been enhanced by the new Mk.IX ocean-going craft, and the portents were not good.

Since September 1939 crews of Coastal Command had made 233 U-Boat sightings, 164 of which had resulted in an attack. The Command had been credited with one 'kill'* plus two shared with the Royal Navy. A further 25 U-Boats had been assessed as damaged as a result of attack by the Command's aircraft, three of these in conjunction with surface vessel action. It was a pretty dismal story but the Command now had a total of 40 squadrons, most of which had some anti-submarine capability. The recent expansion programme had very nearly reached its target of 15 extra squadrons, improved weapons, equipment and tactics had been introduced, and perhaps most important of all—the decision had been taken to go on the offensive. Most of the credit for the steady development, achieved in the face of great difficulty and heart-breaking set-backs, must go to Air Chief Marshal 'Ginger' Bowhill who had brought the Command from little more than a naval reconnaissance force at the beginning of the war to a position where it was poised to take on the enemy on its own terms. It was at this point, on 14 June 1941, that he handed over to a new AOC-in-C, Air Marshal Sir Philip Joubert.

*Subsequently withdrawn.

CHAPTER 4

War of Attrition– Anti-Shipping Operations 1941-42

DESPITE SET-BACKS for the 'strike' concept, the anti-shipping campaign was gaining momentum when Air Marshal Joubert took command of Coastal Command in June 1941. The 'Channel Stop' had restarted, offensive reconnaissance by single Coastal Command aircraft was being undertaken along enemy occupied coasts from Northern Norway to Western France, and free-lance patrols by Beauforts and Hudsons were scouring the English Channel and North Sea, while No.2 Group, Bomber Command, were keeping up their strong attacks on shipping. The Germans reacted strongly, giving their convoys increased fighter cover and special flak ship escort. To be effective, crews had

to bomb from mast height, and the comparatively slow Blenheims and Hudsons proved very vulnerable in the face of this formidable defence. Between 1 April and 30 June Blenheims of No.2 Group flew over 1,000 sorties against shipping, resulting in 297 attacks and the loss of 36 aircraft, while Coastal aircraft made 143 attacks and lost 52 aircraft, a staggering 36% of those despatched.

Operation *Barbarossa*, Hitler's attack on Russia, started on 22 June 1941, and for UK forces disruption of his transport system soon became a priority. No.16 Group commenced intensive attacks on Channel shipping using Beaufort and Blenheim Squadrons on 27

Hudsons remained the backbone of the anti-shipping reconnaissance force throughout 1941. Here a Mk.V, AM540/QX-G, of No.224 Squadron goes about its business over the North Sea. (RAF Museum)

June, but the rather *ad hoc* control arrangements soon led to disagreement between Air Marshal Peirse, AOC-in-C Bomber Command, and Joubert. A new plan was hammered out giving responsibility for anti-shipping operations between Cherbourg and Texel to Bomber Command, and the rest of the sea areas around the British Isles to Coastal, with the proviso that either Command could call on the other for additional resources when required. The agreement also provided for the 'Channel Stop' to be increased to two-squadron strength and the loan of No.59 Squadron to Bomber Command until re-equipped with Hudsons. In an effort to suppress the flak ships, Fighter Command agreed to help in the Channel area by providing Hurricanes to shoot them up before the Blenheims went into the attack. The new arrangements came into operation almost immediately, the bombers usually operating in groups of three, heavily escorted. Casualties remained high but they had to be accepted in view of the value of the traffic, much of it carrying iron ore.

The close watch on capital ships in Brest harbour was maintained, anxiety levels within the Admiralty and Coastal Command rising sharply on 21 July when photographs revealed that some of the *Scharnhorst's* camouflage had been removed and it appeared that she was preparing to sail. A visual recce was attempted early the next day without positive result, and it was not until midday that a PR sortie confirmed that the ship had disappeared. A thorough search was mounted on the 23rd, and with much relief the ship was located

at La Pallice. During the night No.217 Squadron Beauforts attacked her with Magnum mines (electro-magnetic sea mines converted for land use), and on the 24th Bomber Command laid on a raid. The crews claimed several hits, but she was back in her old berth at Brest two days later. The 'panic' was over for the time being!

The few crews and aircraft left in Britain by No.252 Squadron were absorbed by a newly-formed No.143 Squadron, but subsequent Beaufighter deliveries to Coastal Command were very slow, and only just sufficient to allow No.248 Squadron to start replacing its Blenheim IVFs in July. During August, No.236 Squadron commenced re-equipment, but when the unit was declared operational in November it was not used for maritime operations but for intruder missions over the Brest peninsula! This was due to uncertainty over the Beaufighter's role, for on 2 September Joubert had issued a new directive confirming that anti-shipping offensive operations were still subsidiary to the primary reconnaissance role, and were to be confined to bombing or torpedo attacks on naval units at sea; torpedo attacks on naval units in harbour; and attacks on merchant ships in convoy, none of which could be carried out by Beaufighters.

Meanwhile, Fighter Command had taken over the 'Channel Stop' operation on 9 October, their new Hurricane IIBs, each carrying two 250-lb bombs, proving much less vulnerable than Blenheims for this dangerous work. On 25 November Bomber Command was relieved of all responsibility for anti-shipping

A couple of 'strike' Beaufighter Is of No.248 Squadron at St Eval in September 1941. The unit was one of the 'mobiles' which spent much of the war on detachments around the British Isles and sometimes further afield. (M.C.B. Anderson)

operations, except that of assisting Coastal with the Wilhelmshaven-Cherbourg sector when specially requested. Peirse conceded that anti-shipping operations were not an easy option, especially with Blenheims—a view long acknowledged by the crews!

The Beaufort torpedo bomber force was nominally increased to four squadrons when No.86 relinquished its Blenheims during June, and to six by the end of August when Nos.415 (RCAF) and 489 (RNZAF) Squadrons formed. In practice, however, personnel shortages resulted in Nos. 415 and 489 remaining non-operational and the other Beaufort units concentrating on mine-laying for the rest of the year, there being only a few torpedo-trained crews available to take advantage of a relaxation of the rules which had previously reserved the weapon for ships of over 6,000 tons.

In November anti-shipping work was further diminished by the Admiralty's understandable insistence on increased 'fleet recce' to cover the *Tirpitz* at Trondheim, and the *Scharnhorst*, *Gneisenau* and *Prinz Eugen* at Brest. Hudson squadrons were combed for aircraft fitted with long range tanks and a special Flight was formed on No.220 Squadron at Wick to operate a 'break-out' patrol up north. The Beauforts of No.217 were moved to Thorney Island with a detachment at Manston known as the *Shipping Interception Flight*. The detachment had the only Beauforts with ASV (installation of which had started in September), the Flight being intended for moonless nights and bad weather attacks using radar to find ships, flares to illuminate them and bombs or torpedoes to attack, assisted by 'Hurri-bombers' from No.11 Group, Fighter Command. The plan never really got underway, for after a couple of experimental attacks the Beauforts were withdrawn from Manston in December 1941 because the force could no longer sustain experiments with only Nos.42 and 86 Squadrons up to strength, and No.22 Squadron preparing for posting overseas. It was a further blow to the strike force concept already suffering from the transfer to the Middle East of the equivalent of 24 Beaufighter crews from Nos.143 and 248 Squadrons, as well as many other aircraft 'diversions'.

In view of the serious shortfall in Beaufort and Hudson strengths (the latter about to be made worse by the transfer of 23 crews and aircraft from Nos.53 and 59 squadrons to Singapore), it was proposed that two of the existing Beaufort squadrons and two of the proposed Target 'E' (an expansion scheme) units should be equipped with Hampdens. This aircraft was considered both versatile and reliable, and amongst its

The fourth Beaufort squadron, No.86 Squadron, at North Coates in September 1941. (Fox Photos)

Hudsons of No.320 (Dutch) Squadron in 1941/42 carrying the unit's 'NO' codes and, just visible on the rudders, the Dutch orange triangle. (Cdr H.J.E. van der Kop RNIN via A.S. Thomas)

planned roles was the armed interception of ships carrying iron ore from Bilbao, Spain, to Bordeaux, France, a task outside the range of the Beaufort and for which the Hudson was judged unsuitable. The plan was very firmly turned down by the Air Ministry on the grounds that all available Hampdens were required by Bomber Command, and in desperation Liberators of No.120 Squadron were used to try to cope with these blockade runners. Two attacks were made by Liberators on a total of four ships, but after one aircraft was badly shot up, such operations had to be abandoned.

One way and another the six months between 1 July and 31 December 1941 had been a traumatic time for the anti-shipping forces of Bomber, Fighter and Coastal Commands. No.18 Group units had attacked 160 vessels of which an assessed 15 totalling 34,700 tons were sunk (verified after the war as 16 of 16,024 tons) for the loss of 33 aircraft. In the No.2/16 Group area, 499 ships had been bombed, and 42 totalling 89,400 tons claimed (later verified as 23 of 22,993 tons). Fifty-five bombers, 23 'coastal' aircraft and four fighters were lost, while west of Cherbourg No.19 Group recorded eight aircraft missing in attacks on 36 ships, two of which were claimed. Thus a total of 698 merchant ships were attacked of which 59 were claimed sunk (41 verified) for the loss of 123 aircraft and their crews. The over-estimation in tonnage claimed is not surprising, it being notoriously difficult for even experienced crews to assess results, and aircraft losses of this order ensured that most were newcomers to the role—another reason for the pain-

fully slow build-up of the Command's anti-shipping strength.

On 27 December 1941 British forces carried out a Commando operation on Vaagso, an island midway between Trondheim and Bergen, to destroy installations, capture German troops and embark Norwegian volunteers for Allied service. Hampdens bombed the Vaagso defences to cover the approach of the assault forces, and Beaufighters of No.235 Squadron provided long range fighter cover and were successful in driving off a variety of German aircraft. For some months Hitler had been convinced that the British intended to invade Norway and, against considerable opposition from Admiral Raeder, he advocated that major naval units including the *Scharnhorst* and *Gneisenau*, currently at Brest, should be moved to Norway where they could help defend the country, and would also be less liable to damage from bombing attacks. The raid on Vaagso only served to convince Hitler that Norway was to be the next flashpoint, and he became insistent that the German battleships should be moved north by using the elements of bad weather and surprise to evade British forces. Reluctantly the German air and naval experts agreed to the plan at a meeting on 12 January 1942, six days after the *Gneisenau* had been slightly damaged by Bomber Command for the second time. The Germans made strenuous efforts to disguise preparations for sailing, but with daily air reconnaissance revealing the arrival of torpedo boats, minesweepers and destroyers, the British Admiralty became convinced that a breakout was imminent, issuing a warning on 2 February which correctly

No.415 Squadron worked up at Thorney Island on Beauforts for torpedo operations during the autumn of 1941, their aircraft including L9802/GX-S. (Public Archives of Canada)

assessed the likely German moves, anticipating that the ships would take the short route through the Channel and up the North Sea. Unfortunately the report also suggested that they would attempt a passage through the Strait of Dover at night, and thus would leave Brest in daylight—the reverse of the German intention. The following day Operation *Fuller*, the planned British response, was put into action and stand-by arrangements for additional forces were implemented. These included the strengthening of submarine patrols off Brest, a heightened state of readiness for motor torpedo boat forces at Dover, increased patrols by Coastal Command off Brittany and over the Channel. Some 250 Bomber Command aircraft were also placed on two hours' readiness, though there was little confidence in the

A destructive affair at Wick on 30 December 1941 when Sgt Denley of No.235 Squadron in T3295/LA-S hit Beaufighter LA-O and a Hudson, and then Sgt Cummins in T4725/LA-J ploughed into the wreckage. (No.235 Sqn records)

A snow-covered Bircham Newton during the winter of 1941/42—difficult conditions for work on the Blenheim IV and Hudson of No.500 Squadron. (via A.S. Thomas)

bombers' ability to do more than damage the German battle cruisers, the main hope lying in the small torpedo bomber force, Beauforts of Nos.42, 86 and 217 Squadrons and the Swordfish of 825 Squadron, FAA. No.86 and part of 217 Squadrons were at St Eval, the remainder of 217 still at Thorney Island, while No.42 Squadron were at Leuchars in case the *Tirpitz* sailed from Trondheim.

On the evening of 8 February Joubert issued an appreciation from Coastal Command HQ indicating that a breakout was likely between the 10th and 15th of February, and he ordered No.42 Squadron to fly south to North Coates. It was a remarkably accurate assessment, but the strain of *Fuller* was already beginning to tell on both Bomber and Coastal Command. With only the Hudsons of Nos.224 and 233 squadrons available for the patrols off Brest, Joubert found it increasingly difficult to fulfil the task in the face of bad weather, enemy fighters and repeated ASV failures, while Peirse was unable to keep virtually his entire bomber force at what amounted to 'immediate readiness' indefinitely. On 10 February he reduced the state, keeping 100 aircraft on four hours standby and ordering the rest to stand down. When PRU pilots were unable to cover Brest because of appalling weather the tension increased, but after a nail biting day they got through on the 11th to find all three major units (*Prinz Eugen* was the third) present and no obvious signs of imminent sailing.

The German commander, Vice Admiral Ciliax, had prepared for the dash to Norway very thoroughly, but he also had his share of luck. He had intended to sail

at 19.30 hrs on the 11th, but an air raid delayed him and the force did not form up outside Brest until 22.45 hrs. At that time a Hudson of No.224 Squadron was on the *Stopper* patrol (a barrier across the exits from Brest) and its ASV should have picked up a ship the size of the *Scharnhorst* easily. Unfortunately the aircraft was flying away from the German vessels, and it was not until the last eight minutes of the next sortie that a *Stopper* Hudson came within range of the German force. For reasons unexplained they were not seen. Another patrol, Line South East, a special *Fuller* measure, lay across the path of the German ships, and they crossed it at about 00.50 hrs on the 12th undetected because the ASV in the patrolling Hudson failed and it had returned to base and was not replaced through lack of aircraft. There remained *Habo*, a third patrol flown as a routine measure between Cherbourg and Boulogne. Hudsons of No.233 Squadron maintained this watch, but a forecast of fog over southern airfields caused the aircraft to be recalled early, and so the ships remained undetected. Ground radar stations, primarily the one at Swingate on the cliffs above Dover, began to plot unusual aircraft activity at 08.30 hrs, at first was thought to be an air-sea rescue operation. By 10.20 hrs it was clear that it was a fighter 'umbrella' for ships moving up the Channel at 20–25 knots, an unusual speed for a convoy! Two Spitfires from No. 91 Squadron, the 'Jim Crow' unit, were sent off from Hawkinge to investigate, the pilots sighted the force but in poor visibility failed to identify any of the ships. They were still trying to do so when Gp Capt Victor Beamish, the Station Com-

Beaufort Is of No.42 Squadron en route to the Norwegian coast, 8 February 1942. (via D.R. Francis)

mander at Kenley, and his Wing Leader, Wg Cdr R.F. Boyd, returned from an independent cross-Channel sweep at 11.10 hrs with news of a strong German naval force steaming 'flat-out' up the Channel. The 'panic' was on!

The lateness of the detection completely wrong-footed the British forces. At 11.30 hrs only the six Swordfish at Manston and seven Beauforts at Thorney Island were in a position to attack within two hours, indeed it was essential that the former did so as soon as possible before radar cover was lost. A fighter escort was hastily organized and the Swordfish of 825 Squadron set out on a gallant but hopeless mission, all six aircraft being hacked to pieces and 13 men lost.

Only four of the seven Beauforts at Thorney Island had torpedoes fitted and these aircraft were hurriedly prepared for a rendezvous with fighters over Manston at 13.40 hrs. The timing was impossibly tight and the Beauforts were late, causing the controlling authority to order direct routing to the target for which they gave a new position, course and speed. The Spitfire escort received the message but the Beaufort crews, led by Plt Off T. Carson, did not because the aircraft had been fitted with special R/T equipment for night attacks on Channel shipping. On reaching Manston at 14.00 hrs the Beauforts started circling but the fighters did not appear, so finally Carson and one other crew set off—but to a position calculated on briefing information which had inexplicably given the target as three merchantmen travelling at 8–10 knots. Naturally the crews saw nothing and gained no radar contacts. In the meantime the three Beauforts left at

Thorney were fitted with torpedoes and had taken off. Armed with corrected information, the crews, led by Flt Lt 'Ginger' Finch, found the ships, and while the leader manoeuvred for an attack on the *Gneisenau*, Plt Off T.A. Stewart and Sgt Rout went for the *Prinz Eugen*. All three dropped their torpedoes, but Finch disappeared and the other two were unable to see the results while concentrating on evading enemy flak and fighters. Both aircraft were hit but returned safely. Immediately after this attack two of the original four, flown by Aldridge and Lee, who had landed at Manston after losing Carson, arrived on the scene and got inside the destroyer screen before sighting the *Gneisenau*. They attacked together, dropping their torpedoes from about 1,500 yds. Both were seen running but were lost in the gathering mist.

Of the bomber force, only No.5 Group was at readiness. Frantic efforts were made to mount attacks, the first Bomber Command aircraft getting airborne at 13.30 hrs. 242 aircraft were despatched but most were unable to find the German ships, only 39 claiming to have bombed them, and there were no hits. Fifteen bombers failed to return and another 20 were damaged.

Meanwhile, No.42 Squadron, originally ordered to North Coates on the 10th, had been delayed by snow and 14 Beauforts were actually on the way from Leuchars to Coltishall, a fighter base, when the breakout was discovered. The crews arrived at 11.30 hrs and were told of the 'flap', and that the Mobile Torpedo Servicing Unit ordered over from North Coates had not arrived. Nine of the Beauforts had

Close formation flying by the pilots of three No.59 Squadron Hudsons from North Coates, 1942.
(RP/MAP)

torpedoes already fitted and, led by Sqn Ldr W.H. Cliff, the crews of these aircraft took off at 14.25 hrs, without the weapons having been 'topped up', and headed for Manston where they were ordered to join up with Hudsons (intended for diversionary bombing) and a fighter escort. Arriving over Manston at 14.50 hrs the Beaufort crews found the other aircraft already orbiting and tried to form up behind the Hudsons. But the Hudson crews were equally determined to get behind the Beauforts, and efforts to attract the fighter pilots' attention were unavailing. This chaotic situation, similar to 217 Squadron's experience, lasted for over half-an-hour before Cliff got tired of it and decided to set course, based on information received before leaving Coltishall. As he turned out to sea with his Beauforts in close formation, six of the Hudsons followed but in thick cloud and heavy rain the two formations lost touch.

Both formations found the ships, five Hudsons of No.407 Squadron, RCAF, bombing from heights varying between 400 and 900 ft. They were followed almost immediately by the Beauforts, already down to eight, one crew having nearly attacked a British destroyer by mistake. Flying in appalling weather Cliff suddenly found himself inside the destroyer screen with the *Gneisenau* and *Prinz Eugen* ahead. Two aircraft, flown by Norton and Gee were badly positioned and they elected to turn away and attack from the other side, while Cliff and his wing men, Birchley and Archer, went for the *Gneisenau*, and Dinsdale, Kerr and Dewhurst made for the *Prinz Eugen*. All the crews ran in at heights between 60 and 100 ft, and seven

torpedoes dropped cleanly, the other failing to release. As so often is the case no results were observed—and indeed there was no damage to the ships. Carson and Banning of No.217 Squadron tried again, found the ships, and with the light almost gone made their torpedo runs. Banning's attack looking perfect, but at the last minute the *Gneisenau* turned away and the torpedo slipped harmlessly by!

There remained the aircraft from St Eval. Twelve Beauforts, six manned by No.86 Squadron crews, three by 217, and three by personnel of No.22 Squadron recalled from embarkation leave, took off for Thorney Island shortly before 13.00 hrs. At Thorney the crews were fully briefed, and soon after 16.00 hrs took off for Coltishall where they were to rendezvous with two 42 Squadron aircraft flown by Plt Offs Wilson and R. Manning. Unfortunately the latter were still on the ground when the formation overflew and were unable to contact them in the gathering gloom. Led by Wg Cdr C. Flood, OC No.86 Squadron, who was flying the only ASV-equipped aircraft, the St Eval crews reached the estimated position of the German force without any radar contact. In virtual darkness the formation turned down the expected track, almost immediately coming under fire from minesweepers, and the crews became dispersed and started searching individually. They were unsuccessful and this last attempt at an attack failed as miserably as had all the rest.

No.42 Squadron reassembled at North Coates in readiness for a strike against the ships on the 13th, but following mine damage the ships had diverted into

An encounter with flak by Beaufort II AW375/MW-Y of No.217 Squadron early in 1942 resulted in tail damage. (Bristol Aeroplane Co.)

Kiel and Wilhemshaven during the night. The strike was cancelled, the Beauforts carrying out an offensive sweep off Borkum before returning direct to Leuchars.

The whole affair was a personal triumph for Hitler, proved right in the face of strong opposition from his admirals. It was a tactical success for the German Navy, and an unmitigated shambles as far as the British forces were concerned, though in the long term it could be said to have been a strategic 'victory' for them because it removed the threat posed by the German capital ships lurking in French Biscay ports. A very thorough Court of Inquiry was held and the blame laid firmly on the failure to detect the breakout earlier, though it was conceded that very bad weather was a mitigating factor. There was also insufficient co-ordination between Coastal, Bomber and Fighter Commands—and with the Admiralty. Not mentioned was the excessive security which resulted in personnel at all levels not appreciating the significance of equipment failures or unusual activity, or the need to report them with urgency.

Meanwhile the Air Ministry had suddenly reversed its decision regarding the provision of a Hampden torpedo-bomber force and Nos.415 commenced re-equipment immediately, while 489 found itself with ex-143 Squadron Blenheim IVs, six of which were hastily bombed up on 12 February and crews placed on immediate readiness for action

during the 'Channel Dash' breakout from Brest.

At much the same time the Germans changed tactics with their E-Boats, concentrating on night time mine-laying instead of torpedo attacks on coastal shipping. By mid-February 1942 such operations had reached dangerous proportions, and on 1 March cross-over patrols by ASV-equipped Hudsons were started between East Anglia and Holland with the object of locating, shadowing and illuminating the E-Boats for attack by naval forces or No.16 Group strike aircraft. Code-named *Hoden*, these patrols had little success, however, the E-Boat proving a very slippery customer, extremely hard to detect on the radar of the day.

Efforts to build up the Beaufighter force took yet another knock when No.236 Squadron was stood down in February 1942 and its most experienced crews sent to the Middle East. The rest formed the basis of a new '236' on 14 March for operations in the 'anti-shipping' role from Wattisham, the first rather tentative sorties being flown the next day. No.489 Squadron finally received its Hampdens in March, and on 21 April two complete squadrons, Nos.144 and 455 (RAAF), were transferred from No.5 Group, Bomber Command, to Coastal Command. By the end of the month both were at Leuchars for torpedo bomber training, by which time No.415 Squadron had carried out the first Coastal Hampden

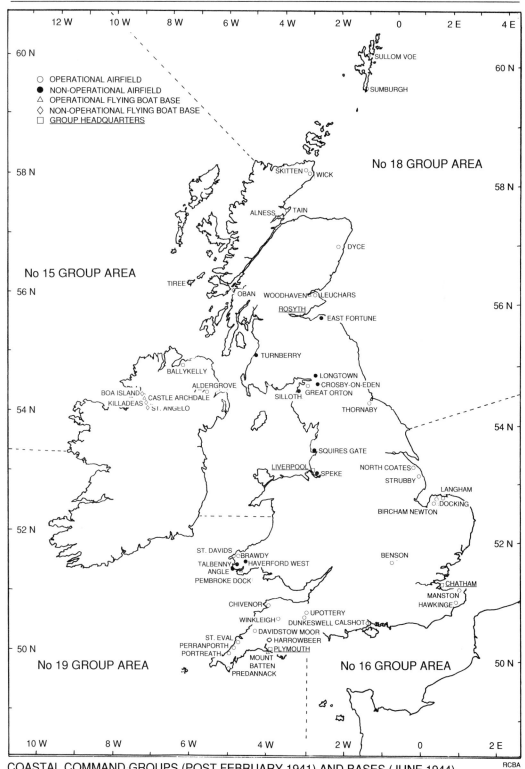

COASTAL COMMAND GROUPS (POST FEBRUARY 1941) AND BASES (JUNE 1944)

RCBA

sorties from St Eval, though the first 'strike' had to wait until the unit moved to Thorney Island, three of the Squadron's aircraft attacking a convoy of six merchantmen escorted by five flak ships off the West Frisian island of Ameland on 29 May. They claimed to have damaged a 6,000 ton ship but lost one Hampden to heavy AA fire. No.489 Squadron was also based at Thorney but had a detachment at St Eval for anti-shipping operations over the Bay of Biscay and was soon in contact with enemy fighters—a very unhealthy occupation!

Unfortunately the increase in Coastal's strength following the introduction of the Hampden was soon diluted by the transfer of No.217 Squadron's Beauforts to the Far East (via the Middle East) in March. This reduced the experienced torpedo bomber force to just two squadrons, Nos.42 and 86, both in No.18 Group, waiting for any move by the remaining operational German capital ships, the *Tirpitz*, *Admiral Sheer*, *Hipper* and the damaged *Prinz Eugen*, all in Norwegian fjords and a threat to Russian convoys.

The Hudson squadrons, helped by the newly arrived Hampdens, bore the brunt of low-level bombing attacks on convoys and independent merchant ships, but though they dramatically increased their operational hours during March/April 1942 results were poor, only two vessels totalling 1,994 tons being claimed as sunk. However, the continual harassment did have its less obvious effect, severe hold-ups being caused while shipments of iron ore from the Kirkenes, Tromso and Narvik areas of Norway awaited the assembly of convoys.

On 6 May No.42 Squadron carried out a sweep of the Skagerrak for the *Prinz Eugen* following reports of a sighting, but within hours the cruiser was relocated in Trondheim harbour. Ten days later reconnaissance aircraft reported the *Lutzow* near the Skaw with a destroyer escort apparently on her way to Norway, and a few hours later a cruiser, undoubtedly the *Prinz Eugen*, and two destroyers were seen heading south-west from Trondheim. All day No.42 were held at readiness for a strike on the *Lutzow*, as soon as the ship came within range, but then another report came in—the *Lutzow* had put about and was steering south. As soon as it was dark the *Lutzow* again turned north and anchored at dawn near Kristiansund, but the ploy had worked for No.42 Squadron had been stood down. Meanwhile, 14 Beauforts of No.86 Squadron had taken off from Sumburgh shortly before midnight and set course for the expected position of the *Prinz Eugen* off Stadlandet. The night was dark, and though the estimate and navigation was good—so good that four of the aircraft were seen by a lookout on the ship—she was not spotted. However, mines dropped by Bomber

Command Hampdens slowed her progress and forced an alteration of course out into the open sea, and at 15.40 hrs on the 17th she was relocated off Karmoy Island.

The AOC-in-C ordered a maximum effort strike using the same pincer action as employed on the *Lutzow* a year earlier. No.42 Squadron were to make for a position 50 nm south of Mandel (southern tip of Norway) and then fly north-west towards Lister, while No.86 made a landfall off Egero Island and turned south-east. Escorted by four Beaufighters of Nos.235 and 248 Squadrons and six Blenheims of No.404 Squadron, RCAF, the 12 Beauforts of No.42, led by Wg Cdr M.F.D. Williams, set off from Leuchars at 18.02 hrs. No.86 Squadron, led by Sqn Ldr T. Hyde, left Wick 11 minutes later, also escorted by four Beaufighters, and with 13 Hudsons of Nos.48 and 608 Squadrons in company. The latter aircraft were acting as decoys and precise timing was intended to bring attackers and quarry all together in the same area at the same time. Williams decided to attack in two waves, 2,000 yards apart, with Sqn Ldr 'Johnny' Dinsdale leading the second one. The Blenheims were to spread out on each beam and make dummy attacks while the Beaufighter crews went in firing cannon to suppress anti-aircraft fire. En route to the landfalls an update of the target position, course and speed was expected from a recce Beaufighter, and it came, but very late because the aircraft had come under attack by Bf109s. The relayed message also included two mistakes—in position and time! As it happened these errors made little difference to No.42 Squadron, it just meant that they came across the ships sooner than expected, but it ruined No.86 Squadron's efforts. In the face of determined fighter attack No.42's Beauforts turned in immediately the ships were sighted, the unexpected position resulting in Dinsdale's formation attacking first, on the starboard bow of the *Eugen*. The Beaufighters swept ahead and almost silenced the destroyers' fire, but the *Prinz Eugen* continued a heavy barrage through which the Beauforts flew. Harried by fighters some crews dropped their torpedoes at extreme range, but others waited agonizingly long seconds— until the ship towered above them. The second formation suffered badly from the flak, the CO and both his wingmen being shot down by the ship's gunners, while the *Prinz Eugen's* captain brilliantly 'conned' all the torpedoes and escaped untouched. Meanwhile No.86 Squadron, in response to the incorrect position report, had turned north from Egero Island accompanied at low level by the Beaufighters. The Hudsons crews, flying at 13,000 ft, saw the ships away to the south but had no way of communicating with the Beaufort force. They bombed, losing one aircraft in the process, and returned to base while the strike force flew vainly on towards Stavanger and its enemy fighters. Bf110s were sighted, but it was a vicious attack by Bf109s that caused the formation to break up, and in the general mêlée four aircraft were shot down, bringing total losses to seven Beauforts and a Beaufighter.

Once again Beaufort torpedo bombers had failed to inflict any damage on a capital ship and it proved to be their last attempt from the United Kingdom, for No.42 Squadron was posted overseas the following month, and No.86 departed in July. It was, however, the first co-ordinated attack on such a target to employ diversionary bombing and anti-flak support for the torpedo bombers—the long discussed 'Strike Wing' concept. Communications had been poor, co-ordination had not been perfect and the results were disappointing. However, the idea had been tried, and appeared to have promise.

Operations against capital ships took the limelight during May and June 1942, but more mundane activities were also taking place off Norway. Hudson, Blenheim and Beaufighter reconnaissance patrols resulted in some 60 sighting reports of convoys or independently routed merchant ships between Kristiansund South and Trondheim, and 13 strikes were made, ten of them by Hudsons of Nos.48 and 608 Squadrons operating from Wick as a Wing. Further south in No.16 Group's region important strikes were

made in the Hook of Holland-Elbe area, employing moonlight or twilight to give some cover. Hudsons from the North Coates Wing (Nos.53 and 59 Squadrons) and Bircham Newton (Nos.320 and 407 Squadrons) carried out most of these attacks, up to 30 aircraft being employed on occasions. The time taken to organize a strike after receipt of the initial sighting report, often as long as five hours, was a problem, but early ASV radar also had its limitations, for it only searched a comparatively small area each side of the aircraft. Any change in the target's course since the report could easily result in abortive sorties, a situation which could only be resolved by improved radar and speedier reaction, both of which were being addressed.

In practice, such attacks were the exception, most operations being armed low-level shipping searches with no specific target, known as *Rovers*. Usually a *Rover* employed three aircraft, but sometimes more, as on 30 May when six Hudsons of No.320 Squadron set off at 23.00 hrs. Two hours later a convoy of seven motor vessels, escorted by eight flak ships was sighted off the Friesian Islands. Hits were claimed on three ships, but heavy flak from the ships and shore batteries plus the attentions of Ju88 night fighters took their toll, two Hudsons failing to return. It took courage and determination to dive through such fire power to release bombs at mast height or lower, for the losses

Beaufort IIA AW350/AW-B of No.42 Squadron departing Leuchars for an attack on the Prinz Eugen, *17 May 1942. (E.F. Birchall via A.S. Thomas)*

A Catalina of No.210 Squadron on Lake Lakhta near Arkangel, North Russia, in July 1942 during the disastrous voyage of Convoy PQ17. In the background is a Beriev MBR-2 patrol flying boat. (British Official)

were frightening, 43 anti-ship aircraft being lost during May alone, though the claims, 12 ships totalling 33,266 tons (ten later confirmed sunk) were an improvement reflecting greater concentration on the 'choke points' off Holland.

Losses escalated during June when a quarter of the aircraft despatched failed to return and, with his resources strained past the limit, Joubert had to order the cessation of low level attacks. The resultant fall in losses was matched by the ineffectiveness of medium

A Hampden TB.I AT255/XA-A of No.489 Squadron turns away to reveal the modified bomb doors required for torpedo carriage—July 1942. (S.B.L. Beattie via R. Haywood)

Hampden TB.I AE201/GX-Q of No.415 Squadron at Thorney Island showing its deepened bomb doors clearly. This aircraft was damaged beyond repair when P2065 caught fire and blew up whilst being refuelled on 26 February 1943. (J.K. Chapman via A.S. Thomas)

level attack, caused partially by the lack of a suitable bombsight, but also by the continuing posting of experienced crews overseas. Attempts to employ Hampdens of No.415 Squadron, RCAF, on armed night patrols in company with radar-equipped Hudsons of No.59 Squadron proved too unwieldy and just as ineffective, and it was clear that the specialized strike force, so long mooted, was essential if the anti-shipping offensive was to be maintained. It was equally clear that the aircraft involved would have to be speedier, more manoeuvrable and have a much bigger punch than the Blenheim, Beaufort or Hampden.

The obvious aircraft was the Beaufighter, already fitted with powerful gun armament, and on which bomb and torpedo trials looked promising. In June No.236 Squadron's Beaufighters were fitted with underwing carriers for two 250-lb HE bombs and, albeit slowly, availability of the aircraft was improving. Re-equipment of No.254 Squadron was commenced in June and No.404 Squadron, RCAF, received the aircraft in September 1942, when the Air Ministry finally agreed with Joubert's submission of the Beaufighter as the Command's principal strike aircraft.

Meanwhile, many miles to the north Operation *Fritham* had taken place. *Fritham* was a series of reconnaissance flights to Spitzbergen which started on 3 May in extreme secrecy and continued until the end

of July 1942. Catalinas of No.210 Squadron were used, two crews landing in Ice Fjord on a couple of occasions to land supplies and take off injured personnel from a naval/army landing party. The original intention had been to set up a flying boat base as well as deny the islands to the Germans, but unfortunately problems experienced by the landing party prevented this and meant that plans to extend the support for Russian convoys already provided by Nos.120 and 210 Squadrons further east by using Spitzbergen had to be abandoned. Instead permission was obtained from the Russians for six Catalinas to operate from Lake Lakhta, near Archangel, to cover convoy PQ17 and over the period 1-4 July No.210 Squadron flew reconnaissance patrols between Iceland and Russia, but without Spitzbergen they could not provide constant cover, a situation made worse by the decision to scatter the convoy.*

At home, Hampden torpedo bombers, unable to operate successfully alongside cannon-firing Beaufighters or with single-seat fighters, were used for limited unescorted operations off the Norwegian coast where convoys were less heavily protected. No.489 Squadron sent a detachment to Wick for this purpose and were soon making their first torpedo attack—against a *Köln* class cruiser lurking in a fjord. It was, however, the disastrous convoy PQ17 that resulted in a major

*See Chapter 6.

challenge for the Hampden crews. It was decided to considerably strengthen British forces in the area before despatching another convoy, and arrangements were made for three PRU Spitfires to be based at Vaenga (Kola Inlet) for visual/photo reconnaissance of fjords and harbours in Northern Norway, Catalinas of No.210 Squadron to go to Grasnaya, principally for the location and shadowing of enemy warships at sea, and for two Coastal Hampden squadrons (Nos.144 and 455) to be detached to Murmansk for torpedo bomber operations—and for an auxiliary aircraft carrier to form part of the escort.

The theoretical range of the Hampden was just 100 nm more than the route mileage from Sumburgh to Afrikanda, where it was intended that the aircraft should refuel before continuing to Vaenga. Thirty-two Hampdens took off during the evening of 4 September for the flight across Northern Norway, Sweden and Russia, the crews without proper maps and only the sketchiest idea of the precise location or appearance of their destination. In view of this and the extremely erratic radio beacons available, it is remarkable that 19 of them landed at Afrikanda as intended. Two landed at Moenchigorsk (escorted by Russian Hurricanes), one followed a Bell Airacobra into Murmachi and another landed at Vaenga. Two force-landed in Russia and one was shot down by a Russian Hurricane pilot having arrived over the Kola Inlet during an air raid. The remaining six were lost en route, three falling to German fighters over Finland, one force-landing and two crashing into mountains, probably due to icing problems.

Operation *Orator* commenced on 11 September when Catalinas of No.210 Squadron started taking off from Invergordon at intervals, spaced to provide continuous reconnaissance over the waters off Northern Norway, before continuing to Lake Lakhta. Each completed an 18-hour sortie which included a box patrol across the expected track of any surface force intending to intercept the convoy. On the same day the Hampden crews started searches from the Russian end, and between 15 and 19 September they escorted PQ18 and also covered the returning QP14 convoy until it was west of 16 degrees east. On 13 September the *Tirpitz* was reported absent from her berth at Trondheim and a major search operation was begun. A combination of communication problems and unserviceability amongst the Catalinas left a gap in the coverage on the 14th, and to contain this a 'reconnaissance in force' by Hampdens was ordered, every available aircraft, 23 in total, being readied. Led by Wg Cdr J. McLaughlin, OC No.144 Squadron, they started taking off at 08.15 hrs and searched from the farthest possible position a German force could have

reached back along the estimated track until the Catalina patrol area was reached. No German ships or submarines were sighted and all the Hampdens were safely back at Vaenga by 15.00 hours. They were immediately prepared for a strike and the crews remained at a high state of readiness for a further three days, for there was still no sign of the *Tirpitz* at Altenfjord or anywhere else.

With PQ18 in harbour *Orator* was complete, and on 1 October the Russians asked for the Spitfires and Hampdens to be handed over to them. This was approved six days later and, after rudimentary instruction for a number of Russian pilots, the detachment embarked in HMS *Argonaut* on 22 October for the journey home. Nothing definite had been gained from this hazardous detachment, but the German capital ships did not try to interfere with the convoys, possibly because of the presence of the Hampdens. However, both U-Boats and the Luftwaffe did attack, the latter sinking eight ships during a furious assault lasting several days, during which they lost 31 torpedo bombers and four other aircraft to AA guns and the Hurricanes of the carrier, HMS *Avenger*.

The 13 Catalinas of No.210 Squadron involved in *Orator* were assisted by a number from No.422 Squadron, RCAF, which had recently converted to the aircraft, and were mainly employed ferrying spares and personnel. None of the Catalinas were lost, but No.210 Squadron had one very unfortunate casualty, Flt Lt D.E. Healy DSO, who had been responsible for many of the successful long range flights to Spitzbergen earlier in the year. Having completed his part in the *Orator* detachment, he was ordered to fly to Spitzbergen to pick up the arctic explorer Lt A.R. Glen, RNVR. Bad weather forced Healy to abandon the flight and return to Murmansk, but when still some 200 nm from the Russian coast the Catalina was intercepted by a Ju88. Shots were exchanged and a number of shells smashed into the cockpit of the Catalina, and Healy was fatally wounded.

Back in the United Kingdom the other Hampden units were active. On 17 September Flg Off A. Mottram and crew of No.489 Squadron found two large merchantmen escorted by five flak ships off Egersund, and managed to torpedo the *Karpfanger* which was later confirmed sunk—the Squadron's first shipping success. No.415 continued its operations off the Dutch coast, and also ran a detachment in the south-west for action between Brest and Cherbourg.

Beaufighter Strike Wing planning went ahead during the autumn of 1942, but considerable work was still required on the torpedo fighter version of the aircraft, and training was hampered by the shortage of practice torpedoes with 'blowing' heads. There was also still the overseas reinforcement 'drain' to contend

The twin Vickers 'K' dorsal gun position of the Hampden. (via A.S. Thomas)

with, but despite all the difficulties the first Strike Wing, consisting of Nos. 143, 236 and 254 Squadrons, was formed at North Coates during November, and the first attempt at a combined strike was made on 20th by Nos.236 and 254 Squadrons on a convoy. Led by Wg Cdr H.D. Fraser, OC No.236, 25 Beaufighters, nine carrying torpedoes, took off for an attack on a convoy off the Dutch coast. After fruitlessly circling Coltishall where they were supposed to meet their fighter escort, the formation left without them and four of the anti-flak aircraft which missed the departure signal. The attack was a shambles, bad weather and inexperience resulting in a lack of cohesion, and the loss of three aircraft, one to fighters, the others to flak. Seven more were damaged, two of which crash-landed at base. One tug was destroyed. Joubert, bitterly disappointed, immediately withdrew the Wing from operations for intensive training in the tactics needed to make a success of what was becoming widely recognized as a complex business requiring precise co-ordination and experience, it being essential for the flak-suppressors to attack just prior to the strike aircraft.

Formation of the other Strike wings was delayed, the squadrons, which included Nos.144 and 455 equipped with replacement Hampdens, continued operations independently. Two of the 'ex-Russia' crews of No.144 Squadron were lost during an attack on

two heavily-escorted merchantmen on 13 December, but a third aircraft flown by F/Sgt J.W. King torpedoed the *Theano*, which subsequently sank. Successes were few, however, and it was with relief that the Squadron re-armed with Beaufighter VIs in January 1943, handing over most of its Hampdens to No.455 Squadron, and preparing for the delayed formation of the Wick Strike Wing.

In addition to continued imports of iron ore from Sweden and Spain the Germans developed trade with their Japanese allies during 1942. The latter had access to commodities vital for German war production, notably rubber, tin and edible oils, which were exchanged for precision instruments, tools and sample equipment. Chosen for their speed and varied appearance a fleet of some 24 fast modern freighters was built up for the Japanese trade, and by travelling well clear of recognized shipping routes and Allied air bases, their captains had some initial success avoiding both surface and air patrols during their voyages to and from Biscay ports. With increasing strength of the air patrols over the Bay, however, their chances of reaching port undetected decreased, the first sighting being made on 20 April 1942 when a *Fujiyama*-class vessel of 6,200 tons was located off the coast of north-west Spain. It was not attacked, and the 6,400 ton *Münster*-class freighter intercepted off Spain on 15 May also survived and reached Bordeaux safely, these

No.144 Squadron aircrew at Leuchars during 1942 prior to detachment to Vaenga, North Russia, in September. (W.D. Barrett via C. Bowyer)

well-armed and well-manned ships proving just as difficult to deal with as iron ore carriers.

On 19 August the SS *Corunna*, a tanker of 12,000 tons, was sighted and it was decided to make a determined effort to sink it, using Lancasters of No.61 Squadron, a Bomber Command unit currently on detachment to No.19 Group. The crew of the first aircraft, captained by Flg Off A.L. Searby, apparently found the ship but failed to return, Sqn Ldr G.E. Weston bombed it but missed, and F/Sgt C.P. Shriner's crew also attacked it before going 'missing'. F/Sgt N.E. Turner and crew claimed to have hit the vessel, but F/Sgt G.E. Dale was driven off by accurate flak and F/Sgt O. Haynes and crew failed to return from the final sortie of the day. It was not an auspicious start, compounded by failure to relocate the vessel during sorties by both Nos.50 and 61 Squadrons during the next two days. *Corunna* reached port safely and No.50 Squadron returned to Swinderby and No.61 to Syerston. The latter had flown 96 sorties totalling 878 hours during its six weeks with Coastal Command—and had sunk one U-Boat.* No doubt 'Bomber' Harris thought that these figures supported his view that such detachments were not 'cost-effective', though in fact they were statistically pretty good. However, it was not short term detachments of bomber-trained crews that Joubert wanted but more long-range aircraft flown by maritime-trained personnel. The roles were completely

different—a fact little understood outside the Command.

'Heavies' used over the Bay for anti-shipping patrols during the summer of 1942 even included Sunderlands and Catalinas on occasions, though the damage they caused to two ships was little recompense for the losses experienced. Closer to France No.612 Squadron's Whitleys were used for target indicating and bombing of tankers in and around the Cherbourg and Le Havre areas—a dangerous occupation but one which succeeded in sinking the *Soglint* in harbour on 13 September. The Germans certainly thought blockade running was well worth the risk, for during October six such vessels sailed from Biscay ports and five ultimately reached their destination. It was obvious that increased efforts would have to be made to stop the trade, the key being closer air/sea co-operation. A scheme enabling aircraft to work with Vice Admiral Barry's submarines patrolling off the north coast of Spain was evolved and had some success though it was still difficult to predict the arrival of inbound vessels in the Bay, and outbound they always took full advantage of long dark autumn/winter nights and bad weather. Allied forces had better luck with the five 'blockade busters' which started out during November/December, for only one arrived in the Far East, and the fortunes of inbound vessels were

*See Chapter 5.

North Front, Gibraltar, at the time of Operation Torch, October 1942. At full stretch over 600 aircraft were accommodated! (Author's collection)

similarly varied. The *Tannenfels* (5,567 tons), *Dresden* (7,840 tons) and *Kulmerland* (7,363 tons) were all sighted and identified—and the latter was subjected to sustained attack by aircraft of Nos.59, 304, 311, 502 Squadrons and No.10 OTU as she approached the Gironde estuary early in November. In total twelve of the 15 ships which ran the blockade during 1942 were intercepted by aircraft, but not one was sunk.

Anti-shipping operations of all types during the year, by Bomber, Fighter and Coastal Commands, proved disappointing statistically. Forty-two ships, totalling 61,000 tons, were assessed sunk for the loss of 251 aircraft—which cannot be considered a good return. However, there were what Joubert called 'hidden assets', primarily that of keeping the enemy's sea supply lines under pressure as a necessary adjunct to attacks on land communications. Additionally, the Germans were forced to protect their ships with ever increasing numbers of guns, fighter aircraft and escort ships—all of which they would have liked to have employed elsewhere.

Ironically, New Year's Day 1943 brought a fillip for Joubert and his hard-pressed anti-shipping force. The *Rhakotis*, a 7,000 ton freighter, was sighted some 130 miles NW of Cape Finisterre by the crews of two No.502 Squadron Whitleys carrying out a night parallel track search. Flg Off A. Hodgson stayed on the scene to shadow, and subsequently 'home in', a Sunderland of No.10 Squadron, RAAF. In turn the flying boat crew directed the cruiser HMS *Scylla* onto the target which she sank by gunfire—a first class example of air-sea co-operation. The British also made another attempt to sink or badly damage the *Scharnhorst* and *Prinz Eugen* on 25 January using Beaufighter and Hampden torpedo bombers, but it was abortive and Joubert decided that such attacks on capital ships were pointless. He directed that the torpedo bomber force, which was progressively becoming an all-Beaufighter organization, should concentrate on harassing German convoys, a move not altogether appreciated by the crews who were keen to take every opportunity to prove their worth, and would tackle anything. Indeed a No.455 Squadron Hampden crew even had a go at a U-Boat on 27 January, but unfortunately the torpedo was set too deep to have a chance against a surfaced submarine.

Air Chief Marshal Sir Philip Joubert left Coastal Command on 5 February under an undeserved cloud and before it was obvious that the anti-shipping force had turned the corner and was poised for success. But that is hindsight and a story detailed in Chapter 6.

CHAPTER 5

The Atlantic Gap– Anti-Submarine Operations 1941-42

AIR MARSHAL SIR Philip Joubert de la Ferte was no stranger to Coastal Command when he assumed command on 14 June 1941, for he had already spent a year at the helm during 1936/37. Probably more important, however, he was also a radio/radar expert for with the development of new submarine detection and location equipment accelerating it was vital that the right choices were made, and the correct tactics evolved. For this task the new AOC-in-C was ideally suited.

By mid-1941 just over half of the aircraft in the Command were fitted with ASV Mk.I or II, but reliability was still poor and effective range limited— so limited that visual lookouts on the submarine usually saw an aircraft before its crew obtained a radar contact. At night, even if contact was made, the submarine was largely immune, a problem being addressed, when Joubert arrived at Northwood, by the Leigh Light which had already been successfully demonstrated,* and he started badly by ordering suspension of work on it in favour of the Helmore Light. The latter, many more times more powerful, had been developed for night illumination of enemy bombers and required the use of heavy batteries which would have seriously affected the weapon-carrying capability of anti-submarine aircraft. Worse still it could not be 'steered', so if the submarine was not directly ahead it would not be seen, nor could it be moved in elevation—essential if the target was to be held in the beam as the aircraft got closer to the 'on top' position. After two months, the new AOC-in-C finally accepted that the Helmore Light was fundamentally flawed, the Leigh Light was immediately resurrected, and after several months spent refining the device it went into production, the first deliveries being made early in 1942.

Experiments with an airborne magnetic detector were also made, but it proved too insensitive, and it was the development of the so-called centrimetric ASV radar which showed most promise and which Joubert considered vital because he feared, rightly, that the Germans would in time produce a receiver which could detect the 1.5 metre wavelength transmissions of ASV MK.I and II. Less technical, but in their way just as important, were camouflage experiments designed to make maritime aircraft less conspicuous. The result was an instruction, issued in August 1941, to paint all operational anti-submarine aircraft white on the undersides and grey on top—just like a herring gull!

At the end of June 1941, with the force increases authorized at the beginning of the year completed, the operational strength of Coastal's anti-submarine component averaged 80 Hudsons, 40 Whitleys, 20 Wellingtons with effective ranges of 250, 310 and 330 nm respectively, 17 Sunderlands with a range of 430 miles and 36 Catalinas which could operate out to 600 miles. It was a force still sadly lacking in long range aircraft, but the recently agreed policy decision to go on the offensive was maintained by Joubert, his intention being to maintain 'barrier' patrols using the shorter range aircraft, Sunderlands on convoy escort, and to reserve Catalinas for 'distant support' operations.

Unfortunately Coastal Command's plans were upset almost immediately, for although the movements of U-Boats were usually known to the British Admiralty, following the partial breaking of the German Naval Code, the number of enemy submarines in the Atlantic was increasing† and all convoys were under direct threat or being shadowed. Sunderland strength, con-

*See Chapter 13.
†63 Operational, 93 in training, and a commissioning rate of 20 a month.

Northrop N3PB floatplanes, originally ordered by the Norwegian government, started operations from Corbett Camp near Reykjavik, Iceland, in June 1941 as No.330 Squadron, RAF, but with Norwegian crews. These aircraft were not fully replaced until June 1943! (British Official)

stantly 'haemorrhaged' by diversion of aircraft to fulfil overseas reinforcement, carriage of urgent freight/VIPs,* and losses from enemy action and accidents, was inadequate to cope and Catalinas had to be used for much of the direct convoy support. The brunt of the offensive patrol work, therefore, fell on Whitleys and Wellingtons, which meant that it was limited to regular sweeps and patrols over the Bay of

Biscay, and the transit route between Scotland and Iceland. The effectiveness of this pressure was soon apparent in the number of increased sightings and attacks which disrupted U-Boat operations because

*A plan to use No.119 Squadron (reformed from G Flight in March 1941) as a special communications squadron operating flying boats was agreed but never properly implemented.

On 27 August 1941 the U-570 surrendered in mid-Atlantic to Sqn Ldr J.H. Thompson and his No.269 Squadron Hudson crew—an almost unique event. This photo of the U-Boat was taken from Catalina AH553 during the successful operation mounted to take the vessel and crew captive. (P. Colyer)

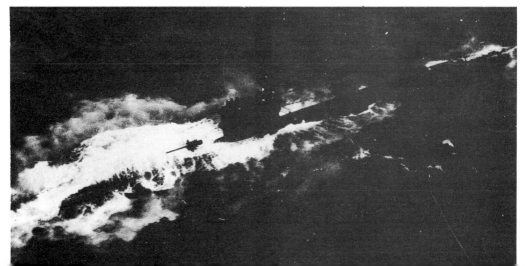

A Catalina of No.413 Squadron coded QL-R on detachment at Woodhaven on the Tay. (Sqn Ldr Hyman via A.S. Thomas)

captains were forced to submerge which slowed their progress, shortened the time on patrol and generally harassed them.

In June 1941 German submarines sank 61 ships totalling 310,000 tons in the Atlantic, but in July came a dramatic reduction to 22 ships and 94,200 tons. In some circles it was felt that the re-organization of the patrols provided the complete answer, though the continued lack of Coastal Command success in 'killing' submarines remained a worry. Trials had shown that unless a 'stick', ideally of six DCs, was laid across the submarine at an angle of about 30 degrees to the track the chances of destroying it were slim, and standardized attack procedures were issued in July. There was no immediate upsurge in the success rate, but there was undisguised relief when the crew of a No.209 Squadron Catalina shared in the destruction of U-452 (Type VIIB) some 220 nm WNW of the Butt of Lewis, followed two days later by high drama. Early on 27 August 1941 Sgt Mitchell and his No.269 Squadron crew had set out on an anti-submarine sweep south of their Icelandic base, and at 06.40 hrs the tell-tale swirl and wake of a diving U-Boat was glimpsed through a rain squall. The Hudson's crew reported the sighting and set up a small area square search, being rewarded 50 minutes later with a surfaced submarine. The pilot attacked from 100 ft, but the four DCs 'hung up' (i.e. did not release) and the U-Boat dived to safety. Other aircraft were soon on the scene, and at 10.50 hrs, over four hours after the original sighting, Sqn Ldr J.H. Thompson's crew (also of No.269 Squadron) saw the

U-Boat in the act of surfacing. The Hudson was immediately turned into the attack and four DCs were released in a 'stick' across the now fast disappearing submarine. Two minutes later it reappeared and crew members were seen on the deck. A burst of fire from the Hudson's turret forced them back into the conning tower and a white flag was waved. Thompson radioed for help, continuing to circle his 'prize' until a Catalina of No.209 Squadron arrived. Shortly after midnight an armed trawler reached the scene but heavy seas prevented a boarding party taking possession and it was not until the following afternoon that the submarine crew were taken prisoner and the vessel was put under tow. It transpired that the depth charges had extinguished the lights and damaged the batteries starting a chlorine discharge, causing some of the inexperienced crew to demand surrender, and the captain had acceded. This surrender of a submarine to the crew of an aircraft was not unique, but it was the first time that it was subsequently captured. U-570 (Type VIIC) later became HMS *Graph* of the Royal Navy.

The U-Boat fleet sank 23 ships of 80,300 tons during August for the loss of three submarines, but in September the toll rose to 53 ships of 202,800 tons, mainly the result of major battles around Convoys SL-97, HG-73 and SC-42, the latter losing 20 cargo ships and one escort. It was notable that only three of the ships were torpedoed within 350 miles of maritime air bases, an indication of the value of aircraft in the deterrent role, and of the desperate need for longer range types. Unfortunately the supply

Bristling with ASV Mk.II aerials, Whitley VII Z6633/WL-G of No.612 Squadron awaits its next sortie. (Aeroplane)

position of the 'long-legged' Liberator remained unsatisfactory. As already outlined,* it had been decided late in March 1941 to reform No.120 Squadron with an establishment of nine Liberators, and at the end of June 20 aircraft had been allocated to Coastal Command (allowing for initial establishment and wastage). Unfortunately this number was almost immediately reduced to 12, of which three were loaned for Atlantic ferry duties, and to make things worse, delivery of those still allocated to No.120 Squadron was desperately slow and the first operational patrol from Nutts Corner could not be made until 20 September.

Meanwhile, the Command's strength in the north had been weakened by the move in stages of No.204 Squadron from Iceland to Bathurst, Gambia, where it joined Nos.95, 200 and a detachment of No.228 Squadron. This steady increase in the strength of anti-submarine forces in West Africa, combined with re-routeing of ships, and the Royal Navy's success in dealing with U-Boat supply ships, had an immediate effect, just two ships being sunk within 600 miles of the African coast during July-September. In September the remnants of No.228 Squadron returned to the United Kingdom to reform with Sunderlands, and the remaining units in the Gambia left Coastal Command on 22 October 1941 when the AHQ was handed over to West Africa Command.

The start of Operation *Barbarossa*, the German attack on Soviet Russia four months earlier (22 June), had little immediate effect on the Atlantic war, but changes in the attitude of the Americans certainly did.

Early in 1941 they had decided that it was pointless sending aid to Britain unless it got there, so their ships and aircraft began searching for German and Italian vessels in the Western Atlantic and reporting them in plain language signals, a procedure very helpful to the British and Canadians. In July, American forces took over the defence of Iceland and on 11 September President Roosevelt announced that United States forces would not merely report the presence of Axis raiders and submarines, but would also attack them. Four days later Congress amended the Neutrality Act to allow American vessels to carry war materials to Britain and the Commonwealth, and by the end of the month the US Navy was escorting convoys two-thirds of the way across the Atlantic. In the meantime, despite the parlous state of British supplies and production, the first convoy carrying war materials to Russia sailed from Britain on 21 August. It took a route west of Iceland then turned east to steer as far north of Norway as polar ice and Spitzbergen would allow, before going south to Archangel and Murmansk. Over the first part of the route the convoy was supported by Nos.269 and 330 (Norwegian) Squadrons, but from 150 miles east of Iceland the ships were on their own, but PQ1 and its immediate successors suffered no losses, the Germans making little attempt to interfere, apparently believing that there would be a rapid collapse of Russian resistance regardless of such support—a view that was to change.

*See Chapter 3.

Sunderland II W3981/ZM-W of No.201 Squadron, 28 October 1941. The installation of ASV Mk.II is now almost universal. (No.201 Sqn records)

Losses to U-Boats were again heavy in October, despite the increasing resources provided by the Americans. This was primarily due to the number of submarines available, for the Germans now had 198, of which 80 were operational, half of them in the Atlantic at any one time. It was notable, however, that this large number was sinking fewer ships than was achieved by the nine U-Boats at sea during the autumn of 1940. Much of the credit for this was due to improved convoy procedures, evasive routeing and the strengthened and much more expert surface forces. But, despite Coastal's continued inability to destroy U-Boats* the Command was helping significantly by forcing Doenitz's submarines to operate almost exclusively in mid-Atlantic outside the range of most aircraft. This in itself meant that each U-Boat was less effective than in earlier months, for they received less help from Fw200 Condors and had a much larger area of sea to search for convoys.

The Command's attempts to close this mid-Atlantic gap suffered another reverse in October when three more Liberators were transferred to ferrying duties, flying crews back across the Atlantic to pick up another aircraft. The AOC-in-C even had to fight off, with Admiralty help, an Air Ministry proposal to transfer the Coastal Whitley and Wellington force to Bomber Command—a situation which now seems almost inconceivable. It reflects ignorance of the Command's activities at the highest level, but also

indicates the constant juggling of resources which went on during 1941 in often mistaken efforts to make the best use of what was available. Conscious that the only way to stop such sniping at his Command's strength was to 'kill' submarines as well as find them, Joubert redoubled his efforts to obtain heavier and more lethal anti-submarine bombs, better bombsights and depth charge pistols.

In October No.19 Group's operations over the Bay of Biscay were strengthened by the move of No.209 Squadron's Catalinas to Pembroke Dock, and of a Hudson squadron, No.53, to St Eval. The latter unit had spent the early part of 1941 at St Eval on anti-shipping work with Blenheims but had been re-equipped with Hudsons, and from August operated a detachment there on anti-submarine duties. The detachment was now brought up to full squadron strength and the Hudsons were soon engaged in Biscay patrols which during November brought them into combat with Fw200 Condors and He115 floatplanes as well as U-Boats.

Allied shipping losses in November were the lowest since the beginning of the war, U-Boats only sinking 13 ships of 62,200 tons in the Atlantic. Unfortunately, this was due more to the diversion of German

*In 245 attacks to 30 September 1941 aircraft had sunk one, captured one, destroyed three in co-operation with surface craft, and damaged about a dozen.

Catalina 1 Z2146/BN-W of No.240 Squadron lifts off Lough Erne in a shower of spray, 1942.
(No.240 Sqn records via P.H.T. Green)

submarines to the Mediterranean and to bad weather than Allied counter measures. Eighteen U-Boats got through the Straits of Gibraltar unscathed, though five were sunk en route and six were so damaged that they had to abandon the attempt. One of the losses, U-206 (Type VIIC), was the victim of Flg Off R.W.G. Holdsworth and his No.502 Squadron crew carrying out a sweep over the Bay on the last day of the month. A *Special Equipment* (i.e. radar) contact turned into a visual sighting on a crash diving submarine and a stick of three DCs across track ahead of the 'swirl' produced Coastal Command's first confirmed unaided 'kill'. The German presence in the 'Med' was soon felt,—HMS *Barham* and the aircraft carrier *Ark Royal* being early victims, but many of the latter's aircraft successfully diverted to Gibraltar, the resultant strengthening of the anti-submarine forces on the 'Rock' being very welcome. Flying from North Front airfield as 812 Squadron the *Ark's* ASV-equipped Swordfish proved very effective in the Straits, and on 21 December achieved the very first successful night attack on a submarine when the U-451 was sunk.

Earlier in the month more permanent strengthening of the forces on Gibraltar had been achieved by sending a detachment—of ten Hudsons from No.233 Squadron—to North Front. At the same time No.200 Group was reformed as RAF Gibraltar, an organization directly responsible to Coastal Command, and a joint Area Combined Headquarters was set up to improve liaison with the Royal Navy. The Hudson's first task was coverage of convoy HG76, it being known that several U-Boats were lying in wait for the 32 merchant ships. Under a strong escort, which included the auxiliary carrier *Audacity*, the ships left Gibraltar late on 14 December bound for Britain. As soon as they entered the Straits the U-Boats made contact, but during the night were beaten off repeatedly by Gibraltar's Swordfish. At 08.15 hrs on the 15th the Hudsons took over, helped rather unconventionally by anti-submarine patrols by *Audacity's* Martlets. As the distance from Gibraltar increased, the Catalinas of No.202 replaced the Hudsons and so successful was the escort in keeping them submerged that the U-Boats lost contact. A day later a Fw200 Condor re-established contact, and during the night of the 16/17th the U-Boats regrouped, and nine of them closed in. Throughout four days of almost continuous attack the escorts, including aircraft from *Audacity*, fiercely protected their charges, destroying four U-Boats and two Fw200 Condors, but could not prevent the loss of two merchant ships, a destroyer and the *Audacity* herself. On 22 December HG76 was met by a Liberator of No.120 Squadron, 750 nm from Nutts Corner. The crew of the aircraft immediately chased off a shadowing Condor, and two hours later attacked a U-Boat before having to depart. After a break of three hours, another Liberator arrived on the scene and during its escort to its 'prudent limit of endurance'(PLE), the crew forced three U-Boats to 'crash-dive', all of them breaking off the engagement. The next day the convoy came under continuous cover from No.15 Group bases and there were no further losses—another striking example of the effectiveness of air support, though yet again largely in the defensive role.

U-Boats operating off Greenland were also tackled, but the task proved very difficult, it being virtually impossible, because of unpredictable weather, to carry out regular landplane sorties from the only available airfield, *Bluie West One*, or flying boat missions from exposed anchorages around the coast.

Shipping losses in December soared to 285, a tonnage of 583,700 tons, but this staggering total over 430,000 tons was sunk in the Pacific, the Japanese having attacked American naval bases without warning on the 7th. Formal declaration of war followed the initial attack within hours, and by the 12th both Germany and Italy were also at war with the USA, and therefore free to attack American shipping wherever it might be. In the Atlantic area the increasing tendency for U-Boat commander's to make use of long winter nights to travel on the surface through the transit areas was the current over-riding concern. Attempts to combat this by increasing night patrols using moonlight, or delayed action flares in conjunction with ASV having proved disappointing, and hopes were concentrated on the Leigh Light (LL). Unfortunately production deliveries planned for January 1942 were delayed, and to make matters worse the Air Ministry ordered the transfer of No.221 Squadron, earmarked as the first unit, to the Middle East. It was decided instead to attach a Flight of LL Wellingtons to the Coastal Command Development Unit, No.1417 (Searchlight) Flight being officially established on 21 February for the purpose. This disappointingly slow progress was matched by the anti-submarine weapon situation. The poor lethal range of the standard 250-lb Amatol-filled depth charge has already been mentioned—the 450-lb AS bomb introduced for carriage by the larger aircraft suffered from a different problem, having to be dropped from a minimum of 600 ft to be effective, a height from which it was very difficult to 'eyeball' a straddle of the target and yet no suitable bombsight was available! Trials with a 250-lb Torpex-filled depth charge were promising, indicating increased lethal ranges, but the explosive was in short supply, and with aircraft attacks producing such poor results the weapon was not given priority—a typical 'Catch 22' situation.

With the USA now officially a combatant, Doenitz despatched six of his large 740-ton U-Boats to the American eastern seaboard for Operation *Paukenschlag* (*Drum Roll*). They arrived during the second week of January 1942, and with the Americans still completely disorganized, German U-Boat commanders sank ships almost at will. Such easy pickings encouraged him to order more U-Boats across the Atlantic, and by the end of the month there were 20 operating in the American coastal area, with another five in transit to the Caribbean. In the first three weeks of *Paukenschlag* 40 ships totalling 230,000 tons were sunk, for despite warnings of the submarine presence ships still sailed independently with lights on at night; lighthouses and buoys were still lit; and many merchant ships continued to transmit their position in clear language. Reluctance to institute any form of 'blackout' along the coast meant that night-time targets were presented in silhouette, and the US Navy refused to take any advice on trade protection offered by the British, insisting on operating their destroyer patrols regularly, and therefore predictably. It was a submariner's paradise, and the result a massacre—but things could actually have been worse had it not been for one of Hitler's premonitions. He had became so convinced that an invasion of Norway was imminent that he insisted on 24 U-Boats being retained in the area for such an eventuality, and they were left largely idle except for an attempt to destroy convoy PQ8 in mid-January which was partially successful, a destroyer and a merchantman being sunk—the first casualties suffered by a Russian convoy.

Meanwhile, the low level of U-Boat sightings in the transit areas convinced both the Admiralty and Coastal Command staffs that patrol patterns had to be altered and the number increased. The latter could not be achieved without more aircraft, and the Admiralty took the opportunity to re-state their requirements during a Defence Committee discussion held in February 1942 on a new policy for Bomber Command. In essence the Admiralty had no objection to the intended switch to area bombing by ever-increasing numbers of aircraft, providing it was not at the expense of naval requirements for long range general reconnaissance over both the Atlantic and Indian Oceans. In essence these requirements meant the immediate transfer of six squadrons of Wellingtons, or their equivalent, from Bomber to Coastal Command, and in the longer term the provision of 81 Fortress/Liberator aircraft.* Joubert went further, pointing out that the loss rate of merchant shipping was such that Britain would not survive another year if it was not cut drastically. He stated flatly that more long range aircraft were required immediately and that if Liberators could not be supplied then Lancasters would have to be provided regardless of the effect on the bomber offensive. A

*In part to replace the three Catalina squadrons the Admiralty wanted moving to the Indian Ocean.

The customers—a British convoy in mid-Atlantic, 1942. (No.120 Squadron records)

week later Air Marshal A.T. Harris took over Bomber Command and, his forthright views being already well-known, it was obvious that no such transfers would be made without a fight! Indeed all Joubert got from the Air Ministry in reply was a proposal to compensate Coastal for the withdrawal of Catalinas for the Far east by a transfer of Whitleys until such time as forthcoming deliveries restored the Command's Catalina strength to 45.

The submarine campaign off the United States seaboard continued during February, when it was also extended into the Caribbean. On the 16th U-Boats shelled oil installations on Aruba Island, a Dutch dependency off the coast of Venezuela, and torpedoed seven tankers in the area. Their efforts were intensified during March when 95 ships totalling 534,000 tons were sunk in Atlantic and Caribbean waters, 46 of them despatched by U-Boats operating at long range. A very ominous development was the sailing of the first 'milch cow' (tanker) submarine at the end of the

A Leigh Light Wellington VIII HX379/WN-A of No.172 Squadron. The light is mounted in the retracted cupola under the fuselage. (RAF Museum)

month, the plan being to refuel and rearm the larger long-range U-Boats at sea, effectively doubling their time on station in the Western Atlantic or off Freetown. It was a plan kept secret for some time following the addition of an extra 'wheel' to the U-Boat's *Enigma* code machine in February.

Many of the losses off the Americas were large tankers, which finally forced a partial convoying system to be adopted. This started on 1 April and gradually became more effective, the only easy pickings for the 18 U-Boats in the area during May being off the coast of Florida where almost unbelievably the shore lights still remained on at night!

By the Spring of 1942 the tactical study of anti-submarine operations put in train by Joubert had been completed and revised plans for coverage of the submarine transit areas agreed. The Bay of Biscay was to be covered by aircraft flying standardized patrols fanning out from the Scilly Isles over both inner and outer parts of the Bay, while the northern transit route between the Shetlands and Faeroes was to be spanned by a series of rectangular boxes within which Nos.15 and 18 Group aircraft would carry out cross-over patrols. At first, shortage of aircraft again prevented full implementation of the plan, but during April Nos.58 and 311 (Czech) Squadrons were transferred from Bomber to Coastal, commencing operations with Whitleys and Wellingtons respectively. Night patrol hours rose rapidly but the results were disappointing, only one sighting and attack resulting from the increased effort during April, and no sightings at all in May.

More transfers occurred during May when No.304 (Polish) Squadron joined No.15 Group for Wellington AS operations from Tiree, and Whitleys of Nos.51 and 77 Squadrons commenced a six-month loan for Bay of Biscay 'sweeps' from Chivenor. It took time for these units to gain expertise in this new and very different role, but there was a perceptible improvement in both sightings and attacks during June, particularly in the Bay.

Up to this point 'Bomber' Harris had managed to minimize the effect on his Command of these forced transfers by nominating his older and less effective aircraft, but the need for longer range aircraft to supplement No.120 Squadron resulted in a direct order from the Air Ministry to detach six Lancasters of No.44 Squadron to Coastal Command. They arrived at Nutts Corner, near Belfast, on 11 June and, accompanied by additional crewmen provided by the resident 220 Squadron, started patrols the following day. On the 15th a surfaced submarine was attacked with depth charges without effect, but the next day Flt Lt T.P.C. Barlow DFC, and crew attacked another which appeared to sink. It was actually 'crash-diving'.

The Squadron returned to Waddington on 6 July after having flown a total of 61 hours on maritime operations.

Torpex-filled DCs (30% more powerful than Amatol) set to detonate at an ideal 25 ft below the surface, were now generally available, and so were rear facing cameras to record the results of attacks. Progress with the Leigh Light was also being made, though by May 1942 there were still only five aircraft operational with No.172 Squadron at Chivenor.* Anxious to score a success, Joubert scrapped his plans to wait until he could obtain maximum surprise by 'swamping the Bay with Leigh Lights' and on the night of 3/4 June ordered the Squadron to commence operations. They managed four patrols, during which the crews had no difficulty in illuminating and identifying fishing boats off ASV homings, but only one was lucky enough to find a submarine—or rather two sailing in company! The pilot, Sqn Ldr J.H. Greswell, had no time to line up for an attack because the aircraft was practically overhead when the first submarine was sighted, and much higher than the 250 ft intended, the forecast pressure being wrong by at least 3 millibars (approx 100 ft). Greswell had hastily reset the altimeter sub-scale and started to turn away when he was amazed to see recognition signals being fired. After a moment of doubt—could it be British?—he decided to attack and closed in again. At three quarters of a mile the co-pilot, Flg Off A.W.R. Trigg, 'struck' the Leigh Light, brought the beam up slowly and there was the submarine. Greswell eased the Wellington down to 50 ft and releasing his four 250-lb DCs achieved a good straddle on the 1,076 ton Italian submarine *Luigi Torelli*. The submarine suffered damage to her steering gear and compass system, and her captain had to make for port on the surface. Two days later attacks by two Sunderlands from No.10 Squadron, RAAF, caused further damage, but the crew put up a spirited defence and inflicted casualties aboard both flying boats before seeking sanctuary in Spanish waters. Fortified by this success, Joubert immediately demanded an increase in Leigh Light production; justifiably so, for during June Wellington crews of No.172 Squadron illuminated seven U-Boats during 230 hours flying over the Bay while ASV-equipped Whitleys using flares flew 260 hours without a single sighting.

Though in use on a very small scale the Leigh Light had a dramatic effect on U-Boat operations, captains showing a growing reluctance to surface at night, with the result that daylight attack opportunities increased. On 24 June Doenitz ordered all U-Boats to proceed across the Bay submerged by day and night, only

*Formed from 1417 Flight.

A much-modified Liberator I AM916/G—with ASV radar and under fuselage gun pack in May 1942 shortly before returning to No.120 Squadron. (RP/MAP)

surfacing to recharge batteries. The resulting slow and uncomfortable transit reduced the detection rate but also decreased the time on patrol, and lowered morale. The first 'kill' using a Leigh Light came on 6 July when Plt Off W.B. Howell and crew sank U-502 (Type IX), and soon afterwards radio altimeters started to be fitted to No.172 Squadron aircraft—making night attacks both safer and more effective.

To take advantage of the opportunities for daylight detections, a detachment of nine Lancasters from No.61 Squadron arrived at St Eval on the 14th. Three days later Flt Lt P.R. Casement and crew on anti-submarine patrol over the 'Bay' sighted a large oil patch and then the conning tower of a U-Boat. The complete weapon load of ten Mk.VIII depth charges and two 250-lb AS bombs were dropped in three runs, a straddle being achieved with one stick of DCs. The submarine crew attempted to bring their guns to bear on the Lancaster, but the aircraft's gunners put down suppression fire until sailors were seen abandoning U-751 (Type VIIC), which then slowly sank stern first leaving about 40 crewmen floating amongst oil and debris. It was a notable 'first' by personnel completely untrained in low level bombing, though unbeknown

The enemy—a U-Boat is attacked in mid-Atlantic by a No.120 Squadron crew captained by the inimitable Sqn Ldr T.M. Bulloch. (British Official via B. Robertson).

Sunderland II W3989/DQ-L of No.228 Squadron on operations from Oban during the summer of 1942. (F. Jackson via J. Evans)

to them they were greatly assisted by the crew of a No.502 Squadron Whitley who had attacked the same target earlier in the day and damaged it so badly that it could not submerge.

Liberators of No.120 Squadron joined No.210 Squadron in providing support for Russian convoys by operating as far east as possible from Iceland and the Shetlands respectively, but for PQ17 which sailed late in June six Catalinas* were based in Russia on Lake Lakhta, near Archangel. They were intended for reconnaissance work against German surface forces, but after PQ17 was ordered to scatter and the ships came under heavy U-Boat attack the Catalinas commenced AS patrols, and in 360 flying hours over Arctic waters sighted four submarines, one of which was attacked.

After months of prevarication the Americans asked for British help in June, and on 3 July 20 Hudsons of No.53 Squadron left St Eval for Quonset Point, Rhode Island, some 150 miles NW of New York. They were really too late to make much impact because U-Boat activity in the area was already lessening as co-operation between the Americans and Canadians improved, and when the submarines moved south into the Caribbean and the Gulf of Mexico No.53 Squadron followed, moving to Waller Field, Trinidad, during August. Detachments were also maintained in British and Dutch Guiana on the South American mainland, and the Squadron achieved limited success, a U-Boat being damaged on the 15th

when caught on the surface off the Orinoco River.

In July it was proposed that a more permanent attachment from a training unit might be more useful than the short Bomber Command detachments sent hitherto, and on 1 August 1942 16 Whitleys from No.10 OTU arrived at St Eval. They were to be used by OTU instructors and student crews during their last three weeks of the course to carry out operational anti-submarine patrols over the Bay of Biscay, armed, but mainly intended to keep the U-Boat commanders under pressure by weight of numbers. The detachment, which was led by Wg Cdr Pickard† in a very dynamic fashion, was tasked with 35 sorties a week and was quickly in action, the crews regularly sighting submarines and sometimes attacking them. They also frequently came under attack by Ju88s, 24 of which had recently been added to the strength of *Fliegerführer Atlantik*'s forces when V Gruppe of Kampfgeschwader 40 arrived at Kerlin Bastard, near Lorient, for fighter operations over the Bay. It was a very real baptism of fire for aircrew just completing their training!

At the end of July Leigh Light operations were really getting into their stride, but then the tunny fishing season started and large numbers of French tunnymen began moving out into the middle of the Bay of Biscay. ASV radar 'returns' from their boats

*Four from No.210 and two from No.240 Squadron.
†Of the film *F for Freddie* fame.

A Whitley VII of No.612 Squadron drops a 'stick' of depth charges, September 1942. (RAF Thorney Island records via P.H.T. Green)

were indistinguishable from those of a U-Boat and much effort and Leigh Light battery power was wasted on them. The use of the searchlights also gave warning to any U-Boat commander in the area, and by mid-August the fishing fleet was so large that night sorties were virtually useless. U-Boats were again able to travel on the surface at night charging their batteries, and often hidden within the fishing fleet. Doenitz was still attracted by easy targets off Brazil and Venezuela, but the opportunity presented by the situation in the Bay was too good to miss and, by the time Brazil declared war in August and offered bases to the Americans, he had already made his initial redeployments and was concentrating on the Atlantic again.

The move was not unexpected but what to do about it was more difficult. The Sunderland supply position had improved markedly, but the aircraft's range was at best only 1,300 nm, and it did not adequately replace the three Catalina squadrons, Nos.209, 240 and 413 which had been transferred overseas. The majority of the Liberators available, Mk IIs and IIIs, were limited to 1,800 and 1,680 nm respectively, while the long-range Catalinas of Nos.202 (Gibraltar) and 210 Squadrons (Sullom Voe) managed 1,840 nm, all of which meant that while there was now no respite for U-Boats attacking convoys within 500 nm of Allied bases, mid-Atlantic cover was still a problem. Plans for carrier-borne anti-submarine aircraft had been made, but there were no Fleet aircraft carriers

available for Atlantic convoy work, and sufficient 'auxiliary' carriers still had to be built. Thus, after nearly a year of operation five hard worked 'very long range' Liberator Is of No.120 Squadron were still the only aircraft which could close the 'gap', and they could only stay a very limited time 'on task' in mid-Atlantic. Recognizing this situation, Doenitz renewed his 'wolf pack' tactics, concentrating his U-Boats in the mid-Atlantic 'Gap'. During August, four night attacks and seven by day were made on convoys bound for Britain, nearly all in mid-Atlantic, and losses were heavy, especially from convoy SC94 which lost 11 ships.

The obvious solution was the provision of more Liberators, and a special mission headed by Air Vice Marshal J.C. Slessor went to Washington to put the case. They succeeded in securing a promise that deliveries would be accelerated despite the American obsession with the requirements of the VIIIth Air Force. It would take time to complete the modifications required to convert them to the VLR configuration, but there nothing that could be done in the short term except eliminate duplication of effort—a recognized problem. Joubert had already decided to centralize control of his longer range squadrons so that he could deploy them to meet the assessed threat regardless of the Group concerned, and in October 1942 he proposed a single supreme director for anti U-Boat operations, with a central planning staff to co-ordinate the often conflicting policies of the

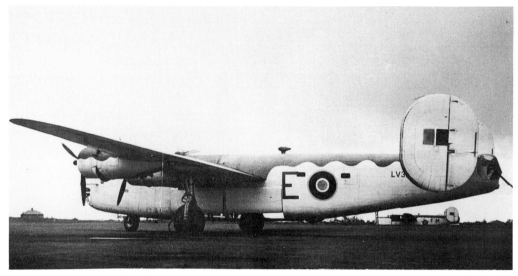

Liberator III LV345/E of No.86 Squadron at Thorney Island shortly after re-equipping from Beauforts, October 1942. (via J.D. Oughton)

British, Canadian and American naval and air authorities, together with those of the Services in the Mediterranean, West Africa, Indian Ocean and Australia. Though the scheme had much theoretical merit, it was too all-embracing to be accepted, but a less ambitious organization, the British War Cabinet Anti U-Boat Sub-Committee, was set up later and despite its unpromising name it did manage to determine priorities and, just as important, ensure that departments acted on them with speed.

No.210 Squadron went to Russia again at the beginning of September 1942 for Operation *Orator* which covered convoy PQ18 and the returning QP14.* Most Catalina operations were concerned with reconnaissance work, only 184 of a force total of 2,320 hours being spent over the convoys in close support. Twenty-seven of the original 40 ships of PQ18 reached Archangel, only three of the losses being attributable to U-Boats, and Convoy QP14 suffered no loss whilst receiving aerial cover from Coastal Command, but four merchantmen and two escorts were torpedoed by U-Boats when without the air 'umbrella'.

Between July and the end of October an additional LL Wellington, two Sunderland and two Liberator squadrons became operational in Coastal Command, and both Nos.206 and 220 Squadrons re-equipped with Fortress IIAs. This welcome increase in strength allowed the cessation of Lancaster detachments and the return of the two Whitley squadrons (Nos.51 and 77) borrowed from Bomber Command, though the continued 'misuse' of No.86 Squadron as a Liberator training unit rankled, especially as most of its prod-

ucts were promptly sent to overseas bomber units. U-Boat sightings in mid-Atlantic also increased steadily during 1942, helped by 'pack' attacks such as the one on convoy SC97 by nine submarines early on 1 September just as it reached the edge of the 'gap'. At midday, Catalinas from Iceland arrived and before nightfall one U-Boat had been sunk, two others attacked and the rest forced to submerge and lose contact. However, the skill of U-Boat commanders was increasing with experience of pack attacks, and they were often depressingly successful. All 13 submarines in a group sent to intercept convoy ON127 in mid-September made at least one attack, resulting in 12 freighters and a destroyer being sunk—a very good return for 'damage' to one U-Boat! It was not always so one-sided though, for naval escorts continued to exact a steady toll, and No.120 Squadron scored their first 'kill' in mid-Atlantic on 12 October when Sqn Ldr T.M. Bulloch DFC, who had already damaged two U-Boats during August, sent U-597 (Type VIIC) to the bottom, and soon after leaving Convoy ONS136 he attacked another submarine on his way back to Iceland.

As the problem of French tunnymen faded in the 'Bay' with the end of their fishing season, a new threat to successful night operations developed, the long anticipated ASV radar detector. Named *Metox*, the equipment had a range of 30 miles—much greater than that of radar—and by mid-September a large number of U-Boats had been fitted with the *Biscay*

*See Chapter 4.

Cross, as it was nicknamed by the crews, and the number of contacts decreased dramatically. The only solution was ASV with a different wavelength and such equipment had already been developed and tested. Unfortunately it used the same basic components as H_2S, a new bombing and navigation aid for Bomber Command, and absolute priority was being given to production for the bomber force. Joubert finally convinced everyone who mattered, except 'Bomber' Harris, that the Germans really had perfected a search receiver, but it took more time for the implications to be fully realized and to get production of ASV Mk III* accelerated.

The strain under which Coastal Command was labouring during the autumn of 1942 was further increased by Operation *Torch*, the Anglo-American invasion of French North Africa. Planning at Coastal Command headquarters had started in August when the stated requirement was the provision of cover for four convoys from Britain, but in the event seven convoys and one naval task force were protected, in addition to maintaining Atlantic operations, anti-shipping, meteorological and photo-reconnaissance.†

The Admiralty believed that some 50 U-Boats would converge on the convoy routes within ten days of the Germans becoming aware of the operation starting, and a further 75 in the following ten days. To meet this threat Coastal Command HQ intended to escort each convoy throughout the hours of daylight, while at the same time maintaining general AS activity in the Bay of Biscay, and the normal patrols from Iceland. By 23 October the plans, which called for maximum co-ordination of effort between Nos.15 and 19 Groups, were laid, and it was obvious that the resources of Coastal Command were insufficient. Loans were therefore requested and Bomber Command provided 20 Halifax aircraft (the whole of No.405

Squadron, RCAF, and part of No.158), which joined No.224 Squadron at Beaulieu. The VIIIth Air Force of the USAAF detached B-24Ds of the 330th Sqn, 93 Bomb Wing, to Holmsley South, the aircraft being modified overnight for carriage of British depth charges. Operations commenced on the 28th, and a day or two later the 409th Sqn, 93rd BW, detached eight B-24Ds to St Eval while, to provide additional AS cover for American convoys, 12 amphibious Catalinas of VP-73, USN, were temporarily accommodated at Ballykelly ready to move to the Casablanca area as soon as it had been occupied. The Bomber Command and VIIIth Air Force units were intended primarily for patrols over the Bay, thus releasing maritime trained units for convoy protection, but some Halifaxes were retained as an anti-submarine strike force for use at short notice if a convoy was threatened by a 'wolf pack'.

The unusual concentrations of shipping in British and American ports did not escape the notice of the Germans, but at first they thought an invasion of Norway was imminent, and then convinced themselves that Dakar in West Africa was the destination. The first convoys crossed the Bay in bad weather which gave them added protection and the only two U-Boats seen close to the convoy route were sunk by No.224 Squadron. In the first incident one of the DCs dropped by Flg Off D.M. Sleep hit the submarine aft of the conning tower and exploded on impact, resulting in the destruction of the U-216 (Type VIID) but also severe damage to the aircraft. It went into a steep climb and nearly stalled, but by moving all the crew into the nose and pushing hard on the control columns the pilots managed to keep the Liberator on an even

*ASV Mk. III had a wavelength of 10 centimetres.
†See Chapter 4, 10 and 11.

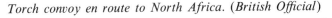

Torch convoy en route to North Africa. (British Official)

keel, later using straps to tie the columns forward. After $1\frac{1}{2}$ hours the flight engineer managed to jettison the remaining DCs and the captain decided to risk a landing at Predannack. Control was lost in the final stages of the approach and the aircraft crash-landed and caught fire, but fortunately all the crew escaped with comparatively minor injuries.

The saturation of the Bay with aircraft for *Torch* appeared to be a great success, but it soon became clear that Doenitz had deployed his main force on an extended patrol line off West Africa covering the approach to Dakar and well to the south west of the Gibraltar convoy routes. Late in October this force intercepted a lightly defended north-bound convoy from Sierra Leone, and 21 U-Boats took part in a ritual slaughter—a sacrifice for *Torch*.

Twelve Catalinas of No.210 Squadron were deployed to Gibraltar, and on 5 November Hudsons of No.500 Squadron arrived at North Front to supplement No.233, which had been on the 'Rock' at squadron strength since July. The first convoys were already within range of Gibraltar's anti-submarine aircraft and by the 7th some 48 sorties a day were being despatched, a flying effort not lost on German agents watching activities from Spanish territory. The general build-up led to a rapid reassessment of the situation by the Axis powers and their submarines started re-positioning in the western Mediterranean, soon totalling 19 German and 21 Italian 'boats'. Intensive patrolling from Gibraltar during 7-8 November brought 15 sightings and nine attacks, the concentration being such that only one ship received any damage. On the 9th, the day after the North African landings, No.608 Squadron joined the other Hudson units on the 'Rock' and No.461 Squadron's Sunderlands, temporarily employed on transport duties, started flying in essential personnel and freight. As the build-up in North Africa continued, operations from the 'Rock' were further increased but room was found on the 18th for LL Wellingtons of No.179 Squadron and soon night patrols were as effective as those during the day.

Between 23 October and 30 November, when the last *Torch* convoy reached North Africa, aircraft operating from the British Isles under Coastal Command control made 29 submarine sightings resulting in 16 attacks, while from Gibraltar and North Africa (No.500 Squadron detachments) 113 were sighted and 60 attacked. Doenitz finally accepted defeat in mid-December and called off the pack, by which time Coastal squadrons at Gibraltar had flown 8,656 hours on *Torch* operations—and not one ship had been lost. The cost was 17 aircraft,* several shot down by 'trigger-happy' gunners on Allied ships.

This major success was gained at the expense of

Atlantic convoys as well as the unfortunate SL125 from Sierra Leone, a total of 83 ships of 508,700 tons being sunk in mid-Ocean during November for the loss of U-132† and U-408 (Type VIIC) sunk by the USN crew of a PBY-5A Catalina of VP-84 operating from Iceland under British control. With the end of the *Torch* convoys, efforts could again be made to regain the initiative over transiting U-Boats in the Bay of Biscay. Some U-Boat commanders were now using their *Metox* receivers to track the aircraft while still well outside ASV contact ranges, and intensive night patrols by flare-dropping Wellingtons and the use of intermittent radar during the daytime proved only palliative. Late in November Coastal Command HQ attempted to make the better use of the forces available while awaiting ASV Mk.III-equipped aircraft. They tried to flood the area of the inner Bay with radar transmissions at night while during the day patrolling it with long-range aircraft supplemented by Beaufighters. The latter were intended to cover the coast where the threat of interception by Ju88s was greatest and were to carry DCs or bombs, though it is doubtful whether this instruction was carried out—not until much later at any event.

With the abandonment of efforts to interfere with the North African campaign, Doenitz returned to the North Atlantic during December with a vengeance. Some 30 U-Boats were positioned in the area and it was obvious that trouble was in store for Convoy HX217 when it came under observation at the mouth of the St Lawrence river. Intensive efforts were made to provide cover by the Canadians and then the British. On 7 December a No.120 Squadron Liberator from Iceland met the convoy when more than 800 nm from base, remaining on task for six hours—a remarkable achievement. In the early hours of the 8th one ship was torpedoed before the close escort Liberator arrived, but it was the only loss that day, for during nearly nine hours on task the crew sighted eight U-Boats and attacked seven of them, ruining their attack plan. The first incident was 27 minutes after joining the convoy, when they attacked a submarine with six DCs, apparently achieving a perfect straddle. Less than $1\frac{1}{2}$ hours later, at 12.45 hrs, another attack was made on a U-Boat using the remaining two DCs, and between 14.26 and 16.43 hrs five more were sprayed with 20mm cannon fire. It almost goes without saying that the captain was the extraordinary Bulloch, but his relief did nearly as well for during an area sweep two U-Boats were attacked with DCs, another two

---

*4 Catalinas, 10 Hudsons and 3 Wellingtons.
†Believed destroyed by the explosion of ammunition aboard a victim.

Fortress II FL459/J of No.220 Squadron, Benbecula 1942. (Author's collection)

with machine gun fire, and a feint made at a fifth!

On the 9th the weather was too bad for flying and another ship was sunk, but on the 10th as HX217 came into range of aircraft other than VLR Liberators, Coastal Command's efforts were redoubled. A Fortress and a Catalina both operating at maximum range failed to make contact with the convoys, but six Hudsons of No.269 swept an area ahead and attacked a U-Boat, and the crew of a VP-84 Catalina, one of four on sweeps closer to the convoy, sighted six U-Boats, attacking and sinking the U-611 (Type VIIC) with a single 650-lb USN depth bomb. Three Fortress aircraft of No.220 Squadron were also despatched on close escort, but hardly settled into

their patrol before reaching PLE. Similar cover was provided on the 11th when Sunderlands were also able to take part. One Fortress crew sighted three U-Boats and attacked two, but the party was nearly over, for on the 12th the 'pack' broke off the attack on HX217 and concentrated on SC111, a day's sailing to the rear. This convoy was also well supported by Sunderlands, Fortresses, Liberators and Catalinas—and by area sweeps by Hudsons—and reached port completely unscathed. Of the 70 merchantmen in the two convoys, just two were lost. Twenty-seven sightings had been made from the air, 16 U-Boats attacked (ten with DCs and six with cannon/machine gun fire) and one, probably two, sunk. Thus despite the most

Whitley V Z6795/JL-W of No.10 OTU Detachment at St Eval was reported missing from an anti-submarine patrol on 21 September 1942—one of many losses from the unit. It was recovered virtually intact by the Germans. (H. Nowarra via A.S. Thomas)

determined U-Boat 'pack' yet encountered the operation had been a success for the Allies, the result of adequate forces and extremely good air/surface co-operation.

Later in the month Allied intelligence agencies again managed to completely break the U-Boat cypher code, though it sometimes took several days to achieve, and in some cases it was not possible to re-route convoys away from the threat. That threat had certainly not gone away, for despite the success with HX217/SC111 a total of 60 ships of 330,000 tons were sunk in the Atlantic during December, and over the year Allied losses had not been completely replaced by new construction, nor had imports kept pace with consumption in Britain. The situation was still very dangerous, but air cover along the North American seaboard was now adequate and the gap between patrols from Gibraltar and West Africa had been closed. The North Atlantic 'gap' remained as difficult as ever, however, for VLR Liberators continued to be in very short supply. A request for 30 such VLR aircraft fitted with American centrimetric radar had been turned down by the United States authorities, so instead some of the shorter range Liberators being modified in Britain for maritime work were further delayed to allow ASV Mk.III to be installed. Deliveries started in January 1943 but were very slow, and the presence at St Eval of B-24s of the 1st Anti-Submarine Squadron (Prov), USAAF, which had replaced the loaned bomber units in November was useful even though the crews were very 'green', as were those of the 2nd AS Sqn which arrived in January 1943.

The first successful attack by the hard-working Fortress units occurred on 15 January when the crew of a No.206 Squadron aircraft on close escort in the North Atlantic to convoy ON160, sighted a surfaced submarine. The approach was made at the classic 20 degrees off the heading of the U-Boat, four DCs straddling the target. There was a huge explosion and when the smoke and water subsided one end of the U-337 (Type VIIC) could be seen bobbing up and down 'like a half filled bottle in the middle of boiling foam'. Despite this the attack was assessed at the time as inflicting 'minor damage' but in fact the vessel was sunk.

Joubert's early replacement by Air Marshal Slessor, almost certainly as the result of differences with the Admiral Commanding Western Approaches, was announced in December 1942, but it was delayed by Slessor's commitments and he did not assume command of Coastal until 5 February 1943. Joubert was therefore still at the helm when the Casablanca Conference was held late in January, and it must have been with grim satisfaction that he heard that during 1943 the resources of both Britain and America would be directed first and foremost at the defeat of the U-Boat. Joubert had taken a lot of 'flak' and become extremely unpopular in high places for persistently presenting well-reasoned arguments for anti-submarine priorities and ironically, just as he was leaving, his views prevailed. Included in the priorities were the U-Boat bases in Bay of Biscay ports which were to be Target No.1 for Anglo-American bombers. He had pressed for such bombing while the pens were being built—now it was a year too late, for the U-Boat shelters were virtually bomb proof, and indeed the attacks were to do little more than destroy the towns themselves. Neither did the declaration mean an immediate injection of aircraft, equipment and facilities, but no longer would Coastal Command be automatically placed at the bottom of the priority list—in itself a great morale booster.

When Sir Philip Joubert took over Coastal in June 1941 he inherited a Command in surprisingly good heart but one which was only capable of providing systematic patrols out to 350 nm from the British Isles and had had little success in the anti-submarine field, having shared in the destruction of just two U-Boats. Twenty months later it had destroyed another 27 submarines, 19 of them in the last five months, and in conjunction with American and Canadian forces, had virtually bridged the Atlantic. During the period 825 U-Boat sightings had been made from the air resulting in 607 attacks, and in addition to the 'kills', 120 assessments of 'damaged' had been credited. On the debit side 118 aircraft had been lost to enemy action or were missing, and a further 116 had been destroyed in accidents, but despite this drain on resources and the transfer of some units overseas, the number of long range squadrons in the Command had risen from 6 to 18, consisting of one Halifax, three Liberator and three Fortress landplane squadrons, two Catalina and seven Sunderland squadrons (with two more forming). Additionally there were five squadrons of Hudsons,* three Wellington units (two with Leigh Lights) and a Whitley squadron, all engaged on anti-submarine work. There were problems, in particular the lack of VLR aircraft, a shortfall in the strength of Hudson squadrons, and the temporary nature of the Halifax squadron† and USAAF/USN units. However, the whole force which still included Whitleys of No.10 OTU, was infinitely better able to deal with the submarine threat than had been the case in June 1941. Overall, Joubert could be well satisfied with his efforts even if they did not always appear to be appreciated elsewhere.

*Plus No.53 Squadron in transit from the USA.
†Still on loan from Bomber Command.

CHAPTER 6

The Strike Wings–
Anti-Shipping Operations
1943

BY 1943 THE German mercantile marine had become very highly organized, and the Allies were faced with the task of disrupting a system at the peak of operational efficiency and well-equipped to deal with the forces deployed against it. Their shipping had three priority tasks: the import of iron ore from Sweden and Spain; maintenance of supplies to German forces in Norway; and continuance of traffic to and from the Far East. The latter was performed on a seasonal basis by a comparatively small number of blockade runners against which the Allies were having some success at the beginning of 1943, but the coastal

traffic to and from Spain was proving a headache. These ships spent much of the voyage in Spanish waters and then hugged the French coast where fighter cover was available and operations against them was out of the question for most aircraft at No.19 Group's disposal.

Norwegian and Swedish traffic provided a different tactical problem for Nos.16 and 18 Groups. It was continuous and heavy, and ships plying the Norwegian coastal routes were within range of No.18 Group aircraft for much of their journey. However, they were only really vulnerable between Stavanger and

Hampden TB.I/UB-C of No.455 Squadron low down over a sparkling sea—its natural environment. (G. Lindeman via R. Hayward)

Kristiansund, and here strong fighter opposition could be expected. Off the Friesian cost, where shipping operations were the responsibility of No.16 Group, distance was not a problem either, but the flak defences and the close proximity of several Luftwaffe fighter bases certainly were, and it had been agreed that the only answer was the development of integrated Strike Wings. Plans envisaged a force of ten Beaufighter squadrons, four of them torpedo-carrying and the remainder fighter/anti-flak units, in being by May 1943 and deployed as follows:

No.16 Group	North Coates	One 'Torbeau' Sqn Two Anti-flak Sqns
	Thorney Island	One Anti-flak Sqn (with roving commission with Nos.18 and 19 Groups as required)
No.18 Group	Wick	One 'Torbeau' Sqn One Anti-flak Sqn
	Leuchars	One 'Torbeau' Sqn One Anti-flak Sqn
	Tain	One 'Torbeau' Sqn (for Russia or Iceland in case of breakout by German naval units)
No.19 Group	Predannack	One Anti-flak/ Fighter Sqn

Unfortunately, by the time Air Marshal J.C. Slessor took over Coastal Command on 5 February 1943 it was already obvious that the plan was not going to be implemented by May.

Mediterranean requirements continued to drain away Beaufighters and crews, adding to the difficulties being experienced by the North Coates squadrons in perfecting the 'strike' concept, and in building up the force. The one remaining Hudson unit, No.320 (Dutch) Squadron, which had expected to re-equip with the Beaufighter, was transferred to Bomber Command instead, and the three torpedo-bomber Hampden squadrons [Nos.415 (RCAF), 455 (RAAF) and 489 (RNZAF)] continued to bear the brunt of 'strike' operations against the Norwegian traffic and along the Dutch coast, the latter mainly at night because of the strength of the opposition. No.415 Squadron, a No.16 Group unit, was also responsible for any daylight strike work over the

Bay of Biscay, for which it was detached to St Eval.

The initial sighting of blockade runners was usually by anti-submarine patrol aircraft, typical being the interception 450 nm west of Finisterre of the tanker *Herborg* on 26 February by the crew of a B-24 of No.1 AS Squadron, USAAF, resulting in her sinking by HMS *Sussex*. By the end of April another five had been disposed of whilst outside Coastal Command's operating areas, and just one had reached a French port—the *Pierre Orseolo* which survived being hit by a torpedo fired by an American submarine. Outbound, the *Orsono* and *Portland* got through the Bay, the latter subsequently being sunk in the Atlantic, but the 6,240-ton *Himalaya* was intercepted and forced back to port twice, on the second occasion (10 April) damaged by Hampdens of No.415 Squadron. Demonstrating its versatility, the same squadron hit the Swedish ship *Tom* off Borkum during the night of 14/15 April, and the following day sank the 4,820-ton *Borga* off Ameland.

In April 1943 the diversion of anti-submarine aircraft to look for blockade runners was put on a more formal basis under *Sombrero*, an operation designed to incorporate a high degree of tactical flexibility so that attacks could be mounted at short notice following intelligence reports. The Germans had started to escort blockade runners with *Elbing* class destroyers, and daily reconnaissance of their 'home' ports soon enabled the Allies to establish when preparations were being made for arrivals from the Far East. Crews of anti-submarine aircraft were then briefed on the likely ships and provided with recognition material to enable a positive identification to be made. But except for Nos.58 and 502 Squadrons, whose Halifaxes had Mk.XIV medium level bombsights, they were not encouraged to attack ships. They were to report and shadow, providing information for air or surface strike forces.

Up north, Nos.455 and 489 Squadrons were active, the 6,800 ton *Altair* being destroyed off Kristiansund on 4 April, but such successes were few and far between, for the Hampden was no more suitable for attacks on heavily armed targets than the Beaufort it replaced. It is indeed salutary to reflect that between April 1940 and March 1943 Bomber, Fighter and Coastal Command aircraft made 3,700 attacks on ships at sea, sinking 107 totalling 155,000 tons for the loss of 648 aircraft, while during the same period Bomber and Coastal lost 329 aircraft while laying 160,000 mines—but that those mines sank 369 ships totalling 362,000 tons. Thus, it had cost six aircraft to sink one ship by bombing or torpedo attack, but less than one for each ship by mining!

Mining operations were covert by nature, and so were the activities of a No.18 Group unit which had formed at Woodhaven on 8 February 1942 with the prosaic title of the *Norwegian Detachment*. Equipped with Catalinas, it was involved in clandestine operations on behalf of the Norwegian Government in Exile for which the aircrew's local knowledge was invaluable, such as the ferrying of agents in and out of the country. On 17 February 1943 the unit became No.1477 Flight, and on 5 March reconnaissance patrols in Norwegian waters were added to the repertoire. They proved extremely hazardous in slow cumbersome Catalinas, and at the end of the month Coastal Command managed to obtain six Mosquito IIs for the Flight. They commenced operations from Leuchars on 16 April—the first armed Mosquitoes in the Command. The aircraft was an immediate success and was soon engaged on a variety of tasks loosely termed 'reconnaissance', the unit being upgraded as No.333 (Norwegian) Squadron on 1 May.

Meanwhile, the Beaufighter Wing at North Coates had been practising hard, and on 18 April it was despatched on its first 'strike' since the previous November. The target was a heavily escorted convoy which had left the Hook of Holland early that morning and was re-located off Ijmuiden by the crew of a No.236 Squadron Beaufighter. Nine 'Torbeaus' of No.254 Squadron, six anti-flak Beaufighters of No.143 and another six from No.236 Squadron carrying bombs, set off at 13.30 hrs led by Wg Cdr H.N.G. Wheeler, CO of the latter unit. Over Coltishall they picked up their fighter escort, 22 Spitfire Vs (long range) of Nos.118 and 167 Squadrons, and six Mustang 1s from No.613 Squadron. The operation went almost entirely to the carefully worked out and much practised plan. The fighter and fighter-bomber Beaufighters attacked the escort vessels with bombs, cannon and machine guns, while the 'Torbeaus', flying in pairs, made for the freighters. Two *M* class minesweepers were left on fire, and an armed trawler was hit. At east two torpedoes hit the *Hoegh Carrier*, a large colier, and she subsequently sank. The whole attack was over in four minutes, and no aircraft were lost—just slight damage being sustained by two Beaufighters. The Germans were left bewildered, the British jubilant, hardly able to believe that they had the solution at last.

It was probably just as well that the crews were unaware that the Admiralty was agitating for a strike force in Iceland, and the immediate replacement of Scottish-based Hampdens by Beaufighters. Their concern was over the continued presence of the German capital ships in northern Norway, well placed to threaten Atlantic and Russian convoys alike, but the only way an Iceland force could be provided quickly would be to break up the North Coates Wing and waste all the hard work put into the co-ordinated training. Fortunately the AOC-in-C was successful in resisting the demand, though he did have to commit the Wing to No.18 Group operations if required.

By April, the Beaufighters of No.236 Squadron not only had bomb racks but were also modified to carry

Catalina 'Vingtor' of No.1477 Flight at Woodhaven early in 1943—the unit was redesignated No.333 Squadron in May. (E. Johansen via A.S. Thomas)

HM King George VI and Queen Elizabeth visiting North Coates on 27 May 1943. In the background are Beaufighter XIs of No.143 Squadron. (British Official via P.H.T. Green)

3″ rocket projectiles (RPs). The latter subsequently turned out to be a devastating anti-ship weapon, but special techniques were required and these took time to develop. RPs were therefore not used on the first Wing strike, nor during a repeat performance on the 29th when Wheeler again led the formation, and two merchant ships and an armed trawler were sunk off Terschelling for the loss of a No.143 Squadron aircraft.

Meanwhile, a second Beaufighter Wing was being formed at Wick where No.144 Squadron had restarted operations as a 'Torbeau' unit in March and was joined on 20 April by No.404 Squadron, RCAF. The two squadrons flew their first operation together a week later when No.404 provided cover for four 'Torbeaus' of No.144 during a convoy strike off Norway. They ran into heavy flak, two aircraft being badly damaged, but one vessel was hit by three torpedoes, and all the aircraft returned to base.

Justification for Wheeler's insistence on fighter escort came on 1 May when 31 Beaufighters of the North Coates Wing were sent on a sweep down the Norwegian coast to hunt down the cruiser *Nurnberg* and three destroyers reported on their way south. Out of range of single-engined fighter escort, the Wing was set upon by Fw190s and Bf109s, and had to jettison bombs and torpedoes in the mêlée that followed. Three aircraft of No.254 Squadron and two of No.143 were shot down, the remaining 26 landing at Wick with their crews thoroughly demoralized by the experience. The next attack, made on 17 May under heavy escort, was a great success, however; a merchantman of 2,964

tons, a minesweeper and a flak ship being sunk without loss. It was becoming very clear that the Wing tactics worked if applied correctly—and if the intelligence was good.

The first operational use of the rocket projectile from a Beaufighter was made during a detachment by No.236 Squadron to Predannack, Cornwall, for anti-submarine work* but by mid-June all the pilots of both anti-flak units in the North Coates Wing were practised in its use and were ready to try it operationally. On 22 June the whole Wing set off to attack a convoy of five Swedish vessels escorted by seven German flak ships and five minesweepers. The force consisted of 12 Beaufighters of No.143 and ten of No.236, all carrying four cannon and eight 60-lb rockets, 12 'Torbeaus' of No.254 Squadron, each armed with cannon and an 18″ torpedo, and an escort of three Spitfire and two Typhoon squadrons. The attack was made off Scheveningen, 176 rockets being fired in the face of light and inaccurate flak, but unfortunately the defenders had recovered from their surprise by the time No.254 Squadron were running in for torpedo drops. Two Beaufighters were shot down and four more were hit, three of which crash-landed on return to base. None of the torpedoes struck home and only two ships were hit by rockets and slightly damaged. It was not a very successful RP debut.

Strikes continued during July, though attempts to mount them regularly from North Coates were frus-

*See Chapter 7.

Hampden TB.I AT246/XA-D of No.489 Squadron in the early summer of 1943—probably at Thorney Island. (S.B.L. Beattie via R. Hayward)

trated by events outside the Wing's control, and from Wick by the detachment of No.144 Squadron crews overseas. At the end of July No.236 Squadron re-equipped with the TF.X version of the Beaufighter, the first variant specifically designed for strike operations. They were in action within days, 14 Mk.Xs accompanying ten Mk.VIs of No.143 and 12 Mk.VI 'Torbeaus' of 254 Squadron on 2 August for a strike on a convoy off Texel. Operating under the umbrella of the strongest fighter escort to date, 51 Spitfire VBs from Nos.118, 402, 416 and 611 Squadrons, the 24 rocket-firers dived into the attack, hitting all four flak ships guarding one flank of the convoy. It was then the turn of No.254 Squadron. Four torpedoes apparently struck the sea bed, but two hit the 2,700 ton ore carrier *Fortuna*, and she sank immediately. One of the flak ships was badly damaged, and the Spitfires set about four Bf109s, shooting down two for no loss. All the Beaufighters returned, though five were damaged.

Within days of this successful attack, the whole future of the Strike Wing concept was again in the

Beaufighters of the North Coates Wing attacking shipping off Den Helder, 13 June 1943. (B. Robertson)

Beaufighter XI of No.143 Squadron returning to Portreath after a sortie over the Bay of Biscay, 1943. (N. Carr via C. Bowyer)

melting pot, Sir John Slessor having told the Air Ministry on 8 August that he could no longer justify the 'expensive' North Coates Wing, and that the squadrons would be better employed hunting submarines in the inner Bay of Biscay where Ju88s were causing trouble for his anti-submarine forces. In view of his championship of the Wing earlier in the year, this volte-face was a surprise, but it was based on statistics which did not make good reading, and on worries about the situation developing in the Bay.

The Wing, which absorbed 60 operational crews and aircraft, was expected to carry out an average of five strikes per month, and this number had indeed been planned during the $3\frac{1}{2}$ months period up to the end of July, but six had been cancelled due to poor reconnaissance, and three because fighter escort was lacking. The nine strikes which had been flown since 18 April had resulted in very few sinkings, and the AOC-in-C and his advisors considered them a very poor return for the effort expended, and the losses experienced. Such was the situation in the Bay that he did not wait for the Air Ministry's blessing, but moved No.143 from North Coates and No.235 Squadron from Leuchars to join No.248 Squadron in flying long-range *Instep* fighter patrols over the Bay and south-west approaches. No.248 had on occasion been assisted by No.10 Group Mosquito squadrons, but only when Fighter Command commitments allowed, and Slessor wanted a bigger and more permanent force in the area to carry out interceptions of German aircraft, often made with the help of ship-borne fighter direction radar.

Slessor's letter caused a furore in the 'corridors of power', resulting in a high level conference on 20 August. Representatives from the Admiralty, the Air Ministry, the Ministry of Economic Warfare, Fighter Command, the Nore Command (responsible for Dutch coast operations), and Coastal Command attended and, backed up by many statistics, the pros and cons of the Strike Wing concept were considered in depth. The evidence showed that during the year ending May 1943 only 21 ships had been sunk by strike aircraft (and ten since then), while in the same period mine laying aircraft claimed 79. This appeared pretty damning, but the Commander-in-Chief, Nore, pointed out that the attacks forced most German convoys to sail at night, and this gave his torpedo boats and gunboats a favourable environment for attacking them, while the Ministry of Economic Warfare representatives were able to point to a dramatic reduction in the tonnage passing through the port of Rotterdam; according to them, entirely due to the activities of the Strike Wing. It was finally agreed to continue with the North Coates Wing and establish the other two. Fighter Command was instructed to provide escorts at 'three squadron' strength on all occasions unless there was an exceptional reason for not doing so, and to increase their *Instep* operations—Slessor had probably got what he wanted.

Planning for the two additional Wings went ahead with renewed impetus, though shortages of trained aircrew continued to delay the build-up. The Wick Wing was officially 'born' in November, though in practice its two squadrons had been operating to-

Mosquito II DZ754 of B Flight No.333 Squadron at Leuchars, October 1943. (Norwegian Official)

gether for much of the previous six months. They flew alone because there were no single-engined fighters in Scotland capable of escorting them to the Norwegian coast. Fortunately, the German fighter opposition was weaker than that experienced further south, and it was contained by arranging to deliver attacks while flying away from enemy airfields to reduce interception opportunities. No.144 Squadron, the 'Torbeau' unit, also found torpedo operations in narrow fjords extremely difficult, and they were the first to use rockets to sink merchant ships rather than just suppress anti-aircraft fire, the 25-lb solid warhead type proving best for this purpose.

From Wick, the distance to some parts of the Norwegian coast was such that the range of the Beaufighter was marginal, and much thought went into devising ways of getting large numbers of aircraft off the ground and formed up quickly. The procedure required considerable skill and discipline by both air and ground crews, and the same applied on return to base when damage and/or low fuel states, also threw a heavy burden on flying control staff. The first 'official' Wick Wing attack was against a German convoy off Stadlandet on 22 November. Six 'Torbeaus' escorted by eight cannon-firing aircraft of No.404 Squadron sank a Norwegian freighter of 1,650 tons and damaged two others for the loss of one Beaufighter. Similar operations followed, and by the beginning of 1944 the two squadrons were working together extremely well. The squadrons were also responsible for providing escorts to long range motor torpedo boats on missions off the

Norwegian coast, and for general area reconnaissance.

Meanwhile, Hampden squadrons had soldiered on through the spring into the summer, dividing their time between anti-shipping and anti-submarine work. The latter was more from necessity than ability, but occasionally attacks were made, and on 30 April F/Sgt J.S. Freeth and his No.455 Squadron crew were able to claim the sinking of U-227 (Type VIIC) off the Faeroes. The Leuchars Wing sank the *Kraus Howaldt* (6,000 tons) off Egero Is on 12 May, and an armed trawler off Stavanger on 19 June, but thereafter they had few encounters and, like No.415 Squadron in the south, virtually abandoned Hampden anti-shipping operations.

No.415 Squadron commenced re-equipping with Wellington XIIIs in September and restarted operations at the end of October, tasked with night anti-shipping operations off the Dutch coast and in the Channel. E-Boats became their speciality, *A* Flight converting to Albacores at the beginning of December when they took over the aircraft of 841 Squadron, FAA, at Manston. These obsolescent biplanes were used for Operation *Deadly*, during which *B* Flight Wellingtons located and illuminated E-Boats for the Albacore crews to attack with bombs, a very hazardous occupation.

No.489 Squadron made one of its last Hampden strikes on 16 September when three aircraft attacked two merchantmen and two flak ships off SW Norway, claiming a torpedo hit. The unit was withdrawn from operations in October to convert to Beaufighter Xs, No.455 Squadron plodding on alone with Hampdens until it too started conversion during December in preparation for the formation of the *Anzac* Strike Wing at Leuchars.

During November, preparations for another bout of blockade running by at least eight ships were observed to be under way at various Biscay ports, and it was also known that five were in-bound from the Far East. A major campaign was mounted against them, starting on 13 December when a detachment from No.254 Squadron arrived at Predannack· for operations against a specific ship, the *Pietro Orseolo*— long a thorn in the C-in-C Plymouth's side. A couple of strikes by Nos.248 and 254 Squadrons was abandoned because of bad weather before orders were given to attack regardless of the conditions. Escorted by eight Typhoons of No.183 Squadron, 12 Beaufighters (half with torpedoes) set off at low level on the 18th. Good intelligence and excellent navigation took them straight to the target, sighted off Concarneau surrounded by minesweepers. The anti-flak Beaufighters of No.248 Squadron went immediately into the attack, followed by the 'Torbeaus'. Two torpedoes hit the *Pietro Orseolo* and the ship was badly damaged, sinking three days later under tow.

More action followed the sighting of 11 destroyers by the crew of a LL Wellington on anti-submarine patrol over the Bay on 23 December. Shortly afterwards, an in-bound 6,000 ton freighter was located, obviously a blockade runner. Throughout the 24th the ships were kept under surveillance, and some attacks were made by the crews of Wellington of No.304 (Polish) Squadron, and Liberators of No.311 (Czech) Squadron and VPB110 of the US Navy. Eight No.502 Squadron Halifax armed with 500-lb MC bombs were assembled as a strike force, and claimed hits despite violent evasive action by the ships; and more attacks followed on the 25th, the crew of a 311 Squadron Liberator scoring a direct hit amidships on the freighter. Unfortunately, a force of 15 'Torbeaus' and 29 anti-flak Beaufighters failed to find the target, now identified as the 7,000 ton *Osorno*, but she was later found beached at Le Verdon at the mouth of the River Gironde, obviously badly damaged.

Aircraft were out looking for other 'runners' on the 27th, and the crew of a No.201 Squadron Sunderland proved lucky, sighting the *Alsterufer* returning home from the Far East. Flt Lt L.H. Baveystock commenced shadowing, transmitting homing signals, and two hours later a No.422 Squadron Sunderland arrived and the pilot, Flt Lt Martin, promptly attacked from 1,500 ft in the face of flak. The first run resulted in an overshoot, but the second pair of 500-lb MC bombs only narrowly missed the target. Another two hours passed before Baveystock was given permission to attack from 3,000 ft, a height which almost guaran-

teed failure without a suitable bombsight. Flt Lt Stack and crew of No.201 Squadron then relieved Baveystock and homed in the crew of a 311 Squadron Liberator captained by Plt Off Dolzal. The Czechs went in at low level in the face of intense flak and parachute charges. Despite this distracting refinement, Dolzal fired four pairs of rockets, five of which struck the *Alsterufer*. He also dropped two bombs, one hitting the stern, and soon afterwards the ship caught fire and was abandoned, the 74 survivors standing off in boats and on life rafts. About an hour later two 86 Squadron Liberators attacked the hulk with 500-lb bombs, and by the time four Halifaxes of No.502 reached the scene it was sinking.

The year was rounded off by the sighting of a force of ten destroyers by USN Liberators of Fleet Air Wing 7 on 28 December. Operating under the control of No.19 Group, the Wing sent out a bombing force of 15 PB4Y Liberators and six of them made courageous attacks from under 1,000 ft in the face of concentrated AA fire. No damage was claimed on the German ships, but three of them were subsequently sunk by the cruisers HMS *Glasgow* and *Enterprise* operating under air cover provided by waves of Beaufighters. Though this was by no means the swansong of the aircraft in the fighter role, it had been accepted that the Beaufighter was no longer fast enough, nor sufficiently manoeuvrable for such work over the Bay, and No.248 Squadron was re-equipped with Mosquito FB.VIs during December—the change-over made easier because the unit had been operating a handful of six-pounder gun Mosquito FB.XVIIIs since October, manned by ex-618 Squadron personnel.

All four remaining 'runners' from the Far East were sunk by aircraft or ship, and on 17 January 1944 Doenitz admitted defeat and recommended that all trade with the Far East should be carried out henceforth by special 'freighter' U-Boats—a significant victory for the Allied forces.

The specialist strike squadrons sank 21 and damaged another 23 ships during 1943. Not a great success story by any yardstick, but at last all three Wings, completely equipped with Beaufighters, were in being. The Wick Wing was working well, starting 1944 by sinking two medium-sized freighters, while at Leuchars No.489 was declared operational on 8 January, and No.455 was in the work-up phase. The tactics were right and morale was high—and so were expectations!

A few days later, on 20 January 1944, Air Marshal Sir John Slessor KCB, DSO, MC handed over Coastal Command to Air Chief Marshal Sir Sholto Douglas KCB, MC, DFC after a momentous year spent successfully building on the firm base left by his predecessors.

CHAPTER 7

The Tide Turns–Atlantic and Bay Anti-Submarine Operations 1943

THE ATTEMPTS TO counter the *Metox* receiver instituted in November 1942 met with little success because insufficient aircraft were available, the level of sightings in the Bay of Biscay dropping back to those experienced before the introduction of the Leigh Light. In January 1943 only four day and nine night sightings were made, none resulting in the destruction of a U-Boat, but with intelligence reports indicating that 45 U-Boats would be transiting the Bay during 3–13 February it was decided to try another tack, and Operation *Gondola* was sanctioned on 4 February, the day before Air Marshal Slessor took over Coastal Command. *Gondola* involved intensive day/night patrols over a comparatively small rectangular area of sea lying across the submarine routes. The outer section of the area was swept by Liberators and LL Catalinas, while Sunderlands, Halifaxes, Wellingtons and Whitleys covered the inner Bay section. No.19 Group maintained the operation for 12 days, flying over 300 sorties, many of them by Nos.1 and 2 Anti-Submarine (Provisional) Squadrons of the USAAF operating from St Eval. Their Liberators were fitted with American centrimetric radar (SCR517)—an advantage shared by the newly delivered Halifaxes of No.58 Squadron which had the British equivalent, ASV Mk.III, but not all the 19 sightings and eight attacks were made with the aid of the new equipment. One of the attacks resulted in the destruction of a U-Boat, the U-519 (Type IXC) by the crew of a B-24 Liberator of No.2 AS Sqn captained by 1st Lt W.L. Sandford.

ASV Mk.III was also being fitted in Wellington GR.XIIs, which were entering service with No.172 Squadron, but the new radar took time to function well and it was a LL 'Wimpey' GR.VIII, fitted with ASV Mk.II which Flg Off G.D. Lundon used to score the Squadron's second 'kill' when he surprised the crew of U-268 (Type VIIC) in the early morning of 19 February.

Sunderland III W4004/Z of No.10 Squadron, RAAF, on the slip at Mount Batten shortly before it was posted missing over the Bay of Biscay, 17 May 1943 (Imperial War Museum)

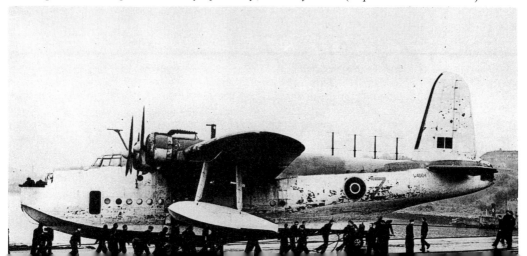

A fully operational Fortress IIA FK212/B of No.59 Squadron in February 1943 when the unit was flying from Chivenor. (No.59 Sqn records)

Undeterred by events in the Bay the German High Command maintained their policy of pack attacks on convoys in mid-Atlantic, and with Doenitz able to deploy a large number of U-Boats during the early part of 1943 it was a tactic which paid off. Convoy ON-166 suffered the loss of 14 ships (85,000 tons) during 21-25 February, and in March, helped by a another change in the German signal coding system which temporarily defeated Allied de-coders the U-Boats came very close to defeating the convoy system. A total of 108 ships grossing 627,400 tons were sunk by German submarines during the month for the loss of 15 U-Boats. The fiercest battle was fought around Convoys SC122 and HX229 during 16-20 March when 20 U-Boats out of a 40-strong pack made attacks on the two convoys after they had merged in an unwieldy mass, the slow SC convoy having been overtaken by HX229. Twenty-one ships, totalling 140,800 tons, were sunk—the U-Boats escaping almost unscathed, though fortunately many were harassed to such an extent that they could not reach attack positions. The majority of the losses occurred during the night of 16/17 March when the convoys were 900 nm from the nearest air base and outside effective cover, but from then on SC122 was escorted by VLR Liberators of Nos.86 and 120 Squadrons, attacks being made on three of the four U-Boats sighted on the 17th. HX229 lost a further two ships early in the afternoon, but then came under the umbrella of VLR Liberators, the crew of one sighting six submarines and attacking three. Two more ships

went down during the next night, and disastrously the four Liberators sent out on the 18th failed to make contact with HX229—which lost another two ships during the afternoon. SC122 was now under almost continuous cover during daylight by a succession of Liberators which between them sighted 24 U-Boats and attacked four. Another ship was lost during the night of 18/19 March, but with both convoys coming within range, Fortresses of Nos.206 and 220 Squadrons joined the VLR Liberators and an A/S sweep around the convoys was made by five Sunderlands on the 19th, the crews of which sighted seven U-Boats and attacked six of them with DCs. The U-384 (Type VIIC) was destroyed by Plt Off L.G. Clark and crew of No.206 Squadron soon after joining HX229. No ships were sunk during the day from either convoy, though one straggler was lost, and the night of 19/20 was also uneventful despite the U-Boats remaining in contact. During the 20th Fortresses again carried out the close escort while Sunderlands made another sweep which resulted in six sightings and four attacks but no definite 'kills'.

The SC122 and HX229 saga provides a perfect example of the problems posed by the 'gap', and highlights the dramatic effect of adequate air cover despite the U-Boat pack remaining in contact for a further two days. It was undeniable, however, that Doenitz and his U-Boat commanders had scored a considerable success, for all except one of the 21 ships lost had been sunk while in convoy, and it was in something of a crisis atmosphere that the Atlantic Convoy Conference was held in Washington. Strong arguments were made for the dispersal of ships but in the end the convoy system was upheld as the only practical method of getting ships across the Atlantic in good order. Some significant changes were agreed, however, North Atlantic convoys becoming a British and Canadian responsibility from 1 April, while to ease organizational problems slower ships were banned from New York and would in future only sail to and from Halifax, Nova Scotia. The thorny problem of Liberator allocation was also raised, for despite the Casablanca Conference* recommendation that 80 VLR aircraft should be deployed to cover the 'Atlantic Gap' no change in the tardy delivery programme was discernible, the Canadians pointing out forcibly that they had trained crews available but only range-limited obsolescent Digbys to fly anti-submarine patrols from Newfoundland.

Intimidated by their Far East interests the American delegates remained adamant that the current distribution was correct, and it was reluctantly decided that the 20 Liberators required to rearm No.10 Squadron, RCAF, for anti-submarine operations out of Halifax, would have to be transferred from the British allocation. Fortunately President Roosevelt, concerned by the losses being sustained in the North Atlantic, insisted on a reallocation, and it was finally agreed that sufficient Liberators would be supplied to maintain the required strength of 80 for operations in the area. The RAF would get 120—though not immediately! Co-incidentally the naval support groups which now included escort carriers, returned to the Atlantic ex-*Torch*, ASV Mk.III reliability increased dramatically, and deliveries of Scottish Aviation-modified Liberators GR.IIIs started to outstrip losses.

While arguments with the Americans over the 'Gap' seemed at least temporarily in abeyance, differences between the Admiralty and the Air Ministry over the conduct of the offensive in the Bay of Biscay rumbled on. Both fully backed the tactics but differed over the necessary resources. Operational Research scientists calculated that 260 long-range aircraft were needed to sustain operations, a figure far in excess of Coastal Command's current resources, while the Admiralty's breath-taking solution was the transfer of 190 Lancasters from Bomber Command! When asked for his views Slessor took a 'diplomatic' line, probably influenced by the 'success' of negotiations over aircraft for Atlantic operation, and suggested that the Americans be asked for six Liberator squadrons (72 aircraft) on loan—as reinforced replacements for those which had just left No.19 Group on transfer to

In March 1943 No.59 Squadron returned to Thorney Island and was again equipped with Liberators, including the Mk.V FL951/T. (No.59 Sqn records)

Morocco. The Anti-U-Boat Committee supported Slessor and the request was made, only to be refused point-blank by Admiral King, the powerful US Chief of Naval Operations, who was still convinced that the war would be won in the Pacific, and that the Atlantic was a comparative backwater!

The end result was that No.19 Group had to fight the Bay battle with reduced forces, though re-equipment of No.502 Squadron with extended range Halifaxes helped somewhat, and 32 LL/ASV Mk.III Wellingtons were now available. *Enclose*, a nine-day operation following the same pattern as *Gondola*, was launched on 20 March and resulted in aircraft making 26 sightings and 15 attacks. U-332 was damaged and U-665 (Type VIIC) sunk, the latter No.172 Squadron's first success with centrimetric radar.

Enclose II followed between 6-13 April when eleven sightings and four attacks were made, one of them resulting in the destruction of U-376 (Type VIIC) by No.172 Squadron. Operation *Derange*, also mounted in April, was concentrated on a different area of the Bay, but despite the use of some 70 Halifaxes, Liberators and Wellingtons equipped with the latest radar it did not produce many positive sightings and was considered a failure by Coastal Command HQ, though in fact the increased number of aircraft undetected by their warning equipment was alarming

*Meeting between Churchill and Roosevelt mid-January 1943.

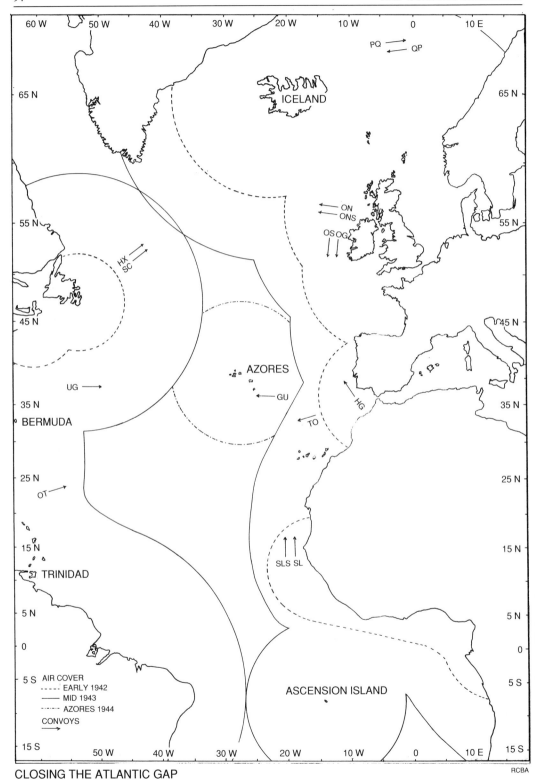

CLOSING THE ATLANTIC GAP

RCBA

Attacks on U-Boats were steadily increasing in number. Here a Type VIIC is straddled by a stick of depth charges. (Public Archives of Canada)

U-Boat crews, and on 27 April Doenitz again changed tactics, ordering commanders to cross the Bay submerged at night and surface to recharge their batteries during the day, until *Naxos*, a German centrimetric radar warning device, came into service.

Despite set-backs in the Bay, the Germans were understandably full of confidence over the eventual outcome of the 'Battle of the Atlantic'. They had increasing numbers of 'boats' on station and, with the ability to partially decipher Allied rendezvous signals, were able to lay plans to intercept convoys in strength. On 26 March 32 U-Boats were in position to attack ONS1, but the weather broke and they lost contact. Attention then turned to Convoys SC123 and HX230,

but as the vile weather abated the submarines were harassed by land-based aircraft and those from the USS *Bogue*, operating as part of the escort to SC123. Only one ship was lost, a poor return for such intensive effort during which two U-Boats, the U-169 (Type IX) and U-469 (Type VIIC), were destroyed by the crews of Fortresses of No.206 Squadron.

A planned delay in the despatch of two Russian convoys enabled the escort groups provided for Atlantic convoys to be further increased during April. A British escort carrier, the *Biter* was deployed,* the ship supporting Convoy ONS4, which made the westbound

*As well as the USS *Bogue*.

Depth charges are loaded aboard a Liberator. (British Official)

Oban was a small but effective base, well positioned for operations off the north-west of the British Isles. Sunderland IIIs of No.330 Squadron occupied the moorings and hardstandings from January to July 1943. (N. Mathisrud via A.S. Thomas)

crossing unscathed though U-Boats were in the vicinity, two of which were sunk. This was not an accurate indication of the effect of an escort carrier, however, because co-ordinated pack attacks were not made on this convoy, but for ONS5, which consisted of 42 ships, a total of 51 U-Boats were on hand and the assault which started on 28 April continuing until 6 May, resulted in running battles with the escorts virtually all the way across the Atlantic. Thirteen ships were sunk, but seven of the attacking U-Boats were destroyed, so neither side could claim it as a success.

Another test was in prospect, however, for on 8 May the Germans again broke the signal code and were able to position 36 U-Boats (out of about 60 in mid-Atlantic) in readiness for Convoy HX237. HMS *Biter* left Argentia on 5 May with the 5th Escort Group to join the convoy which was also covered by the RCAF until within range of VLR Liberators from Iceland. On 12 May three Liberators of No.86 Squadron, each carrying two of the new Mk.24 mines* and four DCs, joined the escort just as the U-89 was being despatched by a destroyer, and it was not long before the opportunity came to use the new weapon. Flt Lt J Wright's crew gained a radar contact which disappeared as he started his attacking run. He dropped a torpedo on the 'swirl' and for two agonisingly long minutes circled the contact position before a small disturbance was seen in the water some 900 yards from the release point. Soon afterwards the damaged U-456 came to the surface and the submarine's gun crew commenced firing at the Liberator as a DC attack was attempted. Short of fuel, Wright was forced to leave the U-Boat wallowing on the

surface. The next morning it was located again by the crew of a Sunderland of No.423 Squadron, RCAF. They called in surface forces, attacking with DCs when it started to submerge—the U-456 (Type VIIC) finally being destroyed by a frigate and a corvette. By now Convoy SC129 was in the same area and both were receiving almost continuous air cover.

Five ships were lost by the two convoys, but five U-Boats were destroyed, a disastrous result for Doenitz. For the Germans worse was to come, an attempted attack by 17 U-Boats on SC120 being thwarted by continuous cover by Icelandic-based Liberators and Hudsons (of No.269 Squadron). The latter sank two U-Boats, the U-646 and U-273 (both Type VIICs), while the crew of a 120 Squadron Liberator captained by F/Sgt W. Stoves dropped two homing torpedoes on U-954 (Type VIIC) on 19 May and she disappeared without trace. The next day another 120 Squadron Liberator crew, captained by Sqn Ldr J.R.E. Proctor, depth charged U-258 (Type VIIC and later a confirmed 'kill') which brought the total during the passage of SC120 to six (two by surface forces)—and not one ship was lost. During ten days in mid-May ten convoys, totalling 370 merchant ships, passed through the U-Boat cordon losing six ships, three of them stragglers. It was a dramatic turn round in fortune produced partially by changed tactics and strengthened escorts, but mainly by filling the notorious 'gap' with a combination of long range Liberators and carrier-based Swordfish/Avengers. As always, the aircraft successfully pinned the U-Boats down, pre-

*A cover name for the *Fido* acoustic homing torpedo.

venting them from getting in position for attacks, but they now also had a weapon capable of destroying submarines which had 'gone deep'. During May 41 U-Boats were destroyed, 23 of them by aircraft, and Doenitz conceded defeat on 22 May, ordering his 'wolf packs' south and west to operate off the Azores, South America and the Caribbean.

This redeployment was not immediately obvious to Slessor, however, and faced with increasing numbers of convoys with no corresponding increase in anti-sub-marine aircraft strength, he informed the Anti-U-Boat Sub-Committee that he could no longer find sufficient escorts for every convoy. He therefore proposed to concentrate his resources on those considered liable to attack, the remainder being left in the care of their surface escorts—a plan reminiscent of one adopted by his predecessor in 1942. In practice this procedure, code-named *Stipple*, had been in operation for some months as an *ad hoc* measure, but it was now put on an official basis, consultation taking place each morning between the U-Boat Intelligence Department of the Admiralty at HQ Western Approaches, Liverpool, and HQ Coastal Command, Northwood.

Meanwhile, the changed German tactics in the Bay had again decreased night sightings drastically and the AOC No.19 Group, Air Vice Marshal G.R. Bromet CBE,DSO, ordered an immediate review of the areas patrolled and an increase in the daylight Operation *Derange* coverage. It was therefore ironic that the first sighting in May occurred a few minutes after midnight on the 1st when F/Sgt P.W. Phillips, captain of a No.172 Squadron Wellington, saw a fully surfaced U-Boat in the glare of his searchlight. The submarine crew were quick to react and commenced firing as the aircraft started its 'run' but six DCs were released in

what appeared to be a good attack. The U-415 had been damaged but not seriously, and she continued on course for base, 550 nm to the east, being spotted some 11 hours later by a No.461 Squadron, RAAF, crew, captained by Flt Lt E.C. Smith. The U-Boat dived before the Sunderland could reach the position but depth charges dropped on the swirl caused further damage. After another six hours she was seen by the crew of a 612 Squadron Whitley and commenced diving with the gun crew still on deck firing at the aircraft. Six DCs were dropped—wide of the sub-marine. The remaining two DCs went down on the estimated position but without success, the U-415 making Brest four days later with a very shaken crew. The next day Flt Lt Smith (of No.461 Squadron) was again in action, stalking a U-Boat from an initial sighting ten miles away. Its gun crew opened up at one mile but the attack was continued and four DCs dropped—with four more on a follow-up attack. Both were well judged and the U-332 (Type VIIC) was mortally wounded, going down for the final time stern first. During the first week of May day-time sightings in the Bay shot up to 71, resulting in 43 attacks, 17 of them in the face of accurate fire from the U-Boats gun crew.

The increasing tendency for U-Boat captain's to remain surfaced and fight back was a disconcerting development for the aircrews, but one which rarely had the desired effect of forcing them to break off the attack. Looking at it from the Commanders' view-point, Slessor considered the 'fight back' policy a positive advantage, taking the line that the increased chances of sinking the submarine were worth the additional losses in aircraft which would result. He abandoned night AS patrols over the Bay early in May

U-Boats were now fighting back. This Type XIVA is heavily armed with an anti-aircraft 'bandstand'. (British Official via B. Robertson)

No.120 Squadron was still flying a variety of Liberator variants. A Mk.III FL923/V flies over Iceland under threatening cloud during September 1943. This aircraft was lost less than a month later when hit by flak from the U-539. (via J.D. Oughton)

and concentrated his forces by day. During the first week's operation three U-Boats were so badly damaged that they had to return to base and two Type VIICs (U465 and U663) were sunk by crews of Nos.10 RAAF and 58 Squadrons respectively. On the 11th, No.58 Squadron were again successful, Plt Off J.B. Stark and crew sending U-528 (Type IXC) to the bottom, and four days later the CO, Wg Cdr W.E. Oulton* got the first 'milch cow' tanker submarine to be destroyed, the U-463(Type XIV). By the end of the month six U-Boats had been sunk in the Bay, Oulton and his crew sharing a third, the U-563 (Type VIIC), with Nos.10 RAAF and 228 Squadrons. Six aircraft had been lost, but it was clear to Doenitz that the 'fight back' tactic by individual U-Boats was not viable, and early in June he ordered his captains to cross the Bay in groups so that they could use their combined fire power on any attacker.

On the British side the fight was not left entirely to the 'heavies'. During February 1943 the U-Boat Warfare Committee had informed the Cabinet that Coastal Command had successfully completed rocket projectile trials, and in May Beaufighters of No.236 Squadron were deployed to Predannack for RP operations over the Bay. F/Sgt A.W.J. Hazell attacked a submarine on the 29th without apparent result, but three days later Flg Off M.C. Bateman, with the U-Boat specialist Lt Cdr F.J. Brookes RN, perched uncomfortably behind him in the narrow fuselage, had better luck. Brookes sighted the submarine through binoculars at some ten miles range, and Bateman turned and dived straight at his quarry. As he selected two pairs of rockets the U-418 (Type VIIC) started to dive. Bateman fired in rapid succession and the RPs were seen to go through the hull taking the U-Boat straight to the bottom.

The 'fight back' policy was not the only hazard

faced in the Bay, for since the beginning of 1943 long range fighters of the Luftwaffe had been operating in greater strength. V Gruppe of KG40 ranged far out over the Bay, co-ordinated attacks by six, or even eight, Ju88s on solitary AS aircraft proving very successful. Some units, among them No.10 Squadron, RAAF, beefed up the already considerable defensive armament of their Sunderlands, but unless the aircraft were able to find sanctuary in cloud their chances were not good. Occasionally, however, they were able to give as good as they got, the fight put up on 2 June by Flt Lt C. Walker and his 461 Squadron crew being an outstanding example. Five hours into their *Derange* patrol over the western part of the Bay the crew were galvanised by the rear gunner's report of eight Ju88s closing rapidly. For the next 45 minutes Walker threw the heavy Sunderland all over the sky as the '88s attacked from various directions, the gunners claiming three fighters shot down and another forced to retire trailing black smoke. The flying boat was riddled with holes, one gunner was killed and other crew members wounded, but the captain got it back to the Cornish coast, setting the Sunderland down on the sea off Marazion, near Penzance, before driving it on to dry sand to prevent it sinking.

For nearly a fortnight the 'convoying' of U-Boats worked well for the Germans, No.19 Group experiencing a sudden reduction in sightings despite the addition of Hampdens of No.415 Squadron, RCAF, to the anti-submarine force. Then late on 12 June a group transit by five U-Boats was discovered 90 nm north of Cape Ortegal, and the reason for the dearth of contacts became obvious. The group was located again the following day by the crew of a No.228 Squadron Sunderland captained by Flg Off L.B. Lee,

*Who sunk the U-663 on the 5th.

and in a hail of fire he attacked and badly damaged the U-564 before crashing into the sea with the loss of the whole crew. The submarine set course for Brest accompanied by U-185 and they were sighted on 14 June by the crew of a 10 OTU Whitley captained by Sgt A.J. Benson. Ordered to remain in the area and carry out homing procedures, Benson got tired of waiting after two hours and attacked U-564 (Type VIIC) on his own in the face of accurate fire. His DCs sank the submarine but the Whitley was damaged and was lost when it came under attack by enemy fighters.

Group transits by U-Boats meant fewer individual targets and more danger from return fire when they were attacked. The only practical response was to increase the number of anti-submarine aircraft in the area so that they could come to each other's aid. Fortunately the reduction in U-Boat activity in the North Atlantic allowed some redeployment of aircraft to No.19 Group and the Bay area, but more were needed, and late in June Slessor made a personal visit to Washington to again argue the case for American help. This time he was able to convince Admiral King of the value of the Bay operations and the 479th Anti-Submarine Group, USAAF, comprising the 4th and 19th AS Squadrons (24 Liberators) were earmarked and they arrived at St Eval during July.

'Fight Back' by U-Boat commanders was not confined to the Bay of Biscay. On 11 June the new CO of No.206 Squadron, Wg Cdr R.B. Thomson, was on patrol over the northern transit route east of Iceland when a U-Boat was sighted and attacked. The U-417 (Type VIIC) was destroyed but not before so badly

damaging the Fortress that it had to be 'ditched'. The whole crew got into dinghies (B-17s floated well), but it was three days before they were rescued by the crew of a Catalina—no joke at 63 degrees north even in the summer.

Three U-Boats from La Pallice successfully fought their way across the Bay early in June, though the almost constant presence of aircraft took its toll of the crews, but a group of five from Brest/Lorient were less fortunate. They were attacked on 14 June by four Mosquito IIs of No.307 (Polish) Squadron, Fighter Command, on detachment at Predannack for *Instep* patrols, the intrepid Poles strafing the submarines with cannon fire and causing so many casualties that U-68 and U-155 had to return to port. One of the aircraft crash-landed at base, but it was definitely a victory for the aircraft because Doenitz was so worried by the incident that he changed his tactics again, and on 17 June ordered his crews to remain in groups but only surface for battery charging, a total of four hours in every twenty-four. He did not completely abandon the idea of an 'Unterseebootfleugzeugfalle' (submarine aircraft trap), however, for he persevered with a plan to fit two armoured 'bandstands' mounting two four-barrelled 20-mm guns and a semi-automatic 37-mm gun on Type VII U-Boats. An experimental installation had already been made on U-441 which, carrying a 67 man crew,* had made a cruise at the end of May during which damage was sustained when a Sunderland crew took the bait and attacked. The

16 more than standard.

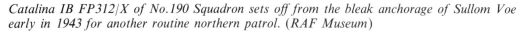

Catalina IB FP312/X of No.190 Squadron sets off from the bleak anchorage of Sullom Voe early in 1943 for another routine northern patrol. (RAF Museum)

aircraft was also badly damaged and had subsequently succumbed to fighters, but one of the 'bandstands' had given trouble and the voyage was not considered a success. On 8 July the repaired U-441 set out again and after being ignored for four days was suddenly confronted by three Beaufighters of 248 Squadron out on an *Instep* patrol. Led by Flt Lt C. Schofield, the aircraft made a synchronized attack, the combined fire power from twelve 20-mm cannon soon reducing the deck of the U-Boat to a shambles, the gun crews and most of the officers being either killed or wounded. The submarine submerged and limped home but it was the end of the anti-aircraft U-Boat. Henceforth they would only fight it out when forced to.

Slessor now decided to play Doenitz at his own game by cutting back on the single-aircraft *Derange* and *Orderly* patrols, and replacing them with sweeps over parts of the Bay, code-named *Musketry* and *Seaslug**. Under the plan, seven aircraft were despatched three times daily to fly parallel tracks through the *Musketry* area, while *Seaslug* was covered by No.15 Group VLR and LR aircraft. The patrols were co-ordinated by the AOC No.19 Group, a crew on the sweep sighting a group of U-Boats being required to make a report and await the arrival of other aircraft before attacking, the advantage of surprise being sacrificed for fire power.

A new weapon, the 35-lb hollow-charge AS bomb, was first tried out on 3 July when the crew of a No.224 Squadron Liberator on a *Derange* patrol obtained a radar contact at ten miles, and shortly afterwards visually sighted the wake of a submarine. The captain, Sqn Ldr P.J. Cundy DFC, immediately attacked, dropping a pattern of the new bombs, the effect of which could not be seen for spray, though the aircraft suffered heavy concussion as they exploded on impact, and was also hit by the U-Boat crew's gunfire. Further attacks were made using DCs, and the U-628

(Type VIIC) sank leaving bodies and debris on the sea surface. With fuel pouring out of a holed wing tank the Liberator limped home, making it to St Eval on three engines. The 35-lb AS bombs were used again four days later by another 224 Squadron crew. Again the results were inconclusive, appearing nothing like so effective as the weapons aboard a trials aircraft which joined the Squadron with the famed Sqn Ldr T. Bulloch when he returned to 'ops' after a seven-month 'rest'. It not only had a Leigh Light, stowage for eight DCs and a Mk.24 Mine, but also mountings for four 60-lb RPs each side of the fuselage. Bulloch was flying this special aircraft on 8 July when the waist gunner spotted a U-Boat travelling alone off Cape Finisterre. The pilot immediately swung the aircraft round into the attack and from 800 yards released two rockets, followed by two more at 600 yds, and then a salvo of four at 500 yds. One of the gunners saw a rocket appear out of the water on the far side of the U-Boat, having apparently gone through the hull as the vessel started to submerge. Bulloch never took chances, dropping the torpedo on the swirl, and when it appeared to have malfunctioned he attacked with DCs. The result was a heavy explosion (probably the torpedo being detonated by the DCs), but in any event U-514 (Type IXC) was the victim of this decisive attack.

The B-24 Liberators of the 4th and 19th AS Squadrons, 479th Bomb Group, USAAF, started operations under No.19 Group control on 13 July, room having been made for them at St Eval by the return to Abingdon of the No.10 OTU Whitley detachment four days earlier. During 11 months with Coastal Command the 'sprog' OTU crews had made 89 U-Boat sightings and 55 attacks. The U-564 had been sunk and three others damaged. Fifty OTU

*See map opposite.

Wellingtons were active in various roles, Mk.X HZ258/S of No.304 Squadron operating with No.16 Group out of Docking mid-1943. (via A.S. Thomas)

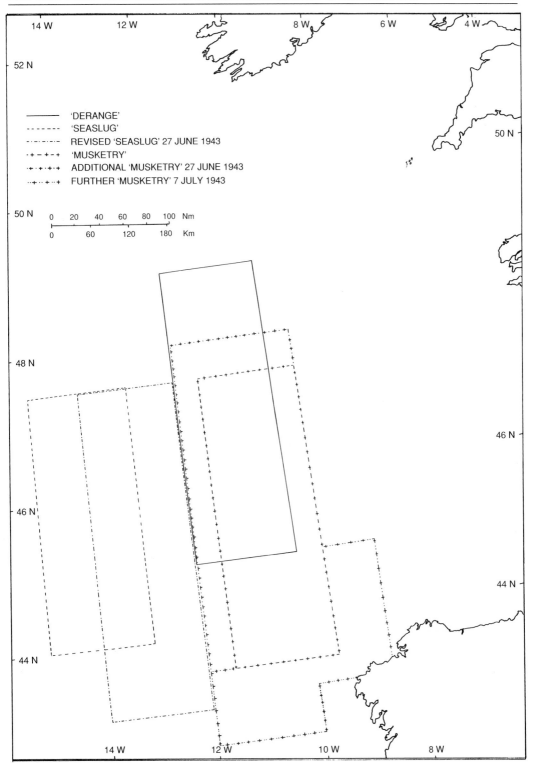

BAY PATROLS — DERANGE, SEASLUG AND MUSKETRY

Down at Gibraltar Catalina IBs still soldiered on alongside Sunderlands during 1943. FP181/L of No.202 Squadron carries standard 250-lb DCs under the wings. (MAP)

aircraft had been lost as a result of U-Boat action, attacks by Ju88s and accidents, during 16,455 operational hours. In statistical terms the results were not impressive, but they made a significant contribution to the number of aircraft which could be put up daily over the Bay, and thus increased the harassment of the U-Boat crews which was so valuable in itself.

The 479 BG's first action came quickly. A 19th Sqn crew sighted two U-Boats in company on 20 July and attacked one of them with DCs. The submarine was damaged but the Liberator was hit by flak and the pilot, Lt C.F. Gallimeir, had to break off and make for base. A 58 Sqn Halifax appeared on the scene at this point and the crew engaged the U-Boat with machine gun fire before attacking with a stick of eight DCs. The U-558 (Type VIIC) immediately started to sink and was abandoned by the surviving crew members. It was a good start by the 479th BG who were to be responsible for the destruction of another three, plus one shared with No.224 Squadron, before relinquishing the AS role to the USN in October 1943. The US Navy unit VP-63 also joined No.19 Group on attachment late in July, operating Catalinas equipped with a Magnetic Anomaly Detection (MAD) device from Pembroke Dock without much success before leaving for North Africa in November.

Meanwhile, Royal Navy support groups had become available for operations in the Bay, and the already excellent rapport between Coastal Command crews and those of the hunter/killer ships reached new heights. The first combined air/sea operation in the area followed the sighting of three U-Boats by the crew of a 53 Squadron Liberator on 30 July during a *Musketry* patrol. A navigational error in the sighting report could easily have ruined the operation,

but fortunately the co-ordinates were corrected by the crew of the first aircraft homed in, a No.228 Squadron Sunderland. It was followed by the 210 Squadron Catalina which was operating with Force *Fisher* (2nd Support Group), a USAAF Liberator of the 19th AS Sqn and a Halifax of 502 Squadron. As this motley collection circled the U-Boats just out of gunnery range the ships steamed at maximum speed towards the datum, but before they could reach the scene the Halifax crew, frustrated by poor communications, decided to attack, dropping three of the new 600-lb AS weapons which fell wide, the crew having been distracted by hits on the aircraft as they made their run. Another 502 Squadron Halifax, flown by Flg Off A. van Rossum, now arrived, closely followed by a Sunderland of 461 Squadron. Van Rossum made attack runs at 3,000 ft and one of his 600 lb bombs fell close enough to damage the U-462 sufficiently to prevent it diving. The 53 Squadron Liberator crew attacked U-461 at low level, the aircraft being so badly damaged by flak that they were forced to land in Portugal, but while the U-Boat gunners were distracted Flt Lt Marrows slipped in unseen and straddled U-461 (Type IV) with seven DCs. The U-Boat split in two and sank. The surface vessels now arrived and opened fire on U-504 which promptly dived. Van Rossum made another attack on U-462 (Type XIV) but she was already sinking and *Fisher Force* spent the next two hours hunting U-504 to destruction. It was not a copybook example of air/sea co-operation—but it had the intended result and went some way to keeping the month's losses in the North Atlantic to 18 ships (97,200 tons).

Four more U-Boats were sunk during the first two days of August, one of them after being badly damaged by the crew of a No.415 Squadron Hampden, and finished off by a USAAF Liberator, the other three victims of Sunderlands. Such a loss rate could not be sustained, and reluctantly Doenitz gave up the 'fight back' transit groupings, ordering U-Boats in the outer Bay to split up and proceed alone, recalled those still in the inner Bay, and rerouted returning submarines via the Spanish coast. During the 97 days of 'fight back' (27 April-2 August 1943) aircraft had sunk 26 U-Boats and damaged 17 for the loss of 12 of their number—plainly an Allied victory due almost entirely to the Germans believing that the majority of aircrew would be deterred from continuing low level attacks in the face of gunfire, and that such fire would always be accurate enough to shoot them down if they did persist. They were also uncertain about the reason for the apparent ease with which aircrews continued to find submarines. They had expected their *Naxos-U* receiver to make them as immune from centrimetric radar as *Metox* had from earlier types of ASV, but commanders of U-Boats fitted with *Naxos* continued to be surprised by the sudden appearance of an aircraft. Often it was a Wellington which they erroneously thought not capable of carrying centrimetric radar, and when the Germans discovered that *Metox* also radiated strong signals they became convinced that the Allies had developed a means of homing onto it. On 3 August Doenitz suspended the use of *Metox*, and the sudden reduction in losses in the Bay area which followed seemed to justify the move. In fact it was due to the change in tactics ordered a day earlier, for no such homing device was in existence, and the real reason for the German failure to detect many of the aircraft was that *Naxos* was nothing like as effective operationally as it appeared to be under trial conditions. Completely confused, the Germans undertook production of a new search receiver currently under development, the W. Anz G.1, 'guaranteed' to be radiation-free.

The use by submarines of Spanish coastal waters between Finisterre and Ortegal was quickly deduced by HQ Coastal Command, and the Admiralty agreed to move two escort groups into the area. Slessor cancelled *Musketry* and *Seaslug* and introduced a series of five patrols code-named *Percussion* 'A' to 'E'. *Percussion* 'A' was a daylight patrol by No.19 Group aircraft covering the outer Bay right down to the Spanish coast; 'B' was also a daylight patrol but flown further out into the Atlantic by No.15 Group aircraft; 'C' was to be conducted at night by LL Wellingtons and Catalinas off the Spanish coast between Ortegal and Finisterre; 'D' were night patrols by flare-equipped Wellingtons of Nos.304 and 547 Squadrons off the Spanish coast, the aircraft illuminating ASV contacts for the escort groups ; and 'E' were day/night

Pembroke Dock in May 1943. Eight Sunderlands can be seen on hardstandings and another on the water. (Gp Capt G.A. Bolland via J. Evans)

patrols further south off the Spanish coast by aircraft under the control of the AOC Gibraltar.* A similar air/surface plan code-named *Rosegarden* covered the transit route through the deep laid mine fields between Scotland and Iceland where the 10th Escort Group was operating, and amongst the forces deployed to cover the area were ten Hampden crews of No.455 Squadron who spent most of August at Benbecula in the Outer Hebrides. Unfortunately the weather was atrocious, and after several unsuccessful weeks the operation was abandoned.

During August, the 479th BG moved to Dunkeswell, and St Eval became host to VPB103, the first USN PB4Y-1 Liberator unit to operate with the RAF. They were followed by VPB105 and VPB110, the three patrol squadrons subsequently forming Fleet Air Wing 7, which replaced the 479th BG at Dunkeswell in September, and was similarly under the control of No.19 Group for operations over the Bay of Biscay. Further south, anti U-Boat operations off the Azores were the almost exclusive concern of the Americans who used surface hunter/killer forces with notable success but at great expense in resources. Land bases in the area were the answer, and with the ever present threat to Gibraltar bound convoys in mind the British Government undertook protracted discussions with the Portuguese, these bearing fruit in August 1943 when permission was given for the building of an airfield on Terceira Island, Azores.

Since the third week of May when Doenitz had largely deserted the 'Gap' for easier areas, not one

*See map on page 104.

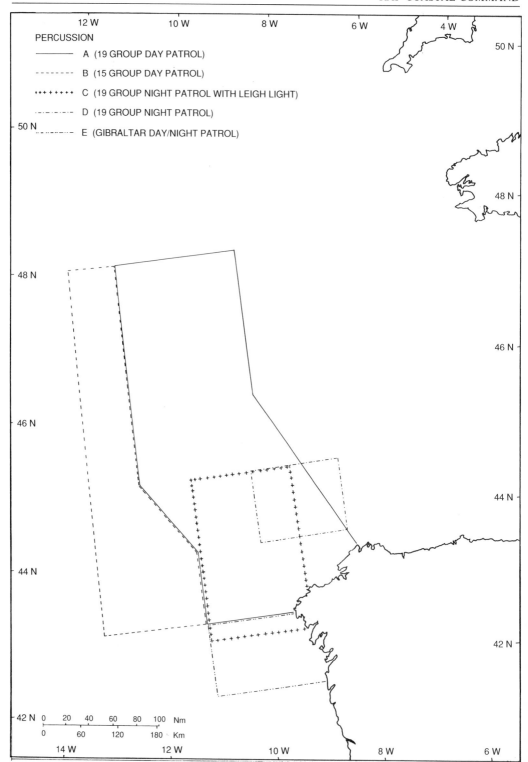

PERCUSSION

——————— A (19 GROUP DAY PATROL)

- - - - - - B (15 GROUP DAY PATROL)

+ + + + + + + C (19 GROUP NIGHT PATROL WITH LEIGH LIGHT)

—·—·—·—·— D (19 GROUP NIGHT PATROL)

·—··—··—·· E (GIBRALTAR DAY/NIGHT PATROL)

BAY PATROLS — PERCUSSION

RCBA

A well-worn Sunderland III—DV960/2-H of No.461 Squadron out over the Bay of Biscay, June 1943. (D. Roberts via A.S. Thomas)

ship had been lost on the all-important North Atlantic. This situation could not last, and at the end of August the Germans decided on a new offensive. Twenty-eight attack U-Boats and a submarine 'milch cow' tanker set out from the Biscay ports and bases in Norway. All had undergone modification to carry increased armour, quadruple gun turrets, *W. Anz* search receiver and two of the new *Zaunkoenig* homing torpedoes, the latter primarily intended for use against convoy escorts. All except the U-669 (Type VIIC), sunk off the coast of Spain early on 7 September by the crew of a No.407 Squadron LL Wellington, reached their patrol area by the evening of the 16th and were soon positioned in a long line across the

convoy routes. Two days later the slow westbound convoy ONS18 (27 ships with ten escorts including the Empire MacAlpine,*) entered the U-Boat area, while 120 miles behind was the faster ON202 (38 ships with six escorts). Warned by *Ultra* intercepts, the Admiralty ordered the 9th Support Group to join in the search for the 'wolf pack' and rerouted the convoys to the north-west. 'Distant support' was provided on the 19th by the crew of a VLR Liberator of No.10 Squadron, RCAF, returning to Newfoundland from Iceland after escorting HMS *Renown* (carrying the British Prime Minister, Winston Churchill, home from

*One of three merchant aircraft carriers (MAC) then in existence.

A busy scene at Aldergrove in March 1943 soon after No.86 Squadron had joined No.120 at this Northern Ireland base. The Mk.III FK228/M in the foreground belongs to the latter unit, the others to No.86 Squadron. A new ATC tower is being built. (Imperial War Museum)

Wellington VIII LB247/D of No.547 Squadron at Tain. This aircraft flew into a hill near Limavady, 5 November 1943, when with No.7 OTU. (via A.S. Thomas)

the Quebec Conference), and during their patrol they despatched U-341 (Type VIIC). The following day ON202, now only 30 miles north-east of ONS18, came under attack by several U-Boats, one of which remained on the surface and prepared to fight it out when a VLR Liberator of No.120 Squadron approached. Heavy gunfire caused Flt Lt J.K. Moffat to release his DCs too early, and he then held off, circling the U-Boat. At last the U-Boat captain judged it safe to submerge, which was just what Moffat wanted him to do, for his aircraft was carrying a *Fido* homing torpedo. The weapon was dropped on the swirl and duly exploded against the submarine's casing—the U-338 (Type VIIC) sinking with all hands. During the night the convoys joined forces, and a thick fog came down protecting the ships until the 22nd when No.10 Squadron, RCAF, operating out of Gander, was able to provide continuous air cover and damage two U-Boats in the process. The strength of the air cover provided both by Liberators and by Swordfish from the *Empire MacAlpine* forced the Germans to lose contact during the 23rd, but despite this and the destruction of three U-Boats (U-229 to an escort), they considered the new tactics a comparative success having sunk six merchantmen and three escorts.

Any satisfaction Doenitz may have felt must have been short-lived, for the next three convoys evaded the re-grouped U-Boat 'pack' completely by using bad weather, though the latter did not prevent patrolling aircraft claiming three 'boats'. When the submarines did make contact with the eastbound SC143 they were routed by Swordfish from the MAC *Rapana*, and Liberators of Nos.86 and 120 Squadrons operating from Iceland. Almost continuous patrols harassed the U-Boats and prevented most of them getting into position, and on 8 October Liberator crews sank the U-419 and U-643 (both Type VIICs), and a Sunderland operating at extreme range from Castle Archdale successfully depth-charged the U-610 (Type VIIC).

For the first time in mid-Atlantic a VLR Liberator fitted with a Leigh Light escorted the convoy for most of the night, and on the 9th Doenitz broke off the engagement without the anticipated success. Three U-Boats had been lost in obtaining the destruction of one freighter and an escort vessel.

A week later the 'wolf pack' tried again. The target was the westbound ON126, but they failed again, six U-Boats being destroyed, four of them by Liberator crews of Nos.59 and 86 Squadrons. By the end of the month no less than 20 German submarines had been lost in the North Atlantic alone and it began to look as if they were beaten.

British forces landed on Terceira on 8 October, and ten days later the first Fortresses of Nos.206 and 220 Squadrons landed on the hastily prepared airfield at Lagens. Patrols started on the 20th, the Fortresses being joined by nine Hudsons on detachment from No.233 Squadron, Gibraltar, by the end of the month. Air Vice Marshal B.G. Bromet became AOC No.247 Group, Azores, on transfer from No.19 Group, and the following month Coastal's grip on the area became much firmer when AHQ Gibraltar, North Front airfield and its anti-submarine squadrons (Nos.48, 179, 202 and 233) were officially restored to the Command after an acrimonious eight months under American control from Morocco.

Meanwhile another new anti-submarine weapon was introduced, a Mosquito fitted with a six-pounder (57-mm) anti-tank gun. Originally intended for anti-shipping operations with the specialist No.618 Squadron, a small number of Mosquito FB Mk.XVIIIs, complete with crews, joined No.248 Squadron at Predannack in October and were tried out in the anti-submarine role. The first action came on 7 November when Flg Off A.J.L. Bonnett, RCAF, attacked the U-123 when almost in sight of her base at Lorient. Bonnett fired eight rounds and scored several hits on the deck and conning tower. One man

Fortress IIAs of No.220 Squadron soon after arrival at Lagens in the autumn of 1943. (via P.H.T. Green)

was killed, but the submarine made port and the gun had to await another occasion to prove its worth.

Rocket firing Liberators, similar to the trials aircraft tried out by Bulloch earlier in the year, were now in limited use by No.311 (Czech) Squadron, and took part in the eventual destruction of U-966 (Type VIIC) which had been located during the early morning of 10 November by a LL Wellington crew and assaulted by PB4Y-1 Liberators of VPB103 and 110. By the time the 311 Sqn aircraft arrived the U-966 was close to the Spanish coast, but an immediate attack was made and four RPs entered the water close to the hull. The U-Boat slowed markedly, apparently damaged, and was later beached near De Santafata Bay and blown up by the crew.

The capitulation of the Italians in September 1943 posed considerable problems for the German Navy, not least the need to reinforce U-Boat strength in the Mediterranean. The U-223 succeeded in breaching the Strait of Gibraltar, although twice attacked, but U-667 which attempted the passage on 24 September was less successful, being badly damaged by three LL Wellingtons of No.179 Squadron and two Hudsons from Nos.48 and 233 Squadrons resulting in a return to St Nazaire for repairs. Nearly a month later Doenitz tried again, resulting in the sinking of U-431 (Type VIIC) on 21 October and U-566 (Type VIIC) on the 24th (by the same No.179 Squadron crew), U-732 by naval forces, and U-340 (Type VIIC) after being damaged by a LL Wellington crew on 1 November and then hunted to exhaustion by destroyers. One U-Boat slipped through the net, but not only was it a disastrous loss for the Germans but it also renewed their doubts about the equipment being used to detect their submarines. They were convinced that *W. Anz* and *Naxos* receivers should have alerted them to known radars, failing to realise that at such a choke point the Allies were able to concentrate forces way above normal levels, confusing the receiver operators

and producing apparent failure of the equipment.

No.247 Group aircraft started operations by attacking 'milch cow' and supply U-Boats in mid-Atlantic, and it was quite a surprise when it became obvious during mid-November that Doenitz was assembling a large 'wolf pack' in the area. His objective could only be attacks on the previously unhindered Gibraltar-bound convoys, but it seemed a very odd time to start such operations, just when the ships could be properly escorted! Still unable to completely break Admiralty codes, the Germans resorted to reconnaissance aircraft to shadow and report two convoys, SL139 and MKS30. They were successful in this, but the number of anti-submarine aircraft now available to Nos.19 and 247 Groups was such that U-Boats were unable to reach attacking positions and the expected battle did not materialize. The protracted negotiations with the Portuguese were proving very worthwhile!

Doenitz's reaction to this latest failure was typical—he immediately brought the majority of his U-Boats into port for refits and installation of his new 'secret weapon' the *Schnorkel* tube. This device, originally tested by the Dutch pre-war, allowed the operation of diesel engines—and battery charging—at periscope depth, while providing a much reduced detection opportunity on radar or visually. It was a very important development—a potential winner.

The U-Boats remaining at sea were moved to areas off the western coasts of Ireland and Scotland where they remained submerged during the day and searched for convoys at night. There was a lull in activity, but despite severe losses the Germans were still managing to increase the number of operational U-Boats, and as soon as the refits were complete they expected to muster some 60 ocean-going craft in the northern half of the Atlantic and to regain supremacy over aircraft using their 'secret weapon'. Opposing them Coastal Command now had some 430 aircraft engaged in

anti-U-Boat operations. The landplane force comprised ten Liberator squadrons (three of them USN operating under the direction of No.19 Group), five LL Wellington squadrons and two squadrons each of Fortress, Halifax and Hudson aircraft—plus a detachment of three Mosquito FB Mk.XVIII fitted with the 57-mm gun. The flying boat strength consisted of seven Sunderland and two Catalina squadrons and a two-aircraft detachment of MAD Catalinas from VP-63 of the USN. This was a powerful force, but by means oversized for the tasks required of the Command.

At this rather awkward moment the appointment of Air Marshal Sir John Slessor as Deputy Allied Air Commander in the Mediterranean theatre was announced, and Air Chief Marshal Sir Sholto Douglas took over Coastal Command. Slessor had proved a successful commander and a popular one, in many ways the lucky recipient of much hard work by his predecessor. Not an innovator, he was firmly wedded to the widely held view of the Command as a basically defensive organization which should demand as little of the available resources as possible. Nevertheless he 'fought his corner' when he felt it necessary, kept his nerve during the terrible early months of 1943, and went on to engineer the winning of the battle, first in the Atlantic and then in the Bay.

The U-426 sinking after attack by Sunderland III EK586/U captained by Flg Off J.P. Roberts of No.10 Squadron, RAAF, 8 January 1944. (British Official)

CHAPTER 8

Strike and Strike Again– Anti-Shipping Operations 1944-45

AIR CHIEF MARSHAL Sir Sholto Douglas took over Coastal Command at a time when the Strike Wing concept had proved itself, aircraft were becoming available in reasonable numbers and, just as important, crews were more plentiful. Planning for the further development of the Wings was well in hand, the immediate task facing the new AOC-in-C being Operation *Overlord*, in which Coastal Command and in particular Nos.16 and 19 Groups, had a crucial part to play, starting well ahead of the actual invasion of Europe.

No.16 Group saw little activity for the first two months of 1944, though Albacores of No.415 Squadron did attack a number of enemy destroyers and set one on fire the very day Sholto Douglas assumed command. This Canadian squadron was one

of his more immediate problems, for the crews were very restless, considering themselves merely 'stooges' for the Royal Navy. In this they were supported by senior RCAF commanders, strenuous efforts having already been made by Air Marshal H. Edwards, AOC-in-C RCAF Overseas, to get the Squadron, together with Nos.404 and 407, transferred to Bomber Command or the Tactical Air Force. He had been unsuccessful when Slessor was in charge, and Sholto Douglas was to prove just as adamant that they would not be released until properly replaced!

The co-ordination and split-second timing achieved by the North Coates Wing had become so successful that the Germans virtually abandoned the use of Rotterdam and the Ems-Hook section of their shipping routes during daylight. Instead they transferred

Armed with 3" rocket projectiles, Beaufighter X/2-G of No.404 Squadron is readied for a sortie, May 1944. Emphasizing the armament options available on this versatile aircraft are the bomb racks under the fuselage and the doped canvas patches over the cannon ports. (Public Archives of Canada)

A Beaufighter X/2-R of No.404 Squadron fires a pair of 3" rockets. (R.C.L. Fitzwilliams via P.H.T. Green)

most coastal activity to the ports of Emden and Bremen, and this certainly provided problems for the Wing, strikes on ships on the Ems-Elbe route being very dangerous without fighter cover, and requests for Mustangs were to no avail despite earlier promises. However, the release of No.143 Squadron from Bay of Biscay operations in February meant the return of the North Coates Wing to full three-squadron strength, and it was decided to try catching enemy convoys as they entered the Den Helder in the early morning. A convoy was intercepted on 21 February when a merchant ship was seriously damaged, a 150-ton R-Boat was sunk and others damaged, but such opportunities were rare, and this proved to be the

only successful strike during the first two months of the year. With the return of better weather the situation improved, three Beaufighters armed with 25-lb RPs and another nine with cannon, escorted by Spitfires, discovering a 6,400-ton merchantman off Den Helder early on 1 March. It was damaged by RPs, and when 21 Beaufighters from the Wing returned later in the day the ship was still there, stationary and apparently abandoned. It was torpedoed but did not sink until hit by a 500-lb bomb from a No.415 Squadron Wellington.

No.16 Group's answer to night sailings was to try Beaufighter and Albacore/Wellington combinations, the plan being code-named Operation *Gilbey*. No.415

Beaufighters attack a coastal convoy, 29 March 1944. (British Official)

Home from Borkum with flak-damaged hydraulics. Flg Off I. Masson and his observer F/Sgt Knight belly-landed Beaufighter X NE812/2-M of No.455 Squadron at Langham, 14 May 1944. (I. Masson via C. Bowyer)

Squadron was used to locate and then illuminate the target with flares, the Albacores co-operating with a Manston-based detachment of No.143 Squadron, while the Wellingtons worked with the rest of the North Coates Wing. Both combinations proved very difficult to co-ordinate properly, one of the few early successes being on 5 March when the 1,878-ton Swedish ship *Diana* was sunk off Borkum by three No.254 Squadron Beaufighters following an excellent homing and illumination.

Within No.18 Groups's area further north there was more action. The Wick Wing badly damaged a ship off Stadlandt on 26 January 1944 using rockets, and from Leuchars No.489 Squadron sank two merchantmen and severely damaged another off Lister. At least eight escorts were damaged during the month off the Norwegian coast, but torpedo strike successes were patchy, the Wick Wing in particular having trouble with the weapon in the many stretches of shallow coastal water north of Stavanger. A solution had to be found and they turned to the rocket projectile, which though generally disappointing as an anti-flak measure, was showing increasing promise as the means of sinking ships. New procedures were evolved which overcame ranging and sighting problems, and decisively proved that the 25-lb solid head version had better flight and underwater characteristics than the 60-lb explosive shot. In a reversal of roles the 'Torbeau' squadron, No.144, became the Wick anti-flak unit, quelling the opposition with cannon fire so that rocket-firers of No.404 could concentrate on making the main attack. On 1 February a merchantman and an escort were sunk by 25-lb

rockets off Stadlandt, and another was damaged, and indications that the changed tactics were hurting soon came—in the form of strengthened fighter forces in southern Norway. On 5 March Nos.455 and 489 Squadrons recorded their first combined success since receiving Beaufighters, sinking a submarine chaser off south-west Norway; and the following day they officially became the Leuchars Strike Wing, celebrating by torpedoing a 1,000-ton vessel off Stavanger.

The provision of a strong Mustang escort on 29 March enabled the North Coates Wing to attempt a strike against shipping on the Ems-Elbe route at last. Six 'Torbeaus', ten Beaufighters with rockets and another ten anti-flak cannon-firers were despatched, and off Juist, north-east of Borkum they intercepted a convoy. Two merchant ships were sunk with torpedoes and their escorts damaged by a combination of RPs and cannon fire, serving notice that the route was no longer safe in daylight. The next day the Wick Wing made a determined attack on their largest target to date, the 14,000-ton liner *Monte Rosa* and claimed it damaged, but the enemy was becoming increasingly cautious. Opportunities for full scale Wing operations became rare, and even *Rover* Beaufighters operating at dusk or first light found few targets.

In the south-west No.248 Squadron continued operations with Beaufighters and the 'Special Detachment' of Mosquito XVIIIs while crews underwent conversion to the FB.VIs, their primary role remaining fighter-reconnaissance but also responsible for fighter support to strike squadrons. Mosquito fighter operations commenced on 20 February 1944, and ten patrols at Flight strength had been made by the end

Wellington XIII MF639/NH-H of No.415 Squadron at Bircham Newton in May 1944 when employed on night anti-shipping sorties. (via A.S. Thomas)

of the month. The first significant action came on 10 March when two Mk.XVIIIs escorted by four Mosquito FB.VIs sighted a German naval force with Ju88s as air cover. The Mosquito fighters engaged the '88s while the XVIIIs made for a U-Boat and its destroyer escort. Two Ju88s were claimed destroyed for no loss and with such encounters becoming more frequent the long range Mosquitoes were joined at Portreath by No.235 Squadron's Beaufighter Xs at the end of the month.

Preliminary operations in support of *Overlord* started early in April with the Albacores and Wellingtons of No.415 Squadron flying 120 sorties aimed at securing the northern end of the English Channel, while at the southern end the Portreath Wing was also active. Usually little happened, but occasionally patrols ran into trouble, as on 11 April when six Mosquito VIs of No.248 Squadron accompanying two Mk.XVIIIs took on the escorts of a U-Boat—two flak ships, two armed trawlers and eight Ju88s. Hits were claimed on all the ships and two Ju88s were destroyed, but the Mosquitoes did not get off scot-free, two being lost through enemy action and another two as a result of accidents.

Anti-shipping forces in the south increased markedly during April when both Nos.16 and 19 Groups received healthy injections of Fleet Air Arm aircraft. Operating in General Reconnaissance Wings from shore bases, their sorties were increasingly directed at E and R-Boats as *Overlord* approached. At Manston No.155 (GR) Wing was formed to operate 819 Squadron (Swordfish) and 848 Squadron (Avenger), while at Hawkinge 854 and 855, both with Avengers, were controlled by No.16 Group through No.157 (GR) Wing. With No.19 Group, 849 and 850 Squadrons (Avengers) flew into Perranporth on 20 April to operate alongside 816 Squadron's Swordfish, and at Harrowbeer, a No.10 Group station, Coastal Command 'lodged' No 156 (GR) Wing and 12 ASV-equipped Swordfish of 838 Squadron. Oper-

ations on *Channel Stop*, Coastal Command's main invasion task, started on 30 April with an offensive sweep from Perranporth, and soon all the GR Wings were involved.

The North Coates Wing carried out two successful attacks on small naval vessels during April. On the 18th Nos.143, 236 and 254 Squadrons sank two trawler auxiliaries with rockets and cannon and two days later attacked a small *sperrbrecker* and three auxiliaries with torpedo, RP and cannon. The *sperrbrecker* was sunk and the other vessels badly damaged.

The Leuchars Wing moved down to Langham during April and carried out their first strike from Norfolk on 6 May when No.455 Squadron provided anti-flak support for 489's 'Torbeaus'. A 1,500-ton freighter was sunk off Borkum, and eight days later they despatched a 1,900-ton merchantman and a mine sweeper off Ameland. Both units also carried out armed reconnaissance over the North Sea carrying two 250-lb and two 500-lb bombs for opportunist use against shipping.

On 8 May eight Albacores of No.415 Squadron were detached to Winkleigh, Devon, to patrol the amphibious training areas and deter any attempted interference by the dreaded E-Boats. The Albacores remaining at Manston were also busy, attacking targets from barges to ocean-going tankers, though the main interest remained E-Boats. Success was elusive, however, until the night of 24 May when an Albacore crew operating alone bombed and sank a large torpedo boat, a vessel almost the size of a destroyer.

The anti-shipping forces available to No.19 Group had also been strengthened by the re-formation of No.524 Squadron* at Davidstow Moor early in April. It was equipped with Wellington XIIIs for night patrols against E-Boats and submarines off the French

*Previously a Mariner flying boat unit for a few non-operational months.

A bomb-toting Beaufighter X NE788 of No.455 Squadron in D-Day identification markings awaits its crew. (Imperial War Museum)

coast, and a further boost was given when the Wick Wing joined them early in May. Escorted by 28 Spitfires the Wing made its first foray from cloud-laden Davidstow on 19 May, the target two destroyers and four escorts sighted off the Brest peninsula. The 22 Beaufighters met intense flak, and though the attack was pressed home using cannon and rockets the results were disappointing. Most of the 60-lb rockets fell short, the leader of the anti-flak escort, Sqn Ldr P.W. Dunn of No.144 Squadron, was shot down, and many of the Beaufighters were damaged, two having to force-land.

Completing the anti-shipping dispositions for D-Day was the move of No.143 Squadron to Manston on 23 May, and with FAA units maintaining continuous patrols throughout the 24-hour period, Nos.16 and 19 Groups were poised and ready. Finally, on D-Day itself, detachments of Beaufighters from North Coates and Langham, each loaded with two 250-lb and two 500-lb bombs, were sent to southern airfields but they remained, like the Beaufighter units in the south west, at 'readiness' and frustratingly idle. In sharp contrast No.248 Squadron's Mosquitoes were very busy from first light, though there was little sign of the enemy until their fifth operation of the day when three destroyers were sighted sailing north at speed out of the Gironde estuary. A Beaufighter strike was laid on immediately, 16 cannon-firers from No.144 Squadron leading 14 rocket-firers of No.404 Squadron from Davidstow Moor to join up with ten Mosquito VIs of No.248 near Lands End. Positioning so that the aircraft would come out of the sun, the leader, Wg Cdr D. Lumsden, pressed home the attack in the face of intense flak. Two destroyers were hit by several 25-lb solid warhead rockets, but several Beaufighters were damaged by the return fire, one having to 'ditch' on the way home and another belly-landing at Davidstow. Just after midnight 12 Beaufighters set off singly to hunt down the destroyers, and five of them attacked targets which may have

been the ships, though all three reached Brest. Patched up they sailed again on the evening of the 8th in company with a large torpedo boat, but were sighted off Ushant by the crew of a No.547 Squadron Liberator, and three hours later were intercepted by British destroyers. One of the German ships was sunk, another had to be beached, and the remaining two returned to Brest—the end of a desperate attempt to

Swordfish IIIs of No.816 Squadron, FAA, operated from Perranporth under No.19 Group control during Overlord, *June-July 1944. (Author's collection)*

Sound and fury—Beaufighter X NE546/UB-E of No.455 Squadron fires a salvo of rockets.
(RAF Museum)

interfere with cross-Channel reinforcement convoys.

At the eastern end of the Channel, Beaufighter crews saw little action for several days after the Normandy invasion, but No.415 Squadron was busy, Albacore crews laying smoke screens to cover the movement of Allied naval forces, spotting for bombardments and attacking E-Boats. Wellingtons also took part in the destruction of E-Boats, the CO of 415, Sqn Ldr A.W.B. Naismith, sinking one and badly damaging another during an engagement with five of the craft off Ostend on 8 June.

The sighting of a convoy off Rotterdam by a Mustang pilot during the evening of 14 June was the cue for an outstandingly successful strike by the combined North Coates and Langham Wings under

the leadership of Wg Cdr A. Gadd, Wing Commander Flying at North Coates. It was still dark on the morning of the 15th when 19 aircraft from Nos.236 and 254 Squadrons took off from North Coates and flew to Langham where they picked up 23 cannon-firing Beaufighters from Nos.455 and 489 Squadrons. Shortly afterwards they were joined by ten Mustang IIIs of No.316 Squadron, and set course. The convoy, consisting of two large armed ships protected by seven minesweepers and a number of R-Boats, was off Schiermonnikoog, and it was here that the massacre took place. Both the *Amerskerk*, a vessel of 7,900 tons, and the 3,500 ton *Nachtigall* were struck by torpedoes and RPs, rockets also disposing of one of the minesweepers. The defenders were completely over-

Flt Lt S. Nunn of No.248 Squadron flies Mosquito VI LR347/T home to a belly landing at Portreath following flak-damage which put out the port engine, July 1944. The aircraft was repaired and later served with No.8 OTU. (R.W. Simmons via A.S. Thomas)

Beaufighter X NE355/EE-H of No.404 Squadron at Davidstow Moor on 21 August 1944 soon after a wholesale change of unit codes. (Public Archives of Canada)

whelmed by the weight of anti-flak fire power, and there were no losses amongst the attackers though several were damaged and one had to make a belly landing at Langham. It was by far the most devastating Strike Wing attack so far!

To their chagrin No.235 Squadron took little part in activities around D-Day because they were busy working up on their newly received Mosquito FB.VIs and were not operational again until 16 June. By the end of the month, however, they had flown 32 Mosquito sorties and had started operating with No.248 Squadron as a Wing, the first successful combined strike by the two units being on 29 June when 24 Mk.VIs and two Mk.XVIIIs attacked a tanker and its six escorts, leaving the tanker ablaze. The next day 21 Mosquitoes from Portreath and nine RP Beaufighters of No.404 Squadron shot up four naval vessels off Concarneau, sinking a submarine chaser of 530 tons.

With the pressure easing in the south-western approaches Nos.144, 404 and 524 Squadrons transferred to No.16 Group going to Strubby in Lincolnshire on 1 July, the latter unit taking over No.415's night strike duties. The Albacore detachment at Winkleigh returned to Manston on 12 July, and the following day the Squadron stood down on transfer to Bomber Command—relentless Canadian pressure had succeeded! The Wellingtons were absorbed by No.524 Squadron, while the Albacores went to a re-formed No.119 Squadron which continued night anti-shipping patrols over the southern part of the North Sea and off the Dutch coast.

On 8 July the Strubby (Nos.144 and 404 Sqns) and North Coates Wings operating together, attacked a convoy off Heligoland, sinking three freighters, a minesweeper and, unhappily, an air-sea rescue craft. A week later the Langham Wing, operating with No.144 Squadron from Strubby, set the tanker *Irania* ablaze off the Naze, and altogether seven strike wing missions were flown during July, five merchantmen and 17 escorts being claimed 'sunk'.

So effective was the *Channel Stop* that the Germans were 'neutralized' in the area, and the FAA squadrons had little to report until July when the Manston and Hawkinge-based units started night *Rovers* off the Belgian and Dutch coasts, and aircraft from Perranporth were similarly employed off north-western France. On 20 July a 850 Squadron Avenger crew sighted two He177s attacking destroyers off Ushant and, despite the odds, waded in claiming damage to one of the bombers. Four days later a merchant ship was sunk and another damaged off St Peter Port, Guernsey.

On moving to Strubby the Canadians left a small detachment at Davidstow Moor, and when the Admiralty decided that it was time to get rid of the remaining ships of *Marinegruppekommando West* No.236 Squadron was sent down from North Coates on 6 August to join No.404. Within hours the two squadrons were airborne on a sweep off the west coast of France and in the harbour of Les Sables-d'Olonne, near La Rochelle, the fast escort *Jupiter* was sighted. It was sunk, hit by 25-lb RPs ripple-fired in pairs, using a new technique devised at North Coates employing cannon fire to provide accurate ranging as the aircraft was dived at the target from 1,500 feet.

A very smart but short-lived Beaufighter X LZ293/MB-T of No.236 Squadron which crashed at Davidstow Moor on 11 August 1944 during an air test. (Imperial War Museum)

Two days later another armed sweep by 24 Beaufighters from Davidstow caught four M-Class minesweepers in Bourgenelf Bay near St Nazaire. All were set on fire and sunk for the loss of one 404 Squadron aircraft.

The Portreath Mosquito Wing was also active in and around the Gironde estuary, and provided roving escorts for Allied destroyer groups being troubled by Do217s carrying Hs293 glider bombs. On 9 August 12 Mosquito VIs of No.235 Squadron and two XVIIIs of 248 Squadron came across four such combinations, shooting down two and damaging the others. By 20 August the combination of sinkings by Allied surface forces, scuttling of damaged vessels, and the activities of the two Strike Wings had reduced the German naval forces in Western France to just two ships, a destroyer and a torpedo boat, bottled up in the

Gironde estuary. It was decided to lay on a final strike from Davidstow using Beaufighters armed with cannon and 25-lb RPs. The 18 aircraft demonstrated their awesome fire-power as they dived into the attack in the face of intense flak from ships and shore batteries. The torpedo boat, T-24, sank almost immediately, the destroyer, Z-24, took rather longer, finally capsizing whilst repairs were underway. None of the Beaufighters was shot down but several were badly damaged, one 'ditching', while the crews of three others had to crash-land in France.

The constant attention of No.16 Group strike forces resulted in the Germans suspending even limited daytime sailing along the Dutch coast, ships proceeding painfully slowly by night in short 'hops' between ports. On moonlight nights *Rover* patrols by North Coates Beaufighters, Wellingtons of No.524 Squadron

The noise and confusion is almost tangible. Mosquitoes of Nos.235 and 248 Squadrons attacking an M-Class minesweeper off Royan, France, 12 August 1944. (via B. Robertson)

from Bircham Newton and Avengers of 855 Squadron, FAA, sought these 'targets of opportunity'. When there was no moon the Group reverted to Operation *Gilbey*, but it remained a complicated procedure. However, when it did work the results could be spectacular, and in operations with bomb-carrying aircraft on *Swingate* patrols during 11–13 September a large torpedo boat of 2,566 tons and ten assorted landing craft/barges were sunk off the West Friesian Islands.

The virtual end of German naval activity in the south-western approaches and the Bay of Biscay meant that more attention could again be paid to the Norwegian area. It was a favourable time to increase the pressure because the enemy's seaborne traffic with Norway was now more important than ever following the Swedes decision to withdraw their ships from German ports. At a stroke the Germans were denied the use of 450,000 tons of shipping, the situation being aggravated by the withdrawal of another 363,000 tons when Finland signed an armistice with Russia on 4 September, and the closure of Swedish ports to German shipping at the end of the month. Further pressure was caused by the arrival of 100,000 Wehrmacht troops in Norway en route from Finland to Germany and increasing U-Boat operations from the country. Soon, between 20 and 30 ships were passing along the Norwegian coast daily and many more transited to and from Oslo, with the Kattegat a 'choke' point.

The Kattegat was therefore an attractive target area, but it remained a difficult waterway for the Strike Wings to patrol, being an awkward routeing problem for No.16 Group units, and beyond the range of Beaufighters based in Scotland. Carrier-borne aircraft were considered, but wisely rejected by the Admiralty because of the risk from minefields and Luftwaffe attack, and the use of continental bases was also turned down, and in the end the task was left to No.16 Group Beaufighters by day and Coastal Halifaxes at night, the Scottish strike wings being left to concentrate on Norwegian west coast traffic until long-range Mosquitoes could be made available.

Banff, an airfield in Aberdeenshire which had been built for Coastal Command but used for flying training, was hastily cleared early in September to allow the deployment of No.154 (GR) Wing for operations with the Beaufighters of Nos.144 and 404 Squadrons (ex-Wick Wing) and Mosquitoes of Nos.235 and 248 Squadrons (ex-Portreath Wing). Making their first armed recce off Kristiansund on 14 September the Beaufighters intercepted four motor vessels escorted by two flak ships. One of the latter was sunk and a 3,330 ton coastal freighter badly damaged. On the 19th a force of 32 Beaufighters attacked an enemy convoy near Stavanger with RPs and cannons sinking two merchant vessels for the loss of a Beaufighter, two days later a mixed force of 18 Beaufighters and eight Mosquitoes sank a freighter and damaged a coaster off Lister, and altogether nine separate Wing strikes were flown on Norwegian coastal targets during the month.

Long-range Mustangs were seldom available as escorts so the Mosquitoes operated in a dual role, protecting the Beaufighters against enemy fighters and also smothering fire from flak ships. 'B' Flight of No.333 Squadron moved into Banff with their Mosquitoes to continue their reconnaissance work amongst the maze of islands and fjords which make up the Norwegian coast but targets were few after the Germans repeated the tactics used off Holland, and only sailed at night and in the early morning, when

Beaufighters of Nos.236 and 404 Squadrons assault the Sauerland, *a Sperrbrecher* (mine detector ship), *off La Pallice, 12 August 1944. (via J.D. Oughton)*

The next day, 13 August 1944, Nos.236 and 404 Squadrons plaster the Sperrbrecher Magdeburg *off Royan, the 6,128-ton ship sinking, as did the 5,339-ton* Schwanheim *during the same attack. (D. Marrow via B. Robertson)*

it was thought safe because of the long transit flight from Banff. To combat this ploy the Banff Wing tried one of their own. On 9 October 18 Beaufighters and eight Mosquitoes took off singly while it was still dark and rendezvoused on a pattern of markers laid about 100 nm off the Norwegian coast by the crew of a Warwick. The strike crews formed up over the pattern and set off for a position off Egersund where a four-ship convoy was expected to be. It was, and they quickly sank a freighter of 2,000 tons and an escorting submarine chaser. The German gunners soon recovered from their surprise and three aircraft were

damaged, but all returned safely. Six days later 21 rocket-firing Beaufighters from Nos.144 and 404 Squadrons, with 17 Mosquitoes of Nos.235 and 248 Squadrons operating as an anti-flak force, sank the Norwegian tanker *Inger Johanne* and a German flak ship off Kristiansund South, again with no loss, and on 21 October six Beaufighters accompanied by eleven Mosquitoes attacked a convoy in Haugesund harbour with RPs and six-pounder guns, sinking two merchantmen.

The Halifax IIs of Nos.58 and 502 Squadrons, very active on anti-shipping work during *Overlord* moved

En route to Norway at low level. Mosquito VIs of No.235 Squadron in their element. (G.A.B. Lord via A.S. Thomas)

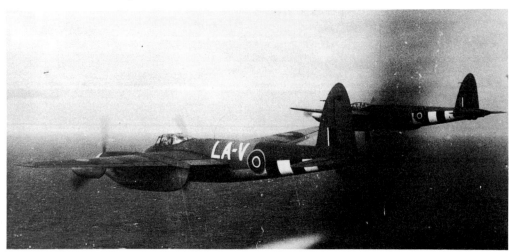

to Stornoway during September 1944 for re-equipment with anti-submarine Liberators. The requirement for continuing night anti-shipping operations over the Kattegat convinced Sholto Douglas that the Halifaxes should be retained, however, and both squadrons resumed the work in October. They operated all along the Norwegian coast and over the Skaggerak and Kattegat, but concentrated on shipping between Oslo, Kristiansund and the Danish ports, making 27 anti-shipping attacks during the month. The aircraft usually operated singly in areas where intelligence sources indicated a high probability of a target, crews obtaining an accurate bombing wind at the attack height of 4,000 feet on arrival in the area and then descended to low level, between 100–200 ft, for the search using ASV radar. On obtaining a contact the crew climbed and dropped flares up wind of the target, then flew half a circuit to arrive downwind as the flares lit and silhouetted the surface contact for an attack with 500-lb bombs using the Mk.XIV sight. The results were difficult to assess but a 58 Squadron crew set a motor vessel on fire on the 25th and two days later a tanker and her escort were hit. Flak was generally not very accurate at the heights used, though Flt Lt J.R. Howard's No.502 Squadron aircraft did receive hits on the 15th resulting in a flare igniting in the bomb bay, a very dangerous situation. Howard headed for Sweden, but with most of the stores jettisoned, and the aircraft functioning satisfactorily, he altered course for Scotland and finally reached Milltown safely.

Sholto Douglas's request for an increase in the establishment of No.248 Squadron's six-pounder gun Mk.XVIII Mosquitoes was turned down because a RP installation was in hand for the Mosquito, and following successful trials in September the AOC-in-C changed his mind. He suggested the immediate abandonment of the *Tse-Tse* (six-pounder) production programme and pressed hard for his Mosquito squadrons to be speedily equipped with RP-modified aircraft. It was a sign of the times that he got them, No.143 Squadron at North Coates converting from Beaufighters during October and providing the opportunity for a re-organization of the strike forces. The Banff Beaufighters were moved to Dallachy where they were joined by Nos.455 and 489 Squadrons from Langham, and the Mosquito Wing at Banff was strengthened by the transfer of No.143 Squadron from North Coates. All three Mosquito squadrons then underwent intensive RP training at Tain and made their first operational sorties with rocket firing aircraft on 26 October.

Up north, attacks were increasingly being directed at shipping at anchor in fjords, and to reduce the risk of the whole force being exposed to attack before a target had been selected, both the Dallachy and Banff Wings started using 'outriders'. Sent ahead of the main force the 'outriders' flew inland parallel to the coast and crossed the fjords close to favourite shipping 'hide-outs'. Any sighting was reported to the Wing Leader who then set up an attack by R/T. This ploy quickly proved its worth, though the more tortuous fjords remained a problem only solved by a pre-briefed attack led in by No.333 Squadron crews using their local knowledge and expertise. Bad weather interfered with operations early in November, but 24 Beaufigh-

Mosquitoes of No.235 Squadron attacking a ship off the Norwegian coast, 26 October 1944. (No.235 Sqn records via P.H.T. Green)

Another dramatic shot of Beaufighters attacking a ship at mast height. The adrenalin must really flow during such moments!

ters of Nos.144, 404 and 455 Squadrons, accompanied by Mosquitoes of No.333 sank two merchantmen in Midtgulen Fjord on the 8th, one of the 'outriders' having led the formation over the mountains into the attack. Missions involving mixed formations of aircraft from the Banff and Dallachy Wings followed, and had some success, but the most important sinking in November was achieved by Nos.404 and 489 Squadrons when the 5,740 ton *Fidelitas* was sunk and another merchant vessel damaged in Sula Fjord on the 27th.

As a follow-up of the Banff 'marker rendezvous' scheme a detachment of four Wellingtons from No.524 Squadron arrived at Dallachy for Operation *Ashfield*. The Wellington crews were tasked with the location of the enemy's shipping at night and marking an assembly point, but it was not very successful because convoys had ample time to sail in the early part of the night and be safely in harbour or moored close in under the shelter of steep fjord cliffs, during the winter, long before first light.

A combined operation by the Banff and Dallachy Wings on 7 December saw 25 Mosquitoes and 40 Beaufighters with an escort of Mustangs from No.315 Squadron (now semi-permanently on coastal strike duty) on an investigation of Norwegian fjords. German fighters had been conspicuous by their absence since the campaign restarted in September, but near Gossen the force was intercepted by about 20 Bf109s and Fw190s. No.315 Squadron claimed four Bf109s and reported two Fw190s colliding, but two Mosquitoes, a Beaufighter and a Mustang were lost.

The Wehrmacht was now moving whole divisions south by rail to Oslo and across the Kattegat by sea,

and despite poor weather in the area throughout December the two Halifax squadrons kept up their attacks. Such were the number of troops involved that it was anticipated that the Germans would also try sailing during the day under strong fighter cover, and debate within Coastal Command focused on how best to deal with such a move. Obviously Mosquitoes were best equipped for the task but it was imperative that they should be kept in Scotland for Norwegian operations, and from Banff the Kattegat was out of range without underwing drop tanks, while with tanks they could only carry four rockets using standard racks. Sholto Douglas applied considerable pressure to get the installation of tiered rockets cleared, but in the meantime the Command had to settle for reduced armament when drop tanks had to be used, and to face reduced activities over Norwegian coastal waters if the anticipated Kattegat operations took place. The Air Ministry was asked to transfer two Beaufighter squadrons from the Mediterranean Allied Air Forces but this was not agreed because of expected Balkan activity during the German withdrawal and Sholto Douglas had to make do with what he already had. In the short term it was adequate because poor weather so hampered operations during December that the Banff Wing could only make seven strikes and the Beaufighters at Dallachy two, but it was not a happy situation.

Most of the FAA units operating with Coastal Command over the D-Day period had returned to Admiralty control during August, but 855's Avengers remained until October and were then replaced by two Swordfish units, 819 and 838, and the Barracudas of 827 Squadron. In February 1945, however, all three

Briefing by Gp Capt Max Aitken in the heavily censored Ops Room at Banff, autumn 1944. (via G.A.B. Lord and A.S. Thomas)

squadrons were disbanded or withdrawn, the aircraft of 819 being offered to Coastal Command. It was an offer eagerly accepted for the ASV Mk.XI-equipped Swordfish IIIs were seen as ideal replacements for No.119 Squadron's Albacores.

Despite the reappearance of the Luftwaffe and seemingly never ending losses to flak, the Strike Wings started 1945 in good spirits, the crews fully convinced that the rocket projectile was the answer to their weapons problem. So versatile was the combination of 25-lb and 60-lb RPs that No.248 Squadron's Special Detachment of Mk.XVIIIs was withdrawn on 15 January and a request made for No.144 Squadron to be re-equipped with RP aircraft because the use of torpedoes was so limited. The Air Ministry agreed,

and recognizing that the employment of strike Mosquitoes as fighter escorts for Beaufighters was uneconomical also provided a second Mustang unit at Peterhead.

German naval forces now started a withdrawal from northern Norway in anticipation of increased operations in the Baltic. On 27 January a No.58 Squadron Halifax crew sighted three *Narvik* class destroyers west of Aalesund travelling south at speed and shadowed them for $1\frac{1}{2}$ hours before attacking from 11,000 feet with 500-lb bombs. No damage was caused, but that night British cruisers engaged the ships, forcing one to return to Bergen, and the following night a small force of No.489 Squadron Beaufighters tried to attack the remaining two in

After moving to Banff, No.404 Squadron aircraft received a new unit code, 'EO'. Beaufighter NV427/EO-L in fighting trim leading EO-S during the autumn of 1944. (Imperial War Museum)

Shipping at Haugesund under attack by the Banff Wing on 21 October 1944. Great care was needed to avoid hitting civilian Norwegian property—achieved by deliberately undershooting and 'creeping' cannon fire onto the target. (G.A.B. Lord via A.S. Thomas)

Brommel Fjord. The circumstances were difficult and two aircraft were lost without damage to the ships, an unhappy story which served to remind the Allies that though the Strike Wings were now 'on top' things could, and did, go disastrously wrong on occasion. Indeed the strike laid on by the Dallachy Wing on 9 February 1945 was another such occasion turning out to be Coastal Command's 'Black Friday'. On that day several worthwhile targets had been reported by No.489 Squadron's reconnaissance Beaufighters, but the choice was easy because one, a *Narvik* class destroyer, was on the priority list. Twenty-two cannon/RP Beaufighters and ten with cannon/machine guns rendezvoused with ten Mustangs of No.65 Squadron over Peterhead and set out for the narrow Fordefjord, east of Vevring, where the destroyer lurked under the cliffs accompanied by a minesweeper and two flak ships. Two of the Beaufighters went ahead as 'outriders' and two ASR Warwicks followed the formation. Led by Wg Cdr C. Milson, the formation made landfall at the entrance of the broad Sognefjord, flew inland and turned north for Fordefjord. On arrival the leader was forced to overfly by the impossible position of the destroyer, and all aircraft had to attack in the face of intense flak and at considerable risk of collision. Surprisingly most of

Swordfish III NF374/NH-M of No.119 Squadron during anti-midget submarine operations early in 1945. The aircraft still carries No.415 Squadron codes. (RAF Museum)

the aircraft survived the attack, though many were hit and several crew members were injured, but the delay gave time for Fw190s to arrive from Herdla, near Bergen, some 65 miles to the south. Within minutes nine Beaufighters and a Mustang had succumbed to either flak or fighters, and many of those that did get back crash-landed and had to be written off. The ships were reported damaged but none was destroyed. Five Fw190s were shot down, at least one by a Beaufighter navigator manning his single rear firing gun, but this was poor recompense for the Wing's losses.

Staff officers at Coastal Command considered that laden tankers and merchantmen were targets of much greater value than small naval vessels, and after this expensive attack Sholto Douglas 'invited' the Admiralty to revise its strike priority list. Rather surprisingly they promptly acceded, and escorts, which included destroyers, dropped to the bottom of the list.

'Black Friday' was a terrible blow, No.404 Squadron being particularly hard hit by the loss of six crews. But young men are resilient and the almost daily battle continued unabated, indeed the Squadron went out on its own on 26 February and damaged a small Norwegian tanker off Kristiansund. No.235 Squadron Mosquito pilots made their first rocket strike during February, but it was March before the long-awaited installation of drop tanks and tiered rockets, and the weather, gave the Banff Wing a chance to intervene in the Skaggerak/Kattegat and supplement in daylight the almost nightly Halifax operations. Fifty-four Mosquitoes from Nos.143, 235, 248 and 333 Squadrons were despatched on the 7th with top cover provided by 12 Mustangs. Two ASR

Warwicks were also in attendance. In the East Skaggerak a large merchantman escorted by a flak ship was sighted close to eight loaded barges. The latter were chosen and four barges plus the flak ship were sunk with rockets and cannon. Unfortunately two Mosquitoes collided during the attack—always a risk, but one which had to be accepted. The next day the Dallachy Wing was out in force and damaged a 4,100 ton freighter and a small ferry, but it was the Banff Wing attacks on 17 and 30 March which were the most effective. At Aalesund, one of the most heavily defended ports in Norway, 31 Mosquitoes attacked six ships in the harbour, sinking three and badly damaging a fourth, while on the 30th Wg Cdr A.H. Simmonds, CO of No.235 Squadron, led 32 rocket-firers accompanied by eight 'fighter' Mosquitoes and a film unit aircraft into a devastating assault on Porsgrunn harbour where five vessels were sunk and a large warehouse shot up.

While most of the activity emanated from No.18 Group's Scottish bases, No.16 Group was still having to cope with the threat of E-Boats whose operations against Antwerp-bound convoys had reached formidable proportions by the end of 1944. They were proving as difficult to intercept or attack as they had been in the Channel, and a conference held at Chatham on 19 January 1945 reconsidered tactics. It was agreed that unless surface vessels commanders had up to the minute information on position, course and speed, and could be vectored from the air, they stood no chance of intercepting the fast and highly manoeuvrable enemy craft. To this end communications were improved, several MTBs having VHF/RT by the begin-

One of the few operational Mosquito XVIIIs, PZ468/QM-D of No.254 Squadron, early 1945. (MAP)

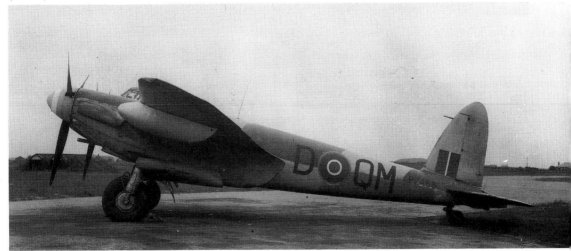

Gp Capt Max Aitken, CO of RAF Banff during the heyday of the Mosquito Strike Wing, 1945. (via G.A.B. Lord)

times British MTBs were brought into contact with illuminated E-Boats, and with the procedure proclaimed a success Operation *Dictator* started on 29 March. Unfortunately it did not live up to its early promise and not until the last few weeks of the war did it start to work well, the ASV Mk.III-fitted Wellington GR.XIV proving the most successful aircraft because its radar display enabled both enemy and 'friendly' surface forces to be seen on the screen at the same time.

In all, over 10,000 tons of shipping was sunk during March 1945 but, with the Strike Wings living up to their promise at last, a new threat to their effectiveness surfaced. A serious manpower shortage caused by the war in Europe lasting longer than forecast, while at the same time forces in the Far East were being built up, meant that the Air Ministry had to make 'domestic' economies. Amongst the proposals was the disbandment of two Mosquito or Beaufighter strike squadrons, a suggestion which Sholto Douglas vehemently opposed, taking the view that the anti-shipping component of his Command was the only completely offensive element and that it was fully stretched and likely to remain so. Knowing that something would have to be sacrificed he made a counter proposal, offering the disbandment of an anti-U-Boat squadron and a

ning of March, and exercises with No.524 Squadron were followed by a trial operation on 17 March conducted by the CO, Wg Cdr R.G. Knott. Three

Wellington XIIIs of No.524 Squadron were employed as flare droppers against E-Boats. Armourers loading these dangerous stores. (A.W. Mills)

Mosquito VI RF838/EO-A of No.404 Squadron taxies out at Banff for a strike, April 1945. (No.404 Sqn records)

reduction in strength of two ASR units as a better alternative. This was agreed and the anti-shipping force remained intact, indeed approval was given for No.404 Squadron to be rearmed with Mosquitoes fitted with 100-gallon drop tanks and tiered rockets!

It was, therefore, ironic that there was considerable diversion of 'strike' effort onto U-Boats during April, though anti-shipping work was not completely neg-

Pin-point accuracy essential! An attack by the Banff Wing on shipping in Sandefjord, 2 April 1945. It resulted in two ships being sunk and four damaged. (No.235 Sqn via P.H.T. Green)

Beaufighters of No.144 Squadron including RD147/PL-U at Langham, 4 May 1945. (via J.D. Oughton)

lected by any of the three Wings. Thirty-eight Mosquitoes from Banff attacked shipping in Sandefjord, sinking two ships and damaging four out of eight, and the pressure was maintained with another successful mission to Porsgrunn when four merchantmen were sunk and two more damaged, for the loss of two of the 35 Mosquitoes despatched.

No.404 Squadron had started conversion to Mosquito VIs in March and moved from Dallachy to Banff on 3 April to resume operations, starting on the 22nd when a Bv138 was destroyed on the water at Kjevik. The remainder of the Dallachy Wing continued to rampage about over Norwegian waters, badly damaging a 3,000 ton merchant vessel on 4 April and sinking the 4,600 ton Oldenburg in Sognefjord on the 7th. The transfer of two more Mustang squadrons for escort duties was agreed and, with improving weather, Coastal Liberators started penetrating the Baltic at night on both anti-U-Boat and anti-shipping work, supplementing Halifaxes. The latter made 101 attacks on ships during the month, nearly all on military traffic, for commercial sailings had virtually ceased. Fifty-one ships were claimed either sunk or damaged during April—a very successful month. No.455 Squadron moved to Thornaby on 3 May for attacks on shipping trying to escape from the Baltic in the face of the Russian advance, the same day as the North Coates Wing entered the Kattegat fray. Briefed to attack anything on sight 12 rocket-firers of No.236 Squadron accompanied by 17 cannon-firing Beaufighters of No.254 escorted by Mustangs, sank a Type XXI U-Boat and four merchant ships in The Belts,

and a 6,400 ton tanker in Kiel Bay. They also damaged the 11,450 ton liner *Der Deutsche* and at least one other vessel for the loss of one Beaufighter and crew. After the operation the Wing landed in south-east Holland for the first time, and the following day flew back over the Kattegat, attacking a selection of ships including a destroyer and four U-Boats, before returning to North Coates. The Banff Wing was also active on 3 May, sending a large formation of Mosquitoes, including for the first time No.404 Squadron, to the Kattegat on the interestingly named *Penetration/Withdrawal* patrol, and the following day returned to the area when Wg Cdr C.N. Foxley-Norris, CO of No.143 Squadron led 48 Mosquitoes escorted by 18 Mustangs into an attack on a seven-ship convoy escorted by an unusually strong force of flak ships. A 3,750 ton merchantman was sunk and two others damaged. All the Mosquitoes returned safely and this proved to be the last anti-shipping strike of the war for Coastal Command, sorties planned for the 5th being cancelled when it became obvious that Germany was on the point of surrender.

It was not the end of operations though, for while most European-based components of the RAF were celebrating VE-Day, Coastal Command had to fly anti-submarine reconnaissance, and for a few days these included the strike units. Within weeks, however, the Strike Wings were decimated, most of the squadrons disbanded and the personnel dispersed, the inevitable but sad end of a small tightly knit force which had started with great hopes, faced disaster, then slowly gained stature as lessons were learnt and

The Langham Wing prior to an attack on shipping in the Kiel area, 5 May 1945. The torpedo carrier on the left is RD425/P6-F of No.489 Squadron. (D. Marrows via C. Bowyer)

successful tactics evolved. From August 1944 until the end of the war, the period during which the 25-lb rocket projectile was the primary anti-shipping weapon, the German Navy had no real answer to the strike squadrons, though remaining a very dangerous adversary with Allied personnel losses still high,

Right up to the end of the war the German flak remained effective, but aircraft got back home despite the damage, as witnessed by Beaufighter X NE605 of No.143 Squadron with half its tailplane destroyed. (via J.D. Oughton)

The most difficult of targets, a ship close in against the edge of a steep-sided fjord. Beaufighters of No.144 Squadron on the rampage in the Fedefjord, 26 April 1945. (A. Hall via P.H.T. Green)

equivalent to those suffered by Bomber Command.

The Strike Wings sank some 215 ships totalling about 300,000 tons out of total German losses from air attack during the period November 1942 to May 1945 of about 450,000 tons. Another 415,000 tons of shipping was lost to air-dropped mines, most laid by Bomber Command but many by Coastal units. German-controlled shipping had been almost completely destroyed by the end of the war—a considerable achievement.

Collision was also an ever-present danger—one such event removing a large portion of the starboard wing of Mosquito VI HR138/Y of No.235 Squadron in January 1945, yet the aircraft returned safely to Banff. (B.H. Quelch via C. Bowyer)

CHAPTER 9

The Battle is Won– Anti-Submarine Operations 1944-45

WHEN AIR CHIEF Marshal Sir Sholto Douglas took over Coastal Command on 20 January 1944, Doenitz, now Commander-in-Chief of the German Navy but still very much in day to day charge, was in high hopes of retaking the initiative and had started concentrating his forces in the western approaches to the British Isles once again. The redeployment was rapidly assessed and the new AOC-in-C moved quickly to counter the threat, transferring two Leigh Light Wellington squadrons, Nos.407 and 612, from No.19

to No.15 Group late in January and arranging for any spare capacity held by AHQ Iceland and the other groups to be declared to No.15 on a daily basis. Further bolstering in the general area was achieved by moving 15 Cansos of No.162 Squadron, RCAF, to Iceland from Canada's Eastern Air Command.

Nos.407 and 612 Squadrons quickly settled in at Limavady but bad weather curtailed operations until the night of 10/11 February when the sea was bathed in moonlight and both units made the most of it.

Leigh Light Catalina IVA JX574/T of No.210 Squadron, March 1944. This aircraft was lost on 9 June 1944 north of the Shetlands. (M.E. Street)

Top: *Liberator V FL982/1-P of No.59 Squadron operating from Ballykelly, June 1944. (via J.D. Oughton)*

Above: *Wellington XIV NB772/P of No.179 Squadron at Predannack during Cork operations, June 1944. (via A.S. Thomas)*

Below: *On the slipway at Castle Archdale looking very spick and span is Sunderland III EK583/3-J of No.423 Squadron, 7 July 1944. (Public Archives of Canada)*

Top: *Sunderland III EK591/2-U of No.422 Squadron landing at Castle Archdale, 15 July 1944. Three months earlier this aircraft had been used by W/O W.F. Martin and crew to sink U-625. (Public Archives of Canada)*

Above: *A Flight Sergeant at the port waist gun position of a Liberator. (British Official)*

Below: *Liberator VI BZ986 at St Eval displaying its Leigh Light installed under the starboard wing. (via C.H. Luke)*

Loading a marine marker in the release chute of a Liberator.

Plt Off M.H. Paynter's No.612 Squadron crew obtained a radar contact and visual sighting of a fully surfaced submarine at one mile. An attack made with the help of the Leigh Light resulted in a perfect straddle and the end of U-545 (Type IXC). Meanwhile Flg Off P.W. Heron and his No.407 Squadron crew on distant support to a convoy, held a radar contact down to a mile and in the glare of the Leigh Light the U-283 (Type VIIC) was sighted with decks awash. Down went a 'stick' of six DCs and the submarine disappeared. It was subsequently confirmed as sunk.

Other units were also keeping up the pressure, and during the first three months of 1944 sixty U-Boats were destroyed in the Atlantic, for the loss of 54 Allied ships—less than a quarter that experienced in the same period of 1942. The 'wolf-packs' had failed again, and on 22 March Doenitz ordered his submarines back into mid-Atlantic to operate singly, making them more difficult to find but also much less effective. With the opposition out of Wellington range and an expected revival of Bay operations, No.612 Squadron returned to No.19 Group

Two operational 'Coastal' squadrons were equipped with Halifax aircraft throughout the second half of the war. HR686/J2 was a GR.II srs IA of No.502 Squadron which failed to return on 3 October 1944. (RP/MAP)

late in March 1944, followed by No.407 in April.

With most of Nos.179 and 233 Squadrons detached to the Azores, the Germans had found it easier to make the passage through the Strait of Gibraltar, all seven attempting it during the period November 1943-January 1944 being successful. Shipping in the Mediterranean had much less opportunity to evade attack than in the Atlantic, and it was obvious that an increase in U-Boat strength in the area had to be prevented. Combined air/sea operations for the Gibraltar area were revised with the object of forcing U-Boats to submerge well to the west of the Strait, so that they would be unable to build up their battery charge before tackling the 'narrows' where the Allied forces now included MAD-equipped PBY-5As of VP-63. The hard-pressed Catalinas of No.202 Squadron and Wellingtons of No.179 Squadron were therefore supplemented by aircraft from the Mediterranean Allied Air Force and Fleet Air Wing 15 of the US Navy, and the effect was immediate.

The two British units were involved in a combined operation on 8 January which resulted in the U-343 being damaged, but the classic example of air/sea co-operation in the Strait occurred on 24 February. It started during the afternoon when one of the two VP-63 'Madcats' flying interminable six minute orbits at 100 feet over the Strait got a firm contact on the MAD recorder. Excitedly the pilot, Lt (Jg) T. Wooley called up the pilot of the other aircraft, Lt H. Baker, who immediately joined in and a line of markers soon established that the contact was moving eastwards at about 2 knots. The destroyer HMS *Anthony* made

contact on asdic, but soon lost it. The Americans regained the submarine and an hour after the initial contact Wooley made an attack with a pattern of 24 AS retro-bombs. A few minutes later Lt Baker made a similar attack and *Anthony* dropped depth charges. Badly damaged and out of control, part of the U-761 appeared briefly above the surface before submerging again whereupon it was attacked by both HMS *Wishart* and *Anthony*. With the situation desperate the U-Boat captain brought the U-761 (Type VIIC) to the surface and it was promptly attacked by a Catalina of No.202 Squadron and a USN PV-1 Ventura of VP-127, both crews attracted to the scene by the contact reports. The 'Madcats' subsequently detected U-392 on 16 March and U-731 on 5 May, and both were despatched by surface forces. Other U-Boats did get through the barrier before the Germans found themselves with more pressing problems to attend to and suspended the operation, but there is no doubt that MAD was a success in the Strait where conditions were ideal for its use.

During March 1944 U-Boat sightings were few and intercepted signals traffic light, important confirmation that the number at sea had been reduced. In part this was due to the fitment of new equipment, in particular the *Schnorkel* tube, but it was also suspected that U-Boats were being held in French Biscay ports in expectation of the Allied invasion of France—a surmise borne out by intelligence reports.

Allied planning took account of German ability to deploy up to 130 U-Boats against any invasion force crossing the Channel by drawing on those in Baltic

Flying Officers D.H. Hormer, G.R. Guess and J.S. McConnell with W/O R.G. Liddell (sitting) in front of Liberator VI/2V-Q of No.547 Squadron at Leuchars, 15 November 1944. (via J.D. Oughton)

The recently re-coded Sunderland IIIA ML884/DG-Z of No.422 Squadron being taxied up to a buoy at Pembroke Dock by Flt Lt F.B. Fallis on 8 December 1944. The front turret is retracted so that the aircrewman in the nose can complete the tricky business of securing the 'boat' to the buoy. (Public Archives of Canada)

and Norwegian waters to supplement those already in the area. It was thought that another 70 could be at sea within a fortnight of the start of *Overlord*, and to counter this very real threat Sholto Douglas intended to maintain day and night patrols over the western Channel and out into the south-western approaches in sufficient strength to ensure that the U-Boats would have to surface, or come up to *Schnorkel* ('snort') depth, to get into an attack position. Similar patrols, though fewer in number, were to be laid on in the eastern approaches and across the northern U-Boat transit area.

The AOC-in-C issued his directive to his Group commanders in April 1944. No.15 Group was to continue covering Atlantic convoys, and in conjunction with No.18 Group cover the northern transit routes. No.16 Group was to patrol the North Sea and eastern Channel, while No.19 Group coped with the big job, the blocking of the westerly approaches. To carry out the plan Coastal Command could muster 36 anti-submarine squadrons, and additionally controlled 3 USN Squadrons, eight Fleet Air Arm units (combining submarine work with their primary anti-shipping role) and a RCAF squadron. The bulk of this dedicated anti-submarine force was in No.19 Group's area—a total of 24 squadrons—while Nos.16 and 18 Groups each had four squadrons, the latter assisted by two in Iceland and part of No.15 Group, to prevent U-boats based in Norway from moving out into the Atlantic. It was a formidable force—so was the task.

The eastern end of the Channel was shallow and was to be extensively mined so it was thought unlikely that U-Boats would attempt to force the Dover Strait. Thus No.16 Group's submarine commitment was expected to be small, and it was to be handled by the three Avenger squadrons in addition to their night anti-shipping operations. To deal with attacks mounted from the west, AVM B.E. Baker's staff at No.19 Group HQ devised 12 interlocking patrol areas, each tailored to the capabilities of a particular aircraft type. The plan envisaged the whole of a 20,000 square mile 'cork-shaped' area being 'illuminated' by radar every 30 minutes, an intensity calculated to produce intolerable strain on U-Boat crews, and a situation whereby they would either be detected or finish up with flat batteries and in no condition to enter the English Channel. The *Cork* patrols were tested in April and found effective against a British submarine attempting the passage, but to maintain the required 30 aircraft continuously on patrol over a sustained period a total strength of some 350 was required. It was only achieved by bringing Nos.179 and 206 Squadrons back to the United Kingdom from Gibraltar and the Azores.

There was little activity on the part of the Germans during April, but considerable concern at both the Admiralty and Coastal Command HQ that Doenitz might suddenly decide to return to 'pack' tactics to attack Atlantic convoys while Allied forces were tied

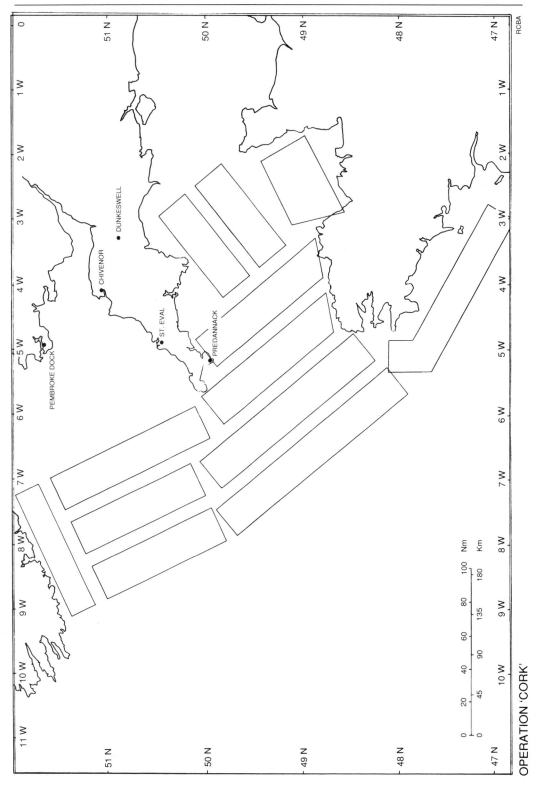

OPERATION 'CORK'

Top: *Liberator VI KG869/2V-B of No.547 Squadron out on patrol during the winter of 1944/45. (D.V. Quinn)*

Above: *Sunderland V RN282/UT-N of No.461 Squadron during the latter months of the war. (Shorts)*

Below: *The final Liberator GR variant, the Mk.VIII, was firmly established alongside the Mk.VI early in 1945. This aircraft, KN753/XB-L of No.224 Squadron, undergoing engine runs, carries the 'Guard' marking, so is probably High Tea (sonobuoy) equipped. (via J.D. Oughton)*

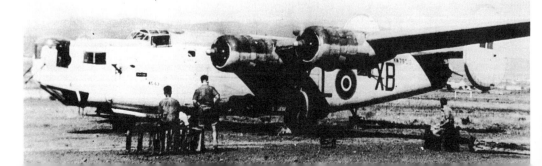

up with invasion preparations, perhaps using those U-Boats (about a fifth of the total strength) now fitted with *Schnorkel* tubes. U-Boat movements were indeed observed in the northern transit area mid-May and No.18 Group mounted a full-scale operation against them. By the end of the month 22 sightings had been made resulting in six U-Boats being destroyed despite a return to the 'fight it out' ploy. No.210 Squadron, which had been reformed from No.190 in January, was in the forefront of the operation. On 18 May, flying at a mere 200 feet Flg Off B. Bastable's crew sighted a fully surfaced U-Boat 250 nm W of Trondheim. As the aircraft closed, the U-Boat crew opened fire, but a perfect straddle with six DCs was achieved and the U-241 (Type VIIC) was later confirmed sunk. The squadron made attacks on the 21st and 22nd without positive result and were again in action on the 24th when Capt F.W.L. Maxwell, SAAF, sighted a submarine 180 nm NW of Trondheim at a range of five miles. During the run in, the Catalina came under heavy inaccurate flak but six DCs were dropped, the last one almost hitting the U-Boat which did a complete circle and stopped, then sank almost vertically, before briefly resurfacing and again sinking stern first. U-476 (Type VIIC) was later confirmed as destroyed. All the activity in the north so depleted No.15 Group that some convoys had to be diverted south so that they would benefit from coverage from the Azores where No.220 Squadron were still operating, together with American units, the Portuguese having allowed joint use from December 1943.

Some twelve hours after the start of *Overlord*, 15 U-Boats set sail from Brest, followed by those based at other Biscay ports. Most were not fitted with *Schnorkel* tubes, and during the night 22 sightings were made by No.19 Group forces, five of them by No.53 Squadron alone. Seven attacks developed resulting in the destruction of U-955 (Type VIIC) and U-970 (Type VIIC), and damage to four others. With the dawn the U-Boats submerged, though not before the 'snort'-equipped U-212 was spotted by two Mosquito XVIII crews of No.248 Squadron, one of which scored six hits out of twelve 57-mm rounds fired, the damage forcing the U-Boat's captain to return to La Pallice. During the night of 7/8 June the 36 remaining non-*schnorkel* 'boats' surfaced for another high-speed 'dash', and fell foul of the Cork patrols. Flg Off K.O. Moore's No.224 Squadron crew obtained a contact at 12 miles, and spurning his Leigh Light the pilot positioned his aircraft 'up moon' from the target and with the radar switched off approached 'silently'. From 40 feet six DCs straddled the U-Boat and virtually blew it out of the water—U-629 (Type VIIC) was doomed. Resuming patrol, Moore is re-

puted to have said: 'Let's get another one', and they did just that, for ten minutes later came another contact. Again Moore made a 'silent' approach down moon and his remaining six DCs despatched U-373 (Type VIIC)—a unique performance!

No.15 Group was dragged in to help with *Cork*, and on 9 June Flt Lt A.K. Sherwood's No.120 Squadron crew was responsible for the destruction of the U-740 (Type VIIC). The following day it was the turn of No.248 Squadron again, four Mosquitoes on a *Yellow* patrol covering the approaches to Brest being perfectly positioned when a submarine surfaced some three miles ahead. Led by Flt Lt S.G. Nunn, the formation climbed to 400 feet and attacked with cannon and machine gun fire, a large explosion occurring in or near the conning tower. The crew started to abandon U-821 (Type VIIC) while the Mosquitoes attracted the attention of a Liberator crew of No.206 Squadron captained by Flt Lt A.D.S. Dundas. His first attack missed but on the second run he laid a stick of DCs across the submarine and when the spray subsided it had disappeared.

The loss of six U-Boats and severe damage to another six was enough for Admiral Krancke, Commander of Naval Forces West in Brest, and on 12 June he ordered the withdrawal of the surviving 22 U-Boats not fitted with *Schnorkel* tubes. During their return to the Bay five were damaged and one sunk, U-441 (Type VIIC) falling victim to the crew of a No.304 (Polish) Squadron LL Wellington captained by Flt Lt J. Antoniewicz. It had been sighted late on 18 June in bright moonlight as it surfaced. An immediate attack with six DCs resulted in a large explosion, pieces of the U-Boat being seen to break away.

Meanwhile six *Schnorkel*-fitted U-Boats had succeeded in breaching the English Channel, and they sank two British frigates and a tank landing ship for the loss of one of their number before being driven out of the area by surface forces. From the air 'snorting' U-Boats were extremely difficult to locate by radar and visual sightings were few unless condensing exhaust gases produced a stream of 'smoke'. Indeed it was not until 18 June that an attack on a *Schnorkel* 'boat' was made—by the crew of a PB4Y-1 Liberator of VPB-110 from Dunkeswell captained by Lt Cdr J. Munson. Only slight damage was caused, however, and it was nearly the end of the month before the destruction of one of these U-Boats could be claimed by Coastal Command—when the U-988 (Type VIIC) was sunk by No.224 Squadron with the help of surface forces. By the end of June a further three U-Boats had succeeded in reaching their patrol area in the Channel, but their commanders were so intimidated by the sheer concentration of the defences that they achieved little.

The crowded maintenance area of Castle Archdale in 1945. The nearest aircraft, NS-W, belongs to No.201 Squadron, ML825/YI-D to No.423 Squadron. (RAF Museum)

From bases in Germany and Norway U-Boats made a determined effort to break out into the Atlantic during June, and No.18 Group was soon very active. No.162 Squadron, RCAF, now operating from Wick, were particularly successful, opening their score on 3 June when Flt Lt R.E. MacBride and crew sank the U-477 (Type VIIC) some 30 nm W of Trondheim in the face of intense and very accurate AA fire. On the 11th Flg Off L. Sherman and crew destroyed the U-980 (Type VIIC) some 250 nm NE of the Faeroes, and two days later the CO, Wg Cdr C.G.W. Chapman, was at the helm when U-715 (Type VIIC) was sunk in much the same area. Intense return fire badly damaged the Canso on this occasion and the crew were forced to 'ditch', five of the eight men aboard surviving nine hours in the water and rescue by an ASR launch. Better known is the attack by Flt Lt D.E. Hornell and crew on the U-1225 (IXC) some 160 nm NE of the Faeroes on the 24th. As Hornell made his attack the U-Boat's gunners poured explosive cannon shells into the Canso, setting fire to the starboard engine and tearing large holes in the wing. The aircraft became extremely difficult to control but Hornell continued the attack, his DCs straddling the target. He then managed to gain a little height but the fire spread to the fuel tanks and the starboard engine mounting which collapsed, the engine falling away from the aircraft. With control almost lost Hornell managed to bring off a successful 'ditching' in spite of a heavy swell and the crew spent 21 hours in one dinghy before rescue, by which time two had

died. Hornell died shortly after being picked up and was posthumously awarded the Victoria Cross for inspiring leadership, valour and devotion to duty. To round off the month, Flt Lt MacBride's crew sighted a U-Boat on the 30th, 210 nm NE of the Faeroes and, unable to attack, homed in a Liberator of No.86 Squadron captained by Flg Off N.E.M. Smith. He straddled the U-478 (Type VIIC) which was subsequently confirmed sunk.

No.210 Squadron made several attacks during June without success, but in July they claimed the unit's sixth and seventh victims. On 17 July the radar operator on Flg Off J.A. Cruickshank's crew obtained a contact at 15 miles and homed the aircraft in, a vessel being sighted at about five miles through patchy fog 240 nm W of the Lofoten Islands and well inside the Arctic Circle. It was identified as a friendly destroyer, but when recognition signals were fired and the letter of the day flashed by Aldis lamp, the vessel started firing at the aircraft, and was then seen to be a U-Boat. On the first attack the DCs failed to release, and during the second run the navigator was killed and the captain seriously wounded. He continued the attack, however, and the six DCs were perfectly positioned, the U-347 (Type VIIC) turning over and sinking immediately. Cruickshank collapsed soon after the second attack but, although bleeding profusely, insisted on taking command again until certain that the damaged aircraft was under control and on course for Sullom Voe. During the five hour return flight the captain drifted in and out of consciousness, but on arrival at base was adamant that he should be propped up in the right-hand seat so that he could advise the co-pilot while the aircraft was flown around the Shetland area for over an hour awaiting better conditions of light and sea state. On landing he directed taxiing and beaching before collapsing yet again, requiring a blood transfusion before being moved to hospital. On examination Cruickshank was found to have 72 wounds. He was subsequently awarded the Victoria Cross for his determination, fortitude and devotion to duty—the only living recipient of the award for a submarine attack.

The following day, 18 July, Flg Off R.W.G. Vaughan and crew had been airborne for eight hours when told to hunt for a U-Boat in an area 180 nm W of the Lofotens. Half an hour later a 'vessel' was sighted at a five mile range and quickly identified as a submarine. The aircraft came under fire as it approached, but the six DCs were perfectly placed and as the Catalina turned away the remains of the U-742 (Type VIIC) were settling in the water. About 30 to 40 survivors and a large number of bright yellow dinghies were also seen, but the crew had their own problems for a serious oil leak had developed on the starboard engine and fuel was leaking from the port tank. After flying for 500 nm on one engine, quite a feat in itself, the aircraft reached base and was beached successfully.

These air patrols in the far north accounted for four U-Boats and damage to six during July, but like nearly all before them the attacks depended on a visual sighting of some part of the submarine or, in the case

of *Fido*, had to be made immediately after the 'boat' had disappeared. To overcome the problem of underwater location the 'boffins' had been working for some time on the development of a 'sonobuoy'. It worked, but production was slow and its debut was still awaited in July 1944.

In August activity up north was much reduced, though Flg Off W.O. Marshall and his No.162 Squadron crew did damage U-300 on the 4th. The majority of the Command's resources remained in the No.19 Group area, the encroachment of the Biscay ports forcing the Germans to send their French-based U-Boats to sea whether they were fit to fight or not. The British expected rich pickings and six, U-107 (Type IXB), U-270, U-385, U-608, U-618 and U-981 (all Type VIICs) were sunk by Coastal Command* but another 31 made their escape via the west coast of Ireland by remaining submerged and using their 'snorts' very circumspectly.

Early in September, with the Bay of Biscay almost devoid of U-Boats, both Nos.15 and 18 Groups were strengthened by transfers from No.19 Group, and during a very quiet period, two of the three successful attacks did occur in No.18 Group areas. The third was 510 nm NW of the Azores where Flt Lt A.F. Wallace and his No.220 Squadron crew, flying a Fortress III fitted with the new ASV Mk.X, caught the U-871 (Type IXD) in the act of surfacing. The DCs were seen to straddle the conning tower, and after an explosion a large oil patch spread out across the sea, followed

*U-385 & U-618 shared with the Royal Navy.

The Leigh Light force at Chivenor was considerably bolstered during the autumn of 1944 by two squadrons from the Mediterranean. Amongst the LL Wellington XIVs received by No.14 Squadron was NB829/CX-O seen here after a sortie, with the crew awaiting transport. (G.E. Jones via C. Bowyer)

Liberator V BZ718/PP-M of No.311 Squadron survived the war and is seen in open storage. It was finally SoC and scrapped in 1947. (via J.D. Oughton)

by debris and bodies. There was little doubt that this was a 'kill'. The U-482, a *Schnorkel*-equipped boat, sank five ships in the shallow waters around the British Isles in September, and it appears that this was a trial voyage, for during October Doenitz reorganized his forces in Norway with the object of concentrating operations west of Cape Wrath, in the Irish Sea, and the Bristol and St George's Channels, all choke points for ships approaching port. To deal with the threat Sholto Douglas further reinforced No.15 Group by moving No.202 Squadron to Castle Archdale and re-equipping the unit with LL Catalinas, replacing it at Gibraltar with the Venturas of No.22 Squadron, SAAF. No.19 Group was also buttressed by Nos.14 and 36 Squadrons which received Wellington Mk.XIVs on joining the Command from the Mediterranean. 'Flooding' the vast area in which ships were at risk as they approached the British Isles was impracticable, so a new form of close air support was given to all east-bound Atlantic convoys for the last 450 miles of their crossing. This took the form of staggered box patrols covering the area ahead out to 60 nm and parallel to the track of the convoy on either beam to a distance of 28 nm, the aircraft stepping forward at the speed of the ships. This plan went into operation during November 1944 under the overall direction of the AOC No.15 Group, AVM Sir L.H. Slatter, aircraft of No.19 Group being at his disposal as required, but there was no immediate improvement in the situation. During September-December 1944 the Command flew 9,126 sorties against U-Boats—a total of 81,327 hours. Sixty-two were sighted but only 29 attacks were made, resulting in the destruction of

five submarines (plus two sunk by surface ships after initial aerial location). The effect of the *Schnorkel* on the attack/loss rate was obvious, indeed submarines fitted with the device remained difficult to locate, never mind attack. Fortunately the weight of air and surface cover and the Germans' comparative weakness* kept shipping losses down. Most of the sinkings that did occur were made by a small number of the more daring U-Boat commanders who were prepared to operate inshore, sometimes within a few miles of air and naval bases. In December, out of some 60,000 tons of shipping sunk in Coastal Command areas, 44,000 tons (seven ships) were in UK coastal waters.

Thus, despite the advantages gained by widespread adoption of the *Schnorkel* tube, the situation remained generally satisfactory from the Allied viewpoint. However, it was well known that two very potent submarines, long delayed by the bombing and mining offensive, were about to become operational and might turn the tables! These were the 1,600 Type XXI U-Boat, 55 of which were in commission at the end of the year, together with 35 of the much smaller 250-ton Type XXIII. Their work-up period was nearly complete and the larger vessel could be expected to operate in the North Atlantic, perhaps in 'wolf packs', while the Type XXIII posed a serious threat to coastal convoys in the North Sea and English Channel.

Development of new equipment had also been pressed forward on the Allied side. The 3-centimetre wavelength ASV Mk.X had entered service in the autumn of 1944 and was not only undetectable by

*Down to 28 U-Boats at sea by the end of the year.

Originally built as a Mk.III, ML827/WH-G was updated to Mk.V standard and served with No.330 Squadron. It was 'ditched' on 12 May 1945 off the Faeroes. (via J.D. Oughton)

submarine receivers but also performed much better than earlier radars against *schnorkels* and periscopes providing the sea state was reasonable. Steady progress was also being made with the introduction of sonobuoy receivers into Liberators, and the training of operators, which had started in July, was going well. This equipment detected underwater sound, particularly propeller cavitation noise, and was expected to be particularly effective against 'snorting' U-Boats because the use of diesel engines increased the general noise level considerably. However, the range of the sonobuoy was quite small in 1944 and it was not so much a primary means of detection as an aid to location after a U-Boat (already sighted on radar or visually) had submerged, enabling *Fido* to be employed more successfully against such a target. Code-named *High Tea* it was in tentative operational use during the autumn of 1944, and by the beginning of 1945 ten squadrons had the equipment. The operational value of both *High Tea* and the Mk.X radar had still to be proved, however, and Sholto Douglas decided to take more immediate measures against the new U-Boats. Their training areas had been reduced by the Russian advance, seasonal ice floes in the Baltic and extensive mining by Bomber Command, and now lay off the island of Bornholm, almost due north of the German/Polish border. It was a very heavily defended part of the Baltic, but he was determined to attack the 30 or so submarines reportedly exercising in the area nightly with the LL Liberators of Nos.206 and 547 Squadrons assisted by Halifaxes of Nos.58 and 502 Squadrons making diversionary attacks. Operation *Chilli I* took place on

3 February when 13 Liberators, avoiding night fighters by flying at low level, combed the 900 square mile exercise area in two waves on parallel tracks. Two similar *Chilli* operations followed during March, and a total of 15 attacks were made on U-Boats and 20 more on surface craft, but the results were disappointing, for no damage was done to U-Boats and only two surface craft were sunk.

Meanwhile the first Type XXIII U-Boat into action had quickly proved its ability to evade destruction at a time when both sea and air forces in coastal waters around Britain were at their peak and the older Type VII and IX 'boats' all but beaten. To further complicate the issue a new threat to Antwerp-bound convoys appeared off the coasts of Belgium and Holland—midget submarines carrying two torpedoes or mines. Three types of these submersibles were encountered, the long-range *Seehund* (Type XXVII), which had a crew of two, and the much shorter range single-seaters, the *Biber* and the *Molch*. They had been intended for action against assault convoys during *Overlord* but were not ready in time, and their first success had been on 23 December when a *Biber* sank the SS *Alan A Dale* off Flushing. More intensive operations followed early in January 1945 and, though largely due to inexperience and bad weather they proved a disaster for the Germans, they were taken very seriously by the Allies. No.16 Group started Albacore box patrols across their transit routes from bases in Holland, and a line patrol from Overflakkee to the Hague countered the possibility that they were being towed for at least part of their journey. The first contact was on 23 January but the

Attached to No.19 Group was the US Navy Fleet Air Wing 7 at Plymouth and its units at Dunkeswell and Upottery. This PB4Y-1 Liberator is on a dispersal at Dunkeswell in 1945. (ATP/B. Robertson)

midget survived the subsequent attack, and by the end of the month ASV-equipped Swordfish had replaced Albacores with No.119 Squadron, their first operational patrol being made on 6 February. Initially the Swordfish flew at night, day box patrols being carried out by Beaufighters of Nos.236 and 254 Squadrons, but these proved vulnerable to fighter attack and, when available, Spitfire XXI of No.12 Group were used instead.

Swordfish patrols were gradually increased and they took over some of the day operations, searching for both E-Boats and midgets, the latter being very active in March, especially on the Thames/Scheldt convoy route. The North Coates Beaufighter Wing (Nos.236 and 254 Squadrons) were tasked to fly another box patrol closer to the British coast, and the number of sightings and attacks increased significantly. Sixteen attacks were made during the month and seven midgets submarines were assessed as sunk, the first, on 11 March by the crew of a No.119 Squadron Swordfish using depth charges. Other weapons also took their toll, the thin-skinned boats

The only operational Warwick GR squadron in Coastal Command was No.179 at St Eval which used Mk.Vs from November 1944 onwards, including PN807/OZ-R. (via C.H. Luke)

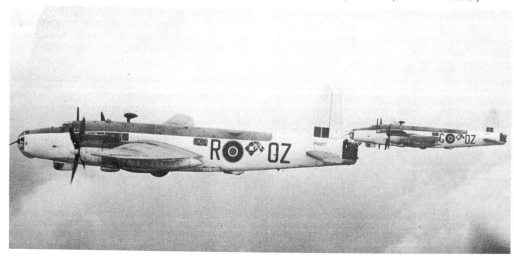

proving vulnerable to cannon fire, and even the crew of an unarmed Anson of No.119 Squadron (used for ASR work) were able to claim one after making a dummy attack which caused a *Molch* to be abandoned! At the end of the month a new patrol between Ostend and North Foreland was introduced, flown throughout the daylight hours by Swordfish of No.119 Squadron based in Belgium when requested by Dover Command. They landed at Manston at the end of each patrol, returning to Knocke via the Thames/Ostend convoy route. Small Battle Units, as the midgets were called by the British Admiralty, on occasion penetrated the Dover/Calais route and even attacked shipping off Dungeness, resulting in No.119 Squadron becoming responsible for dawn and dusk patrols in this area during April. In addition Barracudas of 810 Squadron operating from Beccles flew a daylight patrol from Great Yarmouth northwards along the East Anglian convoy route, and when it became obvious in April that *Seehund* midget submarine sorties emanating from Ijmuiden were setting out under cover of darkness, three LL Wellingtons of No.407 Squadron, equipped with Mk.VIA radar, were detached to Langham to carry out one sortie each night over the area. On 21 April 822 Squadron, FAA, equipped with Barracudas, became available to No.16 Group and the Swordfish then replaced the Beaufighters.

From 23 December 1944 until 11 May 1945, the period of midget submarine operation, aircraft under the control of No.16 Group flew 1,191 sorties (3,008 hours) on operations against them. Eighty sightings resulted in 64 attacks and 16 assessed 'kills' plus ten 'possibles'. Surface forces, sometimes helped by aircraft, accounted for another 50. Assessments of the damage they caused, by torpedo and mine, vary considerably but it would appear that they sank some 16 ships totalling about 19,000 tons for the total loss from all causes of 105 submarines—not a good return except in the amount of air/surface effort expended on them.

U-Boats were not inactive either and were becoming very successful in evading air attack, not a single German submarine being lost during passage to and from their operating areas during January 1945, though six were destroyed by surface forces once in contact with convoys. This continued inability to detect the new U-Boats was extremely worrying and in the short term the only solution appeared to be even more intensive close support and inshore operations using aircraft fitted with ASV Mk.X radar. Sholto Douglas, therefore, asked the Air Ministry to obtain American agreement for the use of the FAW 7 units at Dunkeswell and Upottery for the latter work, and Admiral King sanctioned the transfer of two Liberator squadrons, a PV-1 Ventura squadron and four Catalinas of VP-63. Doenitz increased the pressure during February, 41 U-Boats sailing from northern bases. Again most were undetected during transit but, by intensive combined air/surface action around the convoys, losses were kept down to eleven merchantmen and three escorts. Twelve U-Boats were destroyed, two by aircraft; the U-327 (Type VIIc) falling foul of a Liberator of VPB-103 and U-927 (Type VIIc) to a Warwick V of No.179 Squadron captained by Flt Lt A. G. Brownsill.

Liberator VIII KK335/PQ-L which served operationally with No.206 Squadron, Coastal Command, during the final two months of war in Europe. (via J.D. Oughton)

The 'strike' units took on surfaced U-Boats whenever presented with the opportunity. Here one comes under rocket attack from a Mosquito VI of No.235 Squadron in the Kattegat on 2 May 1945. (G.A.B. Lord via A.S. Thomas)

While the air activity around convoys was effective in discouraging attacks on shipping, it was not sinking U-Boats—it was in fact a return to defensive operations. Sholto Douglas reviewed tactics yet again and decided that while priority was still to be given to convoy protection, sufficient forces were to be retained for sweeps through the transit areas when the U-Boat plot suggested this would be a worthwhile occupation. The resulting increase in No.18 Group's activity produced an almost immediate return, nine U-Boats being sighted and six attacked during 5,971 hours of patrolling during March.

The sweeps off Norway at night, mainly carried out by Liberators of Nos.206, 224 and 311 (Czech) Squadrons could be hair-raising. On 3 March No.206 Squadron sent four aircraft which between them made attacks on an enemy coaster, two U-Boats and a *Narvik* type destroyer—the latter a very unpleasant sight in the glare of the Leigh Light. It responded with heavy AA fire and the Liberator was hit, though there were no casualties and the crew regained base safely. A more conventional anti-submarine attack, made on the 20th, was the first to bring to bear all the new equipment now available to Liberator crews. Following a tenuous radar contact Flt Lt N. Smith's No.86 Squadron crew laid a standard five sonobuoy

pattern on the datum, and the operator soon heard the sounds of propeller cavitation in his headset—they had a U-Boat. While the sonics operator continued to work on localizing the submarine by comparing signal strengths on the buoys, the radar operator obtained another brief contact and Smith decided to attack along the radar bearing with his two homing torpedoes. Six agonizing minutes later the sonics operator heard sounds of a considerable disturbance, then only normal background 'noise'. There were several U-Boats lost to 'unknown causes' in March, and this may have been one of them, but two days later the crew of a No.120 Squadron Liberator captained by Sqn Ldr L.J. White dropped two acoustic torpedoes on a sonobuoy 'fix' off Malin Head and could be more definite—subsequent explosions leaving little doubt— it was the end of U-296 (Type VIIC). Catalinas had also been fitted with *High Tea* by this time but their crews had little success with it, largely because of insufficient training and lack of practice, for there were few real targets about.

Most of the U-Boats were still being sent to British coastal waters, but in March Doenitz again tried regaining the initiative, ordering six craft into the Atlantic. The US Navy became convinced that they were intending to fire V-2 rockets at American cities

A marvellous sight—though one treated warily by aircrews. A surfaced U-Boat flies the black surrender flag following Germany's capitulation in May 1945. Coastal Command's war was over at last. (*British Official*)

from towed containers, but in fact they were looking for convoys!

In April 15 U-Boats were sighted in the northern transit areas, of which nine were attacked with little to show for it. Events further south overshadowed any disappointment, however, for U-Boats were now being forced out of the Baltic by the advance of Russian forces and they started streaming through the Kattegat in a desperate bid to reach Norway. Forced by mines to run the gauntlet on the surface, they were a tempting target for the Coastal strike squadrons, and the Banff Wing laid on a sweep on 9 April aimed as much at them as surface craft. It was a major effort, 30 Mosquito VIs of Nos.143, 235 and 248 Squadrons armed with cannon and rockets, two No.333 Squadron 'outriders' and a Film Unit aircraft setting off accompanied by Mustangs from Peterhead. In the Kattegat the leader, Sqn Ldr H.H.K. Gunnis of No.248 Squadron, sighted two U-Boats, and one after another the aircraft of Nos.143 and 235 Squadrons fired RPs at U-804 (Type IXC), ten salvoes resulting in the submarine starting to sink. No.248 Squadron then concentrated on U-1065 (Type VIIC) which, struck by at least ten rockets suddenly blew up, debris resulting in the loss of the Film Unit aircraft and damaging three more Mosquitoes so badly they had to

land in Sweden. Soon afterwards Flg Off A.J. Randell of No.235 Squadron attacked the U-843 (Type IXC) in the face of intense return fire, but after two passes the submarine was seen to be on fire and it sank. The next major clash, on the 19th, involved the Banff Wing again when 22 Mosquitoes led by Wg Cdr A.H. Simmonds of No.235 Squadron, and escorted by the usual Mustangs, spotted four U-Boats in line astern behind a minesweeper. As they dived onto their targets the leading U-Boat submerged and it was the second, the U-251, and the fourth, U-2335, which bore the brunt of the attack. U-251 (Type VIIC) was sunk and the minesweeper, U-2335 and U-2502 were damaged but the Germans put up a stout defence and two Mosquitoes crashlanded, one of them in Sweden. Joined by No.404 Squadron, the Banff Wing despatched 33 Mosquitoes on 2 May, again with a strong Mustang escort, and found two U-Boats in the Kattegat. The result was much the same as on previous attacks, the U-2359 was sunk, the other Type XXIII was damaged, and a minesweeper in the area was set on fire and later sank.

The North Coates Wing was also active against U-Boats, twelve rocket-firers of No.236 Squadron accompanied by 17 cannon-firers of No.254 Squadron spotting the U-2524 in the Kattegat during the

Sunderlands of No.201 Squadron make a final flight down the 'corridor' across Eire between Lough Erne and Donegal Bay prior to leaving Castle Archdale in August 1945. (RAF Museum)

evening of 3 May. The brand-new Type XXI was quickly despatched, and the Beaufighters went on to land in Holland. The next day they further demonstrated their superiority when four U-Boats* were found in the Little Belt, and they sank the lot! It was a fitting end to the North Coates Strike Wing's years of endeavour during which it had its fair share of trials and tribulations.

Early in May, Liberators of Nos.86, 206, 224, 311 and 547 Squadrons joined in the slaughter, flying night sorties over the Kattegat. Thirteen U-Boats were destroyed in the area during the period 2–7 May, seven by the Liberators, five by Beaufighters and one by Mosquitoes, but it was only right that the final sinking of the war should follow classic anti-submarine operation lines. At 0.43 hours on 7 May Flt Lt K.M. Murray's radar operator reported a radar contact at two miles. Two minutes later other crew members aboard the No.210 Squadron Catalina sighted a 'snort', a periscope, white smoke and a wake, and Murray attacked with four DCs as the submarine crash-dived. At 05.00 hours a *High Tea* basic 'PO-BRY' pattern† was laid, and just over an hour later positive submarine 'noise' was heard on the Red buoy. This had faded away by 06.40 hours when a large patch of oil appeared on the surface. At 07.41 hours contact was gained on the Green buoy, the noise, sounding like hammering, suggesting that repairs were being carried out. It steadily increased in volume and by 08.34 hours could be heard on the Red and Orange buoys as well. The Green buoy was replaced

by a Yellow and at 09.31 hours the Catalina was joined by a Liberator, the crew of which laid an extension pattern from the Yellow buoy. Contact was again lost but regained at 10.30 hours. At 12.53 a Purple replaced the Yellow buoy but contact was again lost until the crew of another Catalina reported engine and hammering noises. A Green replacement buoy was laid, and with the noise increasing the crew of the second Catalina obtained a datum and dropped four DCs on a north-easterly track. At 15.44 hours Flt Lt Murray set course for base having held intermittent contact for nearly 11 hours. The submarine was the U-320 which later signalled that serious damage had been sustained. On 9 May, hours after Doenitz, as Hitler's successor, had ordered German armed forces to lay down their arms, the U-320 (Type VIIC) went to the bottom off the Norwegian coast—there were no survivors.

Fortunately for the Allies the tribulations which had surrounded the Type XXI, a submarine as fast under water as the average escort vessel, prevented any operational sailings until 30 April when the U-2511 left Bergen on patrol, followed a day or two later by the U-3008. The U-2511 met a hunter/killer group in

---

*U-236 (Type VIIC), U-393 (Type VIIC), U-2338 (Type XXIII) and U-2503 (Type XXI).
†Five-buoy standard pattern, the frequency of buoy transmitters being identified by colour banding, Purple, Orange, Blue, Red, Yellow—hence 'POBRY'. Other colours (and frequencies) were available for extensions.

the North Sea but the captain evaded them easily and there is no doubt that the end of the war in Europe came not a day too soon, for the Type XXI would have posed great problems for anti-submarine forces and the pendulum would have swung decisively in the U-Boats' favour—at least for a time.

Patrols and convoy escorting did not cease immediately Germany capitulated, for there was no guarantee that U-Boat commanders, many fanatically loyal to the Third Reich, would obey the order from Doenitz to surface, display a black or blue flag, and when contacted proceed to a designated Allied port. Coastal Command crews had orders to take no chances, U-Boat crews not displaying the flags, or refusing to obey instructions were to be attacked. In fact, all did

co-operate but it was a tense time, and it was not until one minute after midnight on 4 June when Wg Cdr J. Barrett DFC, CO of No.201 Squadron, received instructions to return to base, that operational patrols ceased.

Since 3 September 1939 Coastal Command had taken part in the destruction of 207 U-Boats* and had sunk 343 ships totalling 513,804 tons, losing 5,866 aircrew and 1,777 aircraft operationally. Over 2,000 decorations had been awarded, among them four VCs, 17 George Medals and 82 DSOs. It had been a very tough fight.

*This figure included 'kills' by USAAF/USN units under Coastal Command control and those shared with surface units.

CHAPTER 10

Meteorological Flying

THE WEATHER HAS been a significant factor in the success or failure of a flight ever since man first ventured into the air. In the early days its impact was immediate, for it determined whether to fly or not, but as the aircraft's range and endurance increased the art of weather forecasting became more important, and special flights were being made solely to obtain information for this purpose before the end of World War I.

The pilot of Gladiator II/E of No.1401 Flight, Bircham Newton, being handed a psychrometer prior to another THUM climb. The instrument measures outside air temperature and humidity. (British Official)

However, it was the formation of the Meteorological Flight at Eastchurch on 1 November 1924 which was the real start of an organization which was to grow vastly in size and importance during World War II. The Snipe-equipped Flight moved to Duxford in January 1925 and started regular vertical ascents to 18,000 feet, temperature, pressure, humidity and the general weather conditions being logged at set levels during the climb, a system which hardly changed during the next 30 years, though the scope certainly did.

The Flight flew a variety of aircraft, having Bulldogs when it moved in September 1936 to Mildenhall, as a 'lodger' on this No.3 Group, Bomber Command station. The same month a similar unit was formed at Aldergrove, the first *THUM* (*T*emperature/ *Hum*idity) ascent being flown over Northern Ireland on 11 January 1937. Both 'Met' Flights received Gauntlets in July 1937 and Gladiators during May 1939, though some Gauntlets soldiered on until December.

The daily *THUM* vertical ascents were useful, but weather systems usually approached the United Kingdom from the west, and to build up complete charts for the country the Meteorological Office relied on synoptic reports from ships in the Atlantic. The procedure worked reasonably well in peacetime but such reports would be virtually non-existent during war, and the obvious alternative—observations by crews of reconnaissance aircraft—were at best patchy. In any case the Meteorological Office considered that specialist observers were needed for the task, and early in 1939, with war clouds already looming, long-range 'weather' units on the lines of the *THUM* Flights were proposed. The need was appreciated by Air Ministry staff but provision of specialist units was 'out of the question' in 1939 when there were not enough aircraft

No.1401 Flight became No.521 Squadron in July 1942 by which time Gladiators had been joined by Spitfire Vs. (Bircham Newton records)

or crews available for offensive operation, and the request was 'pigeon-holed'.

Following the fall of France in June 1940 Bomber Command became increasingly anxious about the accuracy of forecasts generally, and in particular those concerning base landing conditions. Strong representations were made to the Air Ministry, and in response the Meteorological Office repeatedly stated that accurate forecasts depended on information which they were not getting, and pointed out that the Germans were already flying such reconnaissance over the eastern Atlantic. Accordingly three new Flights, Nos.403, 404 and 405, were formed in November 1940 at Bircham Newton, St Eval and Aldergrove respectively, and the *Thum* units at Mildenhall and Aldergrove were redesignated Nos.401 and 402 Flights. The routes requested by the 'Met' Office required a track distance of 1,000 nm, for which the ideal aircraft was the Hudson, but none was available so the Flights had to make do with Blenheims and complete as much of the 'ideal' route as possible.

On 1 March 1941 Coastal Command assumed control of all five meteorological units. They were promptly redesignated Nos.1401 to 1405 Flights and came under the operational control of the Group in which they were based. During August No.1406 Flight formed at Wick (No.18 Group) when a small number of Hudsons became available, and in October No.1401 (Met) Flight moved to Bircham Newton and received Hurricanes in order to increase the altitude attainable on *Thum* flights. Two more new Flights, No.1407 at Reykjavik (RAF Iceland) and 1408 at Wick, were formed in the autumn with Hudsons, but aircraft were in short supply and it was April 1942

before the Icelandic unit was able to make its first sortie.

A requirement for very high level 'met' sorties by Nos.1401 and 1402 Flights resulted in Hurricanes being replaced by Spitfires during 1942. Code-named *PRATA*, this ascent was made at dawn, aircraft remaining within a nominal ten miles of the airfield as the pilots climbed to 40,000 feet, levelling for

An externally mounted psychrometer is fitted on the side of the front fuselage of a Blenheim IV of No.1405 Flight, Aldergrove. (British Official)

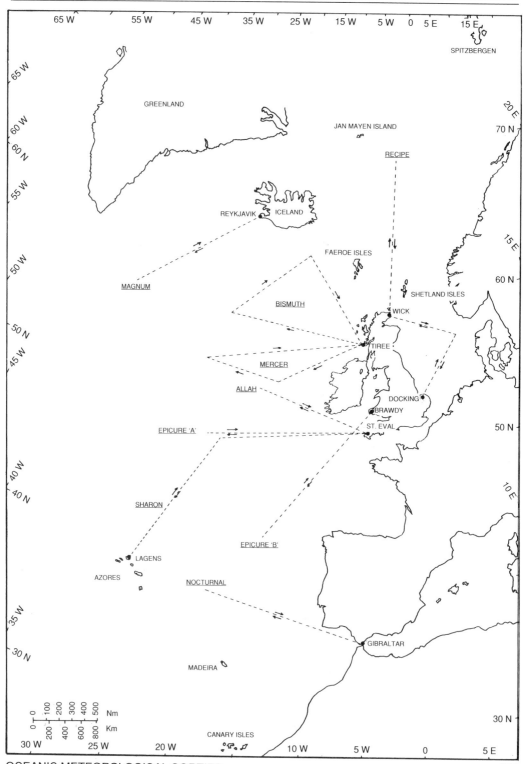

OCEANIC METEOROLOGICAL SORTIES

RCBA

B-17G Fortress 42-31766 of the USAAF Heavy Weather Squadron at St Eval, May 1944. The psychrometer is prominent on the starboard side of the nose. (via C.H. Luke)

readings at 5,000, 10,000 and 15,000 feet, then at 2,000 feet intervals up to 30,000 feet and every 1,000 feet thereafter. At the higher levels a standard aneroid capsule altimeter was not sensitive enough to give accurate readings so a Mk.14B ICAN altimeter was fitted. Each check height had to be maintained for two minutes to allow the thermometer reading to stabilize before recording. Visual observations of the type, base and tops of cloud, formation of icing and condensation trails were also made. Like the Gladiator pilots still flying the *THUM* sorties, the Spitfire pilots flew these tedious ascents almost regardless of the weather, having their own methods of regaining the airfield. In low cloud or fog the usual method at Aldergrove was

Halifax V LK966/P of No.518 Squadron at Aldergrove in 1945. Meteorological instruments are visible on the side of the nose where the 'met station' is installed. (RP/MAP)

Fortress IIA FK213/Z9-G served with No.519 Squadron at Wick and still carries the unit markings though in open storage. It was SoC in March 1947. (J.D.R. Rawlings)

to carry out a VHF D/F homing to overhead, then steer 210 degrees and continue descent over Lough Neagh until visual with the surface, returning to the airfield at low level. At Bircham Newton where the ground was flat No.1401 Flight pilots did an abbreviated D/F let-down procedure, crossing over the wireless station at 100 feet on track for the airfield, the boundary of which was 100 yards ahead. On receiving an 'engines over' message the pilot throttled back, and descended at a set rate at glide landing approach speed (about 90 mph). On reaching the boundary two airmen positioned either side of the approach path fired green very lights which it was hoped would give some help with perspective. The pilot then 'felt' for the ground, a line of glim lamps laid diagonally across his landing track indicating the centre of the airfield. It sounds dangerous, but in practice there were very few landing accidents using this procedure.

Routine reconnaissance sorties by Nos.1403–1408 Flights were flown on pre-set tracks differentiated by code-names such as *Rhombus*, *Bismuth* and *Magnum*.* The flights were made at a constant 950 millibar level (about 1,800 feet altitude) and timed to reach the furthest point of the sortie at dawn. Readings of humidity/temperature, and observations of cloud/sea conditions were taken at 50 nm intervals using instruments and the Mk.1 eyeball. The outside air temperature, wet and dry bulb, was provided by a psychrometer attached to the fuselage side in a position providing undisturbed airflow and allowing readings to be taken from the cockpit.

The Blenheims and Hudsons of No.1405 Flight had flown 291 *Bismuth* sorties in 330 'operational' days by the beginning of March 1942—an extraordinary effort in the bitter weather conditions experienced that winter. It then amalgamated with No.1402 Flight, the enlarged unit retaining the latter title and continuing *Bismuth*, *THUM* and *PRATA* flights. In similar fashion No.1401 Flight, operating Blenheims, Gladiators, Spitfires and Mosquitoes, absorbed the Hudsons of No.1403 Flight—and then in August became No.521 Squadron. Hudsons continued *Rhombus* flights, Gladiators *THUM* and *RHUMP* (a climb to the 400 millibars level 50 miles NE of base), Spitfires *PRATA* and Mosquitoes *PAMPA* sorties. The *PAMPA* was a flight deep into enemy territory, first flown in November 1941 by a Spitfire. It failed to return, further attempts being suspended until the arrival of Mosquitoes in May 1942.

Bomber Command had been unhappy about the priority afforded the *PAMPA* flights ever since the initial failure of Spitfires, and continually agitated for control of 'their' Met aircraft. At the end of March 1943 they got their way, the Mosquito Flight of No.521 Squadron joining No.8 (Pathfinder) Group as 1409 (Met) Flight. Further changes were to follow, the Establishment and Re-equipment Committee deciding that more efficient aircraft were needed for weather reconnaissance. They selected the Halifax V for long-range (1,400 nm) and Ventura for medium range (1,000 nm) work, the new establishments to

*See map on page 150.

No.269 Squadron operated as a composite unit from the Azores, the 'met' element comprising Spitfire VCs, amongst them BL939/HK-M at Lagens in March 1945. (No.269 Sqn records)

come into effect in September as follows:

No.517 Sqn
(from 1404 Flt)	24 Halifax V	Brawdy
518 Sqn		
(from 1405 Flt)	16 Halifax V	Tiree
519 Sqn		
(from 1406/1408 Flts)	12 Ventura V	Wick
520 Sqn		
(from 1403 Flt)	8 Halifax V	Gibraltar
521 Sqn	6 Ventura V	B.Newton
No.1407 Flt	6 Ventura V	Reykjavik

No.1403 Flight had been reformed at Gibraltar during June 1943, initially with Gladiators for *THUM* flights but in August receiving three Hudsons from No.233 Squadron for *Nocturnal* reconnaissance sorties.

The introduction of the Halifax started in July with the formation of No.518 Squadron, temporarily at Stornoway. *Mercer* sorties commenced on 15 September, and ten days later the unit moved to Tiree where it was joined by the newly formed Meteorological Conversion Unit during November. The Halifax allowed a much more useful flight profile to be adopted. As before, readings were taken at 50 nm intervals, but now sea level pressure readings were taken every 100 nm, and at the end of the leg a climb was made to the 500 mb level (approx 18,000 feet). The aircraft was then flown 500 nm due east before carrying out a descent to sea level followed by a return to base at 1,500 feet.

Considerable modification was required to suit the Halifax for meteorological reconnaissance, a task entrusted to Cunliffe Owen Aircraft at Eastleigh. It was the first aircraft large enough to allow a properly laid out observer's station to be installed—in the nose forward of the navigator's position.

Nos.517 and 519 Squadrons formed in August, both equipped at first with Hudsons and Hampdens, because the Halifax V modification programme suffered delays, and Venturas were in short supply. The former was supplemented by a detachment of four B-17F Fortress of the USAAF at St Eval, these aircraft remaining in the far south-west when No.517 Squadron moved to St Davids in November. No.519 received a few Spitfire VIs which were used for *PRATA* ascents while their Hampdens (replaced by Venturas during September) flew long range *Recipe* sorties up past Iceland to latitude 67 degrees N. During September No.520 was formed at Gibraltar with Hudsons and Gladiators, and No.521 reformed at Docking with a mixed bag of Hudsons, Hampdens, Gladiators and Spitfire IXs.

Meanwhile, No.1407 Flight soldiered on at Reykjavik. All three original Hudsons had crashed by late March 1943, Hampdens being received as replacements the following month. They were not very successful in the harsh conditions, and operational commitments were maintained by three long-range Hudsons transferred from No.269 Squadron. In September No.1402 Flight, still at Aldergrove, relinquished its Hampdens and Hudsons and ceased *Bismuth* to concentrate on *THUM* and *PRATA* work, and during the same month No.1407 was notified that Venturas were on allotment, but the first did not arrive until February 1944 and a series of accidents decimated them—the unit having just one Hudson available in May.

Halifax Vs arrived at Gibraltar for No.520 Squadron in February 1944 and the following month the unit was given a new task—night reconnaissance

Top: *Up in Iceland No.251 Squadron was formed from No.1407 Flight, and also had several roles, including meteorological flying. Fortress IIA FK197/AD-E accompanies a Hudson II of the unit under a glowering sky off the Icelandic coast during 1945. (G. Flowerday)*

Above: *'Met' stalwarts Spitfire VII MD159/B and Halifax III LV788/Y3-R of No.518 Squadron in 1945 with Nutts Corner airfield as a backcloth. (RAF Museum)*

Below: *Hurricane IIC PG469/Y3-KI of C Flight No.518 Squadron at Aldergrove in 1946. (R.E. Hilliard)*

of the Strait. Meanwhile from Tiree No.518 Squadron's Halifaxes had taken over the *Bismuth*, one of the most important, and certainly the longest lasting of the standard meteorological reconnaissance sorties. It consisted of a 550 nm leg due West, followed by 400 nm tracking NE before turning for base—a large triangle. The flight content was similar to that described earlier for *Mercer* (which continued) with readings taken at standard heights. When Nos.517 and 520 Squadrons became operational with Halifaxes they flew patrols respectively code-named *Epicure B* and *Nocturnal*, the former covering the Bay of Biscay from Brawdy and the latter out towards the Azores from Gibraltar. Problems with the Halifax soon developed, however, Merlin XX engines proving unsuitable for the type of operation being undertaken. The USAAF's 8th Reconnaissance Weather Squadron (Heavy) had to increase their 'Met' flights to cover the shortfall and by May 1944 they were making four sorties a day from St Eval on *Epicure A*, *Allah*, and *Sharon*, the latter a shuttle to/from the Azores. Despite the problems 91% of the task laid down by the Director of Meteorological Observation at the Air Ministry was met between November 1943 and June 1944, the sorties over the Atlantic on 4 June proving vital in the decision to order the 6th as 'D-Day' of *Overlord*.

More turmoil was caused by a shortage of Venturas in the Spring of 1944. Fortuitously a number of Hudson IIIs became available and No.1407 Flight was re-equipped in June 1944, and with three of the aircraft fitted for ASR duties the unit was upgraded as No.251 Squadron on 1 August. Meanwhile No.1402 Flight had received Hurricane IIs specially modified for 'met' work by Malcolm Bros of White Waltham and down at Lagens in the Azores No.269 Squadron, a composite unit with anti-submarine, ASR and 'met recce' as roles, flew Hudsons for weather work until October when they were replaced by Spitfires and activities were confined to *THUM* ascents.

Back home No.1402 Flight received a Spitfire VII for *PRATA* ascent trials in September and Hurricanes started replacing the long-serving Gladiators on *THUM* flights in November—the unit moving to

Ballyhalbert at the beginning of December 1944. Halifax Vs remained the mainstay of Atlantic operations, despite the unsuitability of their engines, while Nos.519 and 521 Squadron covered the North Sea and the area between Iceland and Norway flying *Rhombus* and *Recipe* sorties with Hudsons. In September it was agreed that the Warwick should replace both Halifax and Hudson aircraft, but the programme continued to slip and it was the Fortress II that re-equipped Hudson squadrons during the autumn of 1944. More trouble loomed in November when it was discovered that Merlin-powered Halifaxes could not maintain height if an engine failed during the first four hours of a 'met' sortie, and it was decided that the Hercules-powered Mk.III variant would be introduced as soon as possible. In the meantime the operational range of the 'met' version of the Mk.V had to be reduced until jettisonable bomb-bay tanks could be fitted, and more frequent engine changes were made, and in spite of these problems No.518 Squadron managed to fly on 363 days during 1944—ice and snow on the other two days making take-off impossible. Halifax IIIs started replacing the Mk.V in March 1945 and joined the Fortresses in carrying depth charges. Several opportunities to attack U-Boats had been missed by the inability of the Ventura and Halifax V to carry weapons on 'Met' sorties.

With the end of the war in Europe the meteorological units were reorganized. No.518 Squadron moved to Aldergrove in September 1945 and absorbed No.1402 Flight and its *THUM* ascents. No.251 Squadron was disbanded in October and No.521 ceased *THUM* flights and moved its Fortresses to Brawdy for *Allah* sorties. No.517 and 521 Squadrons moved to Chivenor during November to continue *Allah* sorties with Halifax aircraft, and No.519 transferred from Wick to Leuchars.

The five 'Met' squadrons, four in the United Kingdom and one at Gibraltar* flew on until most of the Atlantic ferrying was complete—then all but No.518 Squadron quickly faded away. The subsequent story is told in Chapter 14.

---

*And No. 269 'Composite' Squadron in the Azores.

CHAPTER 11

Photographic Reconnaissance

AERIAL PHOTOGRAPHIC RECONNAISSANCE made rapid strides during the latter years of the 1914–18 War, and by the Armistice virtually every use of the airborne camera employed during the next 50 years had been tried out. Trenchard, the great peacetime Chief of the Air Staff, clearly recognized the importance of aerial photography, but unfortunately he disliked specialization, and as far as he was concerned any observer 'worth his salt' could operate a camera when required. Thus, during the whole of the inter-war years the only significant photographic advance was the development of the F24 camera, the first to use roll film instead of plates—and it

appeared in 1925. Photography remained a minor part of aircrew duties and little thought was given to the reconnaissance aspect. It was not until the mid-1930s, when attempts to discover what the Italians were up to in the Mediterranean proved almost completely ineffective, and the British found themselves dependant on the French for coverage of German fortifications, that changes began to be made. In 1936 the RAF set up an organization aimed at obtaining information about German industry, while the British Secret Intelligence Service (SIS), impressed by clandestine French photographs of the area between the Moselle and the Rhine, decided to

Spitfire 'F' X4384 of the PRU at St Eval in August 1941. The operating conditions are not exactly ideal! (M.C.B. Anderson)

enter the aerial photography business themselves.

In January 1937 the Deputy Chief of Air Staff (DCAS) stated that 'we must regard the development of long range photography as highly important and accord it a high degree of priority in research, development and training', but in practice progress was painfully slow within the RAF. The impetus came from Wg Cdr F.W. Winterbotham, Chief of Air Intelligence in the SIS who, in co-operation with the French, arranged the finance and contracted an Australian 'adventurer' named F.S. Cotton, whose many exploits included aerial survey work in New-foundland. A private company, the Aeronautical Research and Sales Corporation, was set up at Heston as a 'front' and the Air Ministry was prevailed upon to purchase a Lockheed 12A, a twin-engined airliner which would not look out of place flying around Europe. The aircraft made its first operational flight from France over Germany on 30 March, but dis-agreements with the French resulted in Cotton going his own way. He fitted a new Lockheed 12A with concealed hatches over standard RAF F24 cameras and in ten days during June flying from Malta, covered in detail Italian airfields, military and naval installations in southern Italy and North Africa, producing prints far superior to obliques obtained by No.202 Squadron who were constrained by being forced to remain in international waters.

By the summer of 1939, Blenheim squadrons of No.2 Group, Bomber Command, had been given a photo-reconnaissance role, and plans for the Air Component of the British Expeditionary Force to France included two similar units earmarked for strategic reconnaissance. Conventional intelligence sources dried up as tension mounted but while the peace lasted, however tenuous, RAF crews could only practice, so Cotton was again despatched to obtain much needed information on German war prep-arations. He was outstandingly successful, but little use was made of his efforts, and the RAF proved on the first day of the Second World War that they had learnt nothing when they despatched a Blenheim of No.139 Squadron to Wilhelmshaven to reconnoitre the naval anchorages prior to an intended bombing raid. At 24,000 feet the camera froze solid and the radio failed, and by the time the Blenheim crew were back and debriefed deteriorating weather prevented the attack. It was a story repeated many times—yet Cotton had already solved frozen camera problems!

Cotton's SIS Flight remained in existence and on 15 September the Air Staff at the Air Ministry swallowed their pride and enlisted his advice, though refusing his offer to obtain the photographs of German naval bases being demanded by the Admi-ralty. Impulsive as ever, Cotton acted on his own initiative, taking his Lockheed across the North Sea to demonstrate his ability by photographing the Dutch coastline. The reaction to this audacious exploit was explosive but the ploy worked—a specialist photographic unit was set up—officially formed within No.11 Group, Fighter Command, on 24 September as the Heston Flight. Cotton was given the

The other PRU stalwart, a Mosquito, visiting the St Eval detachment in September 1941. (M.C.B. Anderson)

F/Sgt A. Dixon poses with his Spitfire 'F' in the spartan surroundings of St Eval, 1941. (A. Dixon via P.H.T. Green)

rank of Wing Commander and put in charge. He immediately asked for two Spitfires, convinced that photographic aircraft should be small and rely on speed and height to escape interception, and hopefully detection, instead of being expected to fight their way to the target and out again.* Not unsurprisingly his request was rejected— he would have to make do with

*A principle first suggested by Flg Off M. Longbottom of No.202 Squadron in a pre-war paper.

A smart Spitfire 'C' N3117—probably painted light green. It served with the PRU from June until December 1941 when it went missing. (via C/Tech Parrott)

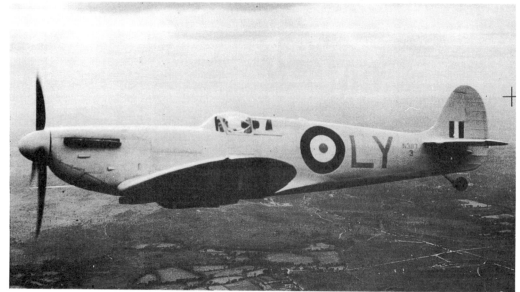

Blenheims—but he did not give up and in October the Spitfires were supplied on the direct instruction of Air Chief Marshal Sir Hugh Dowding, AOC-in-C Fighter Command. Work on the installation of cameras started immediately, and on 5 November, five days after the parent unit at Heston became No.2 Camouflage Unit* a Special Survey Flight was sent to France with one PR Spitfire. Bad weather thwarted the unit, and it was not until 29 December that a successful sortie was flown—over the Aachen-Cologne area of Germany. Trials were concluded on 10 January 1940 by which time the solitary Spitfire had flown 15 sorties and achieved twice the photographic coverage achieved by No.2 Group. Only once had the aircraft been approached by an interceptor and it was easily evaded.

A conference at Heston on 3 January accepted that the use of solitary fighter-type aircraft was the answer to the PR problem, and the unit at Heston† was tasked with translating ideas and one-off 'lash-ups' into procedures and equipment which could be used by operational RAF units. Two days later the Special Survey Flight was back in France and despite considerable opposition and hindrance from the Royal Aircraft Establishment (RAE),‡ Cotton gradually forced through camera installation improvements and increased the fuel capacity of the aircraft. His 'corner-cutting' brought great advances very quickly but his abrasive style engendered opposition and the RAE also had genuine reservations, the extra loads and in

particular its distribution having a serious de-stabilizing effect on the Spitfire. This was probably acceptable on the PDU but not for general squadron use, and that was the RAE's basic remit and the PDU's as well!

On 10 February the detachment in France was re-designated as No.212 Squadron—a further subterfuge—and its strength and that of the PDU itself was steadily built up during 1940, events which more than justified the appointment of Sqn Ldr G.W. Tuttle DFC, as Cotton's deputy.

Following the German breakthrough into France, No.212 Squadron was frantically busy, but by early June the battle had moved so far south-west that it could be covered from Heston, and on the 14th the unit was withdrawn. While these momentous events were taking place another battle was being fought within the Air Ministry. Pressure had been building up for the PDU to be regularized, there being general agreement that the situation was unsatisfactory, for though it was in Fighter Command administratively, and came under the Air Ministry operationally, the choice of targets and the distribution of resources was dictated by Cotton! Bomber Command pressed their case for a take-over, but it was finally decided that as

*An attempt to 'camouflage' its purpose.
†Re-named the Photographic Development Unit (PDU) on 17 January 1940.
‡Responsible for clearing the PR modifications to Spitfires.

Painted PRU blue Spitfire 'F' P9385 is positioned for the camera in September 1941. (via C/Tech Parrott)

Flt Lt A.H.W. Ball getting out of his PRU Spitfire after a sortie—St Eval, June 1942. (M.C.B. Anderson)

the Admiralty was involved control should be vested in Coastal Command, already responsible for visual reconnaissance over the sea and of enemy occupied ports and estuaries.

Accordingly the PDU, Heston, and the Interpretation Unit at Wembley, were placed under the control of Coastal Command on 18 June. No.212 Squadron was disbanded on the same day and, it being obvious that Cotton would not or could not behave as a conventional unit commander, he was dismissed and Tuttle was appointed in his place. In order to emphasize its operational role, the PDU became the Photographic Reconnaissance Unit (PRU) and Wembley was renamed the Photographic Intelligence Unit (PIU), both administered by No.16 Group but operationally tasked by HQ Coastal Command. The scope of the task was vast, for everyone had discovered the value of aerial photography and the PDU was expected to provide both photographs and interpretation for the Combined Intelligence Committee, the Air Ministry, the Admiralty, the War Office and RAF Commands. The threat of seaborne invasion of the United Kingdom launched from anywhere on a 2,000 mile Continental coastline provided the PRU with its first priority, for to accurately predict the size and scope of such an attack regular systematic photographic coverage of every port and harbour was required. In the 'pipeline' were 30 Spitfires with 'bowser' wings, and capable of a round trip of 1,750

miles, which would bring places as far apart as Trondheim and Marseilles within reach from the British Isles, but currently Tuttle had available just 13 aircraft, most of them range-limited to 1,300 miles. It was a tall order!

Four operational Flights were established, each to have three medium and one long range Spitfire (when available), a Hudson and a Tiger Moth. On 1 July *A* Flight went to Wick and *B* Flight to St Eval, and on the 24th *C* and *D* Flights were formed at Heston followed by *E* Flight (with two Wellingtons and four experimental Spitfires) the next day. Further expansion had already been approved, *F* Flight being established with six Spitfires, expressly for PR coverage of enemy airfields in Holland, Belgium and Northern France at regular intervals.

During August 163 sorties were flown, 112 from Heston, 21 from Wick and 30 by *B* Flight from St Eval. At the end of the month the first factory modified PR Spitfire arrived at Heston though RAE conversions continued to be produced and it would be a long time before any degree of standardization was achieved.

The first signs of invasion preparations were noted on 1 September when barge concentrations were seen, and by the 18th 1,044 barges could be counted on photographs covering ports between Flushing and Boulogne. But by the 23rd the barges were being dispersed and the Germans soon announced the post-

The Mosquito PR prototype W4501 in service with the PRU July 1941-October 1942. (Imperial War Museum)

ponement (and eventual cancellation) of Operation *Sea Lion*.

Bombs had fallen on both Heston and St Eval in August, and during September considerable disruption was caused following several attacks on Heston. During a meeting on 2 October to discuss the expansion of the PRU/PIU and the formation of a Photographic Reconnaissance Group, HQ Coastal Command was told to consider alternative locations, and Benson was chosen, being reasonably accessible from London but much less vulnerable.

The 'escape' of the *Graf Spee* into the Atlantic immediately prior to the start of the war and the subsequent damage she caused had been a nasty shock to the Admiralty and, with the threat of invasion diminished, their full attention was turned on to the problem of Germany's other surface raiders. They could now lurk in ports as far apart as western France and northern Norway and the Admiralty needed to know where they were, if preparations were being made to sail and, of paramount importance, early confirmation of a sailing. The St Eval detachment was therefore employed almost exclusively on coverage of the Brittany ports, while Spitfires at Wick kept watch over Scandinavian harbours, and Heston surveyed German anchorages. By early October all the major units had been found in German ports and the Admiralty was able to relax—too much for they allowed a false sense of security to prevail!

The first 'bowser' Spitfire sortie was flown on 29 October, a high level flight to Stettin lasting five hours 20 minutes. Low level operations were also introduced for close-up photography of small heavily defended targets using a variant of the PR Spitfire, known as the 'G', which retained some armament. Compared with the normal high level operation these flights were very dangerous and soon became known as *dicing* (with death), considerable navigational expertise being required, for only one 'pass' could be made if the essential element of surprise was to be retained. Most *Dicer* sorties were made to try to find oft reported *Freya* sites—German early warning radars. These proved extremely elusive, partially because the interpreters did not know exactly what they were looking for, and it was to be several months before the PRU was rewarded with a definite sighting.

Although additional aircraft had been ordered, the build-up of the PRU was hampered by other commitments. An Intelligence Photographic Flight* had been formed in the Middle East, and a Bomber Command PR element† was established at Oakington in No.3 Group—both using Spitfires as basic equipment. During November the number of sorties flown by the redesignated No.1 PRU fell to 133 because of bad weather, though this could not be blamed entirely for

*Subsequently No.2 PRU.
†Became No.3 PRU on 16 November.

it taking several days to discover that the *Admiral Hipper* had disappeared from Brunsbuttel and was loose in the Atlantic. The Germans, not for the last time, had shown considerable acumen in obscuring any of the usual signs of preparation, then raising 'steam' as soon as the 'recce' aircraft had left the area, confident that another overfly would not be made for several days. The shock was amplified by the departure of the *Scharnhorst* and *Gneisenau* from Kiel between 21 December and 9 January,* and the *Hipper* which slipped out again on 1 February. Daily cover was the obvious answer but with the resources available this could only be attempted on a very limited number of targets, and it was only the insistence of Mr Churchill, the Prime Minister, that the RAF concentrate on objectives immediately connected with the 'Battle of the Atlantic' which ensured that the priority list was kept to manageable proportions.

In the meantime the move to Benson had started on 27 December 1940 and was completed on 4 January 1941. Among the aircraft transferred were a handful of Blenheims operated by *F* Flight used for spasmodic sorties over lightly defended airfields. They were replaced by Marylands, by which time two Blenheims and two Spitfires had been badly damaged during an air raid in February 1941. Benson was not proving as safe as had been expected!

The control of photographic reconnaissance resources within the United Kingdom again came under review early in 1941, but changes were confined to the replacement of the PIU by a Central Interpretation Unit (CIU). Early in April the unit moved from Wembley to Medmenham, where it was to remain for the rest of the war.

The *Hipper* appeared in Brest after her Atlantic foray and was joined by the *Scharnhorst* and *Gneisenau* late in March when the ships became the special responsibility of the St Eval detachment, and between 28 March and 30 April over one third of all PRU sorties covered Brest. On four occasions the whole harbour was photographed from 500 feet as a panorama—an exceedingly 'dicey' venture. In addition to the ports, hundreds of airfields were photographed during the first six months of 1941, and at the request of the War Office photographic records were built up of activity at storage dumps and railway marshalling yards—usually from above 20,000 feet but occasionally from low level. Detachments were sent to Gibraltar to observe French naval activity at Dakar and Casablanca and along both north and south coasts of the Mediterranean, while the Flight at Wick continued to record naval activity in Norwegian fjords. The installation of an F8 survey camera (with 14″ or 20″ lens) in some Spitfires allowed larger scale fine definition prints to be obtained from high level

sorties over ship-building facilities in Germany, and at last a check on U-Boat construction could be made. The information gained was alarming, but at least it gave the Admiralty pre-warning of the rapid production build-up being achieved.

The production version of the 'bowser' wing Spitfire, the PR MK.IV arrived in March and was operational on 5 April. Initially delivered in 'duck egg' green, the aircraft underwent much colour scheme experimentation, even white and pink being tried, but finally the decision was made to use a cerulean blue which became known as 'PR blue'. The new Spitfire was soon demonstrating its capabilities, covering Malmo for the first time on 10 April, and the port of Genoa in Northern Italy on the 14th during a flight from Benson which lasted over seven hours—and ended with the aircraft landing in a field near Hawkinge out of fuel.

The *Bismarck* and *Prinz Eugen* had been skulking in port at Gdynia on the Gulf of Danzig for many months, but on 20 May the Admiralty received a report that a naval force had passed through the Kattegat westwards—enough to start any naval staff officer's nerves jangling. The Wick detachment immediately received a priority tasking for a search off the Norwegian coast. Two Spitfires were despatched, Plt Off M.F. Suckling making landfall just south of Sogne Fjord. He photographed shipping in Hjelte Fjord, Herdla airfield and Flatoen seaplane base, then a *Hipper* class cruiser and four smaller vessels off Store Sotra, west of Bergen. Flying closer to Bergen the young pilot spotted a ship which he identified as another *Hipper* class cruiser at the eastern end of the fjord. In fact it was the battleship *Bismarck* and the start of a hunt which finished with the destruction of the ship six days later after a dramatic chase around the Atlantic.† More excitement followed when the *Lutzow* was sighted rounding the Skaw‡ by the PRU, and she was subsequently attacked by a single Beaufort and limped back into Kiel for repairs which took six months to complete.

Reconnaissance cover of German capital ships was now becoming manageable with the *Tirpitz* still being fitted out at Danzig, the *Hipper* and *Scheer* in Baltic ports and the *Scharnhorst*, *Gneisenau* and *Prinz Eugen* all at Brest. They still posed a very real threat, of course, and in periods of bad weather when they could not be photographed the Admiralty Intelligence Centre became a very tense place.

Disagreement over the use of No.3 PRU had started soon after its formation, but when it was

*On 27 December 1940.
†See Chapter 4.
‡Between the Kattegat and Skagerrak.

A typical photograph taken by a PR Spitfire of No.542 Squadron—the eastern entrance to the Kiel Canal at Holtenau. (via B. Robertson)

discovered that the unit was often operating in the same area as No.1 PRU, relations became very strained. The situation was only resolved when the Air Ministry ordered its amalgamation with No.1 PRU on 1 June 1941 despite Bomber Command protestation. A few days later two more Marylands arrived at Benson for *F* Flight but were transferred to the new *G* Flight which left for Gibraltar early in July. The Maryland had proved an excellent aircraft for PR work, especially in the Mediterranean area, but more significant in the long term was the arrival on 13 July of the first PR Mosquito to reach Benson—though it was to be some time before the aircraft was fully operational.

By September 1941 the operational strength of No.1 PRU was 37 Spitfires, two Marylands and two Mosquito PR.1s—and it was on the 17th that the first photo 'recce' was attempted with one of the latter aircraft. Electrical trouble prevented the cameras from functioning, but on the 20th a successful four-hour sortie was flown during which the Sylt/Heligoland area was covered. It was obvious that the Mosquito was going to be most useful for the long distance targets, but for the present the Spitfires were still covering the *Tirpitz* at Gdynia, it falling to Flt Lt D. Salwey during a 7 hour 50 minute flight on 23 September to discover that the ship had sailed—for gunnery trials in the Baltic. The St Eval detachment was now concentrating exclusively on the port of Brest, a nervous Admiralty requiring twice daily photographic proof that the German capital ships

remained in port. This caused the PRU great problems for the advantage of surprise was largely lost by such regular visits, but all that could be done was to vary the height and direction of approach in the hope that this would enable solitary unarmed Spitfires to evade the standing patrol the Germans put up at 30,000 feet over Ushant.

During October three Mosquitoes were sent up to the Wick detachment, and the following month the whole Norwegian coast including the fjords was regularly covered for the first time. The first operational Mosquito loss was on 4 December 1941 when an aircraft failed to return from Norway, and it turned out a bad month, for five Spitfires were also posted 'missing'—four of them on Brest missions. These grievous losses were not completely in vain for the PRU did provide the first indications that the capital ships were preparing to sail from Brest. This was on 11 February 1942 when Flg Off Ball caught on film the *Scharnhorst, Gneisenau* and *Prinz Eugen* all with smoking funnels, accompanied by six destroyers, numerous minesweepers and torpedo boats. Unfortunately the British Admiralty was still caught out because they had convinced themselves that the Germans would not risk the Channel in daylight which meant that they could not leave Brest under cover of darkness. The German Admiral Raeder had other ideas, however, and the ships left at 23.00 hours that very night.*

*See Chapter 4.

Mosquito I W4060 of No.540 Squadron, late 1942. This aircraft went missing on 20 February 1943. (No.140 Sqn records via P.H.T. Green)

Many *Freya* early-warning radar sites had been discovered by the end of 1941, but until interpreters noted suspicious tracks at Bruneval leading to other sites nothing had been found of the associated *Wurzburg* azimuth and height finding radar reported to be in service. A *Dicer* on 3 December failed to obtain close-up photographs but a repeat two days later was successful and a parabolic dish aerial fitting the tentative 'intelligence' description of the equipment was identifiable together with a large 'control' building. Positive identification could only be obtained by examining the equipment, however, and on

28 February Commandos raided the Bruneval site and captured parts of the installation—a dangerous venture made somewhat easier by a scale model prepared from the PRU's photographs. By the end of the year 70 such sites had been identified, together with over 700 radio stations of various types.

Meanwhile the lack of useful post attack photographs of Bomber Command operations was worrying the new AOC-in-C, Air Chief Marshal Sir Arthur Harris, anxious as he was to confirm the claims of his crews. He was not afraid to say so in very firm terms, and fortunately the departure of German capital ships

Spitfire XI MB787 of No.541 Squadron, St Eval during the summer of 1944. (J. Olver)

Another view of the superb Spitfire XI, this time EN664/0 of No.541 Squadron in September 1944. It was named 'Brenda'! (J. Olver)

from Brest meant that more attention could be paid to the bombing campaign. From March 1942 target and damage assessment photography received higher priority, the famous '1000 bomber' raids of May/June being particularly well covered, 'before' and 'after' photographs proving the success of the attack on Cologne—and also the less than perfect bombing of Essen and Bremen.

The first Mosquito PR Mk.IV had been received by the PRU in April, but deliveries were very slow and it was July before a permanent detachment of three aircraft could be sent to Leuchars for long-range PR capable of covering both Northern Norway and the Baltic from the same base. The shift to PR coverage of Bomber Command raids was noted with apprehension by the Admiralty who insisted on regular photography of the *Tirpitz* in Trondheim Fjord being maintained. Trondheim was the limit for Spitfires but the Mosquito PR Mk.IV could cover Narvik as well and 'alarm bells' sounded when the *Sheer* and *Lutzow* were found there on 15 May. The *Tirpitz* had, in fact, been sent to Trondheim because Hitler was convinced that an attack on Norway was imminent, but by the spring Raeder was planning *Rösselsprung* (knight's move), a co-ordinated attack by Norwegian-based surface ships and the Luftwaffe on Russia-bound convoys. His first opportunity followed the sighting of the ill-fated PQ17 convoy, and on 6 July it was established that the German ships had left port and presumed that they had gone north out of range of Mosquitoes operating from Britain. Arrangements for the PRU to refuel in Russia were made, and on 8 July Flg Off Bayley and F/Sgt Little left Leuchars on the

first such sortie. They located the *Tirpitz* steaming back to Narvik from North Cape, refuelled at Vaenga and returned direct to Leuchars.

The information gleaned by the PRU did not prove of immediate help, but it established the practicality of operations from Russia, and for the next convoy, PQ18, plans were laid much earlier. A ground party left by sea on 13 August and on 1 September three PR Mk.IV Spitfires flew from Sumburgh to Vaenga via Afrikanda. One aircraft was badly damaged by Luftwaffe bombing of Vaenga on 9 September but the other two were able to confirm that the *Sheer, Hipper* and *Köln* were still in Alten Fjord on the 11th. All efforts to find the *Tirpitz*, reported missing from Narvik by a British-based PR Mosquito, proved unsuccessful, however, and the Admiralty reasonably assumed that she had again sailed north. Spitfire and Mosquito PR sorties were concentrated on fjords and the open sea up to the North Cape, without success, the ship having merely been on sea exercises in Vest Fjord and on the 18th returned to Narvik—Hitler having refused permission for his capital ships to be deployed against PQ18 because of his continued conviction that Norway was about to be invaded. Another Spitfire and a Mosquito were sent to Vaenga to assist in the photographing of the whole Norwegian coast in the far north, after which the aircraft and equipment were handed over to the Russians, the British leaving by sea on 23 September—the day that the *Tirpitz* returned to Trondheim and back in range of PR flights from Leuchars.

The steady improvement in the PR service afforded Bomber Command did not satisfy Sir Arthur Harris, or his staff, who consistently underestimated the problems caused by weather, and demanded cover within hours of every major bombing attack. In October 'Bomber' Harris again wrote a pointed letter to the Vice Chief of Air Staff on the subject of control of the PRU resources but, though the Air Ministry were a long time considering, Harris did not get his way. The PRU had grown 'like topsy' by the summer of 1942 when it had eight Flights with a total strength of over 70 aircraft flying from six bases— Benson, Leuchars, Mount Farm, North Front, St Eval and Wick—plus a large technical component which not only serviced the aircraft but also modified them for photographic use. In July the Chief of Air Staff, Air Chief Marshal Sir Charles Portal, accepted that the organization was now too large for split control by the Air Ministry and No.16 Group, and that a separate PR Group should be formed which would take complete control of all PR assets in the United Kingdom. The proposal immediately attracted strong opposition from the Chief of Naval Staff, who insisted on retaining responsibility for all reconnaissance north of 54 degrees N, and from the Chief of the Imperial General Staff who would not countenance No.140 Squadron being removed from Army Co-operation Command. The plan was temporarily dropped, but the unwieldy PRU was disbanded on 18 October and the following day, still within Coastal Command, the two Mosquito Flights (*H* and *L*) became No.540 Squadron at Leuchars with a detachment at Gibraltar, the six Spitfire Flights became Nos.541 (ex-*B* and *F* Flts), 542 (ex-*A* and *E* Flts) and 543 (with detachment at St Eval), all nominally at Benson. No.544 Squadron was formed from the Night Photography Flight and other elements at Benson to operate Spitfire Flights at Leuchars and Gibraltar—and as Operation *Torch* progressed from Marrakesh and Agadir in North Africa. The Mosquito detachment at Gibraltar photographed the French fleet at Toulon during *Torch* while the Spitfires covered the invasion beaches, ports and installations along the North African coast.

The Spitfire PR Mk.IV was now subject to interception by Luftwaffe fighters, aided by improved performance and better ground radar. An updated Spitfire, the Mk.XI, was on the stocks but would only trickle into service, and in the meantime a camera-fitted Mk.IX was introduced, the first reaching No.541 Squadron at the end of November 1942. An alternative, strongly advocated, was the replacement of virtually all PR Spitfires by Mosquitoes, and with the PR MK.VIII due to enter service early in 1943, and the production PR MK.IX to follow soon afterwards, the idea was certainly attractive. The staff at Benson remained strongly pro-Spitfire, however, and were backed by

the AOC-in-C, Air Marshal Slessor who argued in a paper presented in March 1943 that the Spitfire had a better rate of climb which allowed it to remain low level until closer to enemy territory thus reducing radar warning time; was less vulnerable to AA fire at low level, while increased manoeuvrabilty made it more difficult to intercept at high level; and that its small size and comparative quietness improved the chance of escaping detection altogether. He concluded by stating that the Spitfire was more economical over short ranges, more versatile for low level work, and that there would never be enough Mosquitoes for all the tasks envisaged for it. He considered the ideal UK-based PR force to be two squadrons of Spitfires and two of Mosquitoes. The Vice Chief of Air Staff was swayed by these arguments, and instituted priority production of the Spitfire PR Mk.XI which, after problems with canopy icing had been solved, was a great success. It was able to 'outfly' the opposition in altitude and was usually faster.

The German capital ships in Norwegian waters continued to give No.540 Squadron steady work during 1943, and to worry the Admiralty, especially when they suddenly disappeared from their usual haunts late in March. The Russians were asked to reconnoitre the North Cape, and at the end of April they discovered the *Scharnhorst* and three cruisers in Alten Fjord—joined early in May by the *Tirpitz*. The position of the ships resulted in Russian convoys from Britain being held in abeyance throughout the 'long day' summer months, and efforts to find the remainder of the German surface navy were intensified. They were finally discovered in the Baltic, but still 'disappeared' at irregular intervals, forcing the PR effort to be maintained throughout the year. Despite this the overall PR demands from the Admiralty had decreased considerably, and when Army Co-operation Command was disbanded on 1 June, and the Second Tactical Air Force was formed, complete with a PR Wing, the CAS took the opportunity to renew the proposal for a separate PR organization to fulfil all other tasks. This time the Admiralty and the War Office put up little opposition, and on 26 June No.106 (PR) Wing was formed at Benson—still as part of Coastal Command. With Air Commodore J. Boothman AFC in command, the Wing controlled Benson and its four operational squadrons, No.309 Ferry Training Unit, the Air Despatch Unit, and No.8 OTU at Dyce.

Work for Bomber Command continued to increase in quantity and quality. By the Spring of 1943 the Battle of the Ruhr was in full swing aided by 'pathfinder' techniques based on new navigation and bombing aids. At the beginning of the year coverage of the Mohne Dam had been requested on a regular basis so that a large scale target model could be

The photographic reconnaissance squadrons of Coastal Command kept special watch on German submarine construction. This photograph of the Deschimag Yard, Bremen, provides evidence of the extensive pre-fabricated building programme for the Type XXI U-Boat in 1944. (British Official)

made—and water levels and the defences assessed. Early in April the Sorpe and Eder dams were added to the tasking list, and sorties covering other possible targets in the area were flown so that German suspicions were not aroused. The final pre-attack photos arrived at Scampton on 16 May—the day of the famous Dambusters raid—and a few hours later No.542 Squadron Spitfires were photographing the damage to the dams and the countryside and towns downstream. It was just the sort of service that 'Bomber' Harris had been calling for, and he used it shrewdly in his campaign in support of his bombing policies. It worked, too; his critics being all but silenced by irrefutable evidence that both specialist targets and main force attacks on cities and towns were effective.

Still very concerned about the remaining German ships in Northern Norway, the Admiralty decided to mount an attack, code-named Operation *Source*, in Alten Fjord during September using newly available British midget submarines. Precise details of the ships and their anchorages were required, and Spitfires were again sent to Vaenga, three aircraft of No.543 Squadron making a successful transit from Sumburgh on 3 September. They flew 31 sorties from Vaenga, 25 of which were successful, and enabled the operation to go ahead, though unfortunately the pre-attack sortie

had to be cancelled because of bad weather. During the interval the *Lutzow* sailed for Germany and the *Scharnhorst* left her berth for gunnery exercises, but the *Tirpitz* was temporarily put out of action by the crews of three of the tiny craft. The Vaenga detachment, in the now time-honoured fashion, handed over their aircraft and equipment and returned to Britain on 1 November, only to find that their Squadron had been disbanded a fortnight earlier! At the same time No.544 Squadron was brought up to full strength, all four PR units being standardized at 20 aircraft.

A Flight of No.540 Squadron remained responsible for the Norwegian anchorages and the Baltic, while from Benson *B* Flight covered central and southern Europe—the latter by refuelling in North Africa. On 28 November, almost by accident, Sqn Ldr J. Merifield of 540 Squadron provided the link between the experimental station at Peenemünde and the mysterious 'ski' sites rapidly multiplying in France. Rumours had long suggested a connection but it was obvious that the large rockets associated with Peenemünde could not be accommodated on the 'ski' ramps, and suspicion fell on a small 'aeroplane' seen on the airfield on 3 November. Now Merifield's photographs of Peenemünde revealed similar 'ski' ramps—and, after further interpretation, one of the small 'aeroplanes' alongside a ramp. No cockpit was visible—it

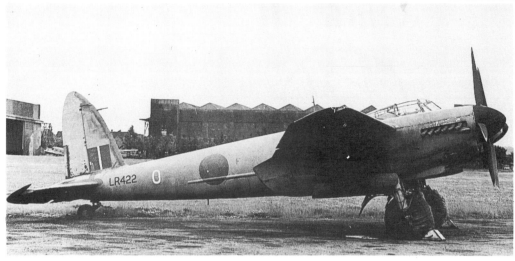

Mosquito IX LR422/0 of No.540 Squadron at Benson in 1944. (Author's collection)

was plainly some kind of flying bomb. Over France the hunt for more *Crossbow* sites, as they were code-named, was intensified and from 5 December onwards they were attacked by both Bomber Command and the United States VIIIth Air Force, resulting in their almost complete destruction by the beginning on 1944.

Meanwhile the Russian convoys started again in November, and it was hoped to tempt the *Scharnhorst* out of the fjords and keep her under surveillance. The plan worked, the battle cruiser leaving Lang Fjord late on 23 December bent on attacking the second December convoy. She was engaged by a well-warned British surface force and sunk on the 26th—the end of one of PR's longest serving targets!

Between mid-November 1943 and mid-February 1944 persistent cloud cover prevented all but two attempts to provide post-raid photographs of Bomber Command targets, but as the priority moved from German cities and production facilities to the dislocation of the communications system of Western Europe so the weather improved. The devastation caused was then plain to see on the photographs brought back by the Spitfires of Nos.541 and 542 Squadrons—and was awe-inspiring.

No.106 Wing was now working well and after much dithering the Air Ministry decided to bring the CIU at Medmenham into the organization. On 14 April 1944 the Wing was upgraded to become No.106 (PR) Group, and in May the newly established Joint Photographic Reconnaissance Committee took over the allocation of priorities and tasking, much to the annoyance of the AOC-in-C Coastal Command who was still charged with administering the Group and

thus had responsibility but little authority.

Cover of *Crossbow* sites continued and when repaired they were attacked again, though the Germans had actually abandoned them as being too conspicuous, and simplified ramps were developed which could be set up virtually anywhere. These were very difficult to locate, and it was not until 27 April that one was positively identified by CIU personnel on a photograph. Within a few days 12 more had been discovered and No.106 Group was ordered to re-photograph the whole of Northern France. Bad weather and the demands of *Overlord* slowed the work, but by early June some 69 ramps had been located, some of them the scene of considerable activity. Unfortunately the *Diver* signal, which indicated that the CIU considered the sites were ready for action was misplaced in the Air Ministry and the first 'flying bomb' arrived in England without warning on the 13th. Concentrated bombing of the sites, suspected V-1 storage areas and factories restricted the German offensive to about one-third of its capacity, and by September most of the ramp sites had been overrun. It was, therefore, a considerable shock when a massive explosion occurred at Chiswick early on 8 September 1944 apparently caused by a rocket carrying a substantial warhead, for none of the sites seen at Peenemünde had been discovered in France or elsewhere in Europe. Indeed it was not until 26 February 1945 that a V-2 was actually spotted in a vertical launching position alongside its transporter—by Sqn Ldr J.E.S. White of No.544 Squadron—and its elusiveness became obvious: it was free-standing on its four fins!

For over four years the photo-reconnaissance crews enjoyed almost complete immunity from attack during high level sorties, but on 25 July 1944 a No.544 Squadron Mosquito XVI, flown by Flt Lt A.E. Wall and his observer, Flg Off A.S. Lobban, was intercepted over Munich by a Me262 jet fighter. The manoeuvrability of the Mosquito saved the day, but it was a shaken crew who landed safely in Northern Italy, and during August four Benson-based aircraft were similarly attacked, and one was shot down. Increasing the height at which the aircraft flew over enemy territory would make interceptions more difficult, but neither the Mosquito PR Mk.XVI, which had a pressure cabin and was in small scale service with No.106 Group, or the first Griffon-powered Spitfire XIXs* re-equipping Nos.541 and 542 Squadrons had a much increased ceiling over earlier variants, the latter limited to 38,000 feet to prevent physiological problems for the pilots.

The AOC-in-C Coastal Command called for pressure cabin Spitfires to be introduced as soon as possible, but difficulties were experienced with the aircraft, and production deliveries were not made until November 1944 when altitudes of 42,000 feet became the norm. The specially lightened Mosquito Mk.32 with increased span appeared in very small numbers (a total of five) and had a ceiling 5,000 feet above the Mk.XVI, but most crews of Nos.540 and 544 Squadrons continued to fly Mosquito PR.IX or XVI and to be subjected to interception by Me163 or 262 fighters, particularly over southern Germany. The PR MK.34 Mosquito, which had a ceiling of 43,000 feet and was expected to solve the problem, was delayed and did not enter service until the war in Europe was over.

No.540 Squadron operated a detachment from Yagodnik in September to cover No.5 Group Lancaster bombing of the *Tirpitz* and then returned to its old stamping ground covering Scandinavia and Northern Germany until the end of the war. No.544,

its operational area shrinking as the enemy withdrew, became involved in Operation *Frugal*, flights to the Soviet Union carrying mail during the Moscow Summit Conference, 9–20 October, which both the Prime Minister, Winston Churchill, and the Foreign Secretary, Anthony Eden, attended. Similar flights were made to Cairo and Naples—and to Yalta between 31 January and 20 February 1945 while the Conference was in session.†

The Spitfire units, Nos.541 and 542 Squadrons, were also kept busy. No.541 carried out 262 sorties during August 1944 and in September extensively covered the Arnhem area in preparation for Operation *Market Garden*, the airborne landings. Both units then concentrated on building up a picture of movements in the rear of the enemy lines systematically covering the communications system, ports, fuel refineries and storage facilities—operations which continued until the end of the war.

Suddenly the tasks which had daily sustained the Group for so long were not required. No.540 Squadron, which had moved onto the Continent at the end of March 1945, was given the job of photo surveying the whole of France, and when this was completed in September the unit returned to Benson for more survey work. No.541 Squadron concentrated on flying diplomatic mail between Britain and France/Germany, as did No.542 until disbanded in August, while No.544, which had been earmarked for the Far East as part of Tiger Force, instead found itself on photo survey over Belgium and Holland before disbanding in October 1945. Thus No.106 (PR) Group entered the post-war era with two operational squadrons, Nos.540 and 541, plus the OTU at Benson, and the CIU at Medmenham.

---

*Which did not have pressure cabins.
†Operation *Haycock*.

CHAPTER 12

Air-Sea Rescue 1941-45

PRIOR TO THE Second World War there was no British rescue organization for aircrew forced down or abandoning an aircraft at sea, and they relied on the Royal National Lifeboat Institute, salvage tugs, vessels in the vicinity or, if in range, the high-speed launches (HSLs) established at flying boat bases. New HSLs with a range of 500 miles* had been developed by the mid-1930s but only seven were in service around United Kingdom coasts in 1938, and there were uncomfortable gaps in the coverage they provided. Self-help equipment aboard aircraft varied consider-

ably. General reconnaissance, torpedo bomber and FAA aircraft had dinghies and distress signals, but other crews rarely had more than a life jacket, and sometimes not even that basic aid!

As a result of Bomber Command representations, a meeting was held at the Air Ministry during February 1939 to consider the situation. It was decided to provision another 11 HSLs, and from July the co-ordination of searches was rather vaguely made the

*250 miles radius of operation.

Representative of early Coastal Command ASR squadrons is Anson I EG500 seen dropping a dinghy. (Imperial War Museum)

responsibility of the AOCs of Coastal Command Groups. Lack of proper communications made this a difficult if not impossible task, and liaison with the various civilian rescue authorities was minimal. Concern over mounting losses at sea during the early months of the war resulted in an attempt by Fighter Command's Movements Liaison Section in April 1940 to involve all the emergency services, but it only had patchy success. It was the upsurge in fighter pilot casualties during June/July 1940, most of them drowned or 'missing at sea' between south-east England and the Continent, that 'triggered' the action which finally resulted in a proper air-sea rescue organization being formed.

At the end of July, Air Vice Marshal K.R. Park, AOC No.11 Group, Fighter Command, in co-operation with Vice Admiral Dover (Vice Admiral Sir Bertram Ramsey), organized a local English Channel rescue service using a number of RAF HSLs, light craft of the Naval Auxiliary Patrol, and twelve Lysanders on loan from Army Co-operation Command—the latter purely in the role of 'spotters'. The value of this small force was immediately apparent, and late in August the Air Ministry officially approved the combined operation and the retention of the 12 Lysanders on a permanent basis. The aircraft, transferred to Fighter Command, were to be used for sea searches around the coast from the Wash to Milford Haven out to 20 miles. Outside this area responsibility

was still vested in the unit losing the aircraft, and while not completely satisfactory the new organization was successful in saving many aircrew, and led directly to the setting up of a Directorate of Sea Rescue Services on 14 January 1941.

The Directorate commenced work on 6 February and immediately started developing ways of supply dropping to 'ditched' aircrew, additional to the dinghy installation already being fitted to Lysanders. Three of the many proposals received were thought worthy of development, the *Thornaby Bag*, the *Bircham Barrel* and the *Lindholme Gear*. The first operational use of the *Thornaby Bag* and the *Lindholme Gear* was during the rescue of a Whitley crew in April 1941, and the *Bircham Barrel* followed in June. The equipment was used, when available, by the crews of Bomber and Coastal squadrons, but it was soon apparent that specialist training and expertise was required both for a successful search, and the dropping of supplies in the right place for recovery by the survivors. The *Lindholme Gear* proved the most successful of the equipments, and in a revised form is still in use today.

Under certain circumstances flying boats and amphibians could alight on the open sea, and long term plans were made for the use of the Supermarine Walrus to be used in-shore when conditions allowed. Sunderlands very dramatically demonstrated their potential off-shore on 18 September 1939 when the

Many of the rescues of 'ditched' aircrew were performed by RAF high speed launches. Several types were in use, but 2734, seen here travelling at speed, was typical. (British Official)

The airborne lifeboat was developed to help in long-range rescues. Hudson III V9158/OS-T of No.279 Squadron was one of the first aircraft so equipped. (British Official)

crews of two of them saved the 34 survivors from the SS *Kensington Court* sunk by a U-Boat some 70 miles west of the Scillies. A year later, on 17 October 1940, Flt Lt I. Podger and crew of No.10 Squadron, RAAF, stumbled on a lifeboat containing 21 survivors from the *Stangrant*, sunk four days earlier, and despite a 'lumpy' sea the captain decided to alight. After embarking the seamen he returned safely to Oban, but the take-off had been hair-raising and subsequent

events were to prove that such open sea rescues by flying boats were extremely hazardous—the Sunderland in particular being prone to accident.

The recovery rate of aircrew from the sea had risen to 35% by June 1941 but it was still felt that the organization could do better. Investigations showed that lack of co-ordination was still a major problem, especially outside the area covered by Fighter Command. In August, executive control of air sea rescue

Despite official disapproval, open sea rescues by Sunderland crews continued throughout the war. Here two of the crew of Liberator FL947/R of No.224 Squadron, shot down on 13 May 1943 by Ju88s, are rescued six days later by the crew of a No.10 Squadron RAAF Sunderland captained by Flt Lt C.G. Rossiter. Unfortunately, Plt Off R.G. Barham died in hospital, leaving Plt Off G.B. Willerton, the Liberator pilot, as the sole survivor. (No.10 Sqn RAAF records)

more than 20 miles from the coast was therefore vested in the AOC-in-C Coastal Command, the Directorate of Air Sea Rescue at the Air Ministry being absorbed by a new organization, the Directorate of Aircraft Safety, at the same time. In order to pull everything together it was decided to appoint a very senior figure as Director General, Marshal of the RAF Sir John Salmond accepting the post on 23 September. He wasted no time, the Fighter Command units being upgraded in size and status, and their operating range from the coast increased to 40 miles in October. They were re-designated Nos.275–278 Squadrons, and for off-shore ASR work two additional Hudson squadrons were established in Coastal Command with a total of 40 aircraft (32 UE plus 8 IR). An Air Sea Rescue Officer was appointed to each Maritime Group HQ for direct liaison with the office of the Flag Officer-in-Charge—the man directly responsible for the operation of all surface craft.

No.16 Group was authorized to commence the formation of No.279 Squadron on 24 October; the unit officially forming at Bircham Newton on 16 November with aircraft equipped with ASV and *Lindholme Gear*, the latter consisting of a set of five buoyant containers comprising a large *M* Type dinghy and four ration/survival packs. The second Coastal

unit, No.280 Squadron, was formed on 28 November 1941 but Hudsons were in short supply and early in January 1942 the Directorate of Aircraft Safety reluctantly accepted Ansons as substitutes. So desperate was the operational situation that No.279 Squadron had nine of its Hudsons withdrawn for distribution to operational Coastal units and also received Ansons in their place. The result was a delay in the unit's operational debut until March 1942, with No.280 following in June; the latter quick off the mark with the location of a 'downed' crew later that month.

As the ASR organization was being extended so improvement of the life-saving equipment aboard RAF aircraft was pressed ahead. During the Battle of Britain the Mae West inflatable jacket was the universal safety equipment carried in fighters, while larger aircraft had dinghies stored in the fuselage. By 1941 the *K* Type single-seat dinghy was in production and saved the lives of many fighter pilots during sweeps over Northern France, while multi-seat dinghies of larger aircraft were provided with proper stowages, usually in the wings and with automatic inflation. These changes gave a much better chance of initial survival of a 'ditching' and, therefore, time for the rescue services to locate the distressed aircrew. The *Q*

On 26 May 1943 Flt Lt W.S.E. Dods of No.461 Squadron tried to rescue the crew of a Whitley in the Bay of Biscay but crashed on alighting. The survivors were located three days later by another No.461 Squadron crew captained by Flg Off G. Singleton who got down safely and picked them up but then could not take off because of the additional weight. The Sunderland was taken in tow by the Free French sloop La Canattante, *but the flying boat was damaged in a collision and Singleton elected to get airborne and land on Angle airfield. (RAF Pembroke Dock records)*

Type sailable dinghy was also introduced, the idea being to give those who had gone into the sea close to enemy territory the chance to sail to freedom.

During 1942 the sailable dinghy was developed into the Mk.1 Airborne Lifeboat. Designed for the Hudson, it underwent preliminary trials during July 1942, the results being sufficiently encouraging to proceed further, and its provision was given added impetus by the circumstances surrounding a rescue in August. On the 12th a Wellington of No.172 Squadron experienced engine failure over the Bay of Biscay and was forced to 'ditch'. A large-scale search was put in operation by No.19 Group and the survivors were sighted in their dinghy by the crew of a No.461 Squadron Sunderland captained by the CO, Wg Cdr N.A.R. Halliday. Despite a heavy swell and a 30-knot wind, Halliday jettisoned his DCs and some fuel and attempted to alight. Unfortunately a huge wave cracked open the hull, an attempted 'overshoot' failed, and the Sunderland broke up. All the crew escaped, but a dinghy burst and only one man of the six men aboard it survived an exhausting swim to another dinghy. A Whitley crew from St Eval relocated the dinghies but was shot down by three Arado 196 floatplanes, and the survivors of the original 'ditching' were not found again until the 16th. The next day three rescue launches reached the scene under the cover of three Hudsons and their Beaufighter escort, the latter driving off Arado 196s attempting to investigate the motor boats. Survivors from both the Wellington and Sunderland were finally picked up, but it was clear that if a lifeboat could have been dropped to the Wellington crew in the first place the incident would have been much less traumatic! On 19 September it was decided to carry out service

acceptance trials of the lifeboat, and its adoption was virtually assured, an order for 24 being placed on 13 November.

There were other problems to be resolved, the Director General of Aircraft Safety (DGAS) drawing the attention of the Air Staff at the end of October to the unsatisfactory types of aircraft in use by most of the ASR squadrons. Criticism was levelled at the Defiant used by Fighter Command, but the Anson was also patently unsuitable. The DGAS also asked for four more 'deep search' squadrons in Coastal Command, though well aware that there was little prospect of additional Hudsons. The Wellington and even the Albemarle were considered for the 'lifeboat' role, but it was the Warwick which was selected for trials, and on 21 January 1943 the Air Ministry announced the decision to go ahead with an ASR version of the Warwick to equip four 20-aircraft squadrons. Progress with the Warwick was painfully slow, plans being prepared for two versions, one carrying *Lindholme Gear* only, the other a lifeboat-carrying variant. The latter attracted an order for 100 production aircraft in May 1943, instructions also being given for the immediate conversion of 40 surplus Mk.1 bomber Warwicks to 'interim' ASR standard—each carrying two *Lindholmes*.

It was recognized that a successful rescue usually depended as much on the survivors as the rescuers, and to improve knowledge of procedures and equipment at least one officer on each station underwent a course at the School of Air Sea Rescue and became responsible for maintaining the standard of aircrew instruction. The effort plainly paid off on 5 May when No.279 Squadron made the first operational drop—to the crew of a Halifax which had 'ditched' 50 miles

Warwick I of No.280 Squadron carrying an Airborne Lifeboat Mk.II—at either Langham or Beccles. (ATP/B. Robertson)

east of Spurn Head. The survivors boarded it successfully, as did the recipients of the second operational
drop which was made in much more difficult conditions on 14 July. On both occasions the dropping
procedure worked well and the boat proved very
seaworthy.

During the last week of May a series of Bomber
Command and VIIIth Air Force attacks on Germany
resulted in a spate of distress calls and No.279
Squadron, based at Bircham Newton, took part in the
rescue of 156 airmen. One of the sorties on the 25th
was flown by the CO, Wg Cdr B.G. Corry DFC, in
response to a sighting report of a 'ditching' only
65 nm from enemy occupied territory. He was only
35 nm from the English coast, however, when a
Fortress was sighted in the sea with men on the wings.
Corry immediately set up a drop which was completely
successful, the boat splashing down just 100 yards
from the American dinghies. Ten minutes later the
occupants of one dinghy were aboard, followed by the
others. Leaving another Hudson circling overhead, the
CO went back to Bircham where he found that two
more Hudsons were already on the way to the original
sighting. Again they were distracted by flares en route,
one Hudson dropping a *Lindholme*, the dinghy of
which the Americans climbed into and were duly
collected by Walrus aircraft. The other aircraft resumed course and was near the original search area
when intercepted by a Halifax and led to five dinghies
tied together. The lifeboat was dropped within 30
yards of the survivors who boarded it just as three
Fortresses arrived to give top cover. Later they were
taken aboard a Danish trawler which was 'persuaded'
to continue west and to dock at Yarmouth. Reports
of survivors continued to pour in, and it became very

difficult to decide which of the incidents justified the
despatch of a lifeboat-equipped Hudson, though it was
basically a matter of survivor numbers and their
position. The Squadron was out again on the 27th,
a successful drop being made to an American crew who
transferred from their dinghies to the 'boat' within
five minutes. They were given a course to steer by
Aldis lamp, but after 40 miles the engines failed.
Re-located the next day, supplies, including fuel, were
dropped and retrieved by this very resilient crew who
were soon on their way again. Similar sorties continued for five days during which No.279 alone flew 163
operational hours. The rescue squadrons had their best
day, however, on 6 September when 131 were saved,
most of them Americans from 20 B-17s which ran out
of fuel on their way back from Stuttgart and had to
'ditch'.

Dropping trials of the Mk.1 Lifeboat from an ASR
Stage A Warwick were completed during July 1943
and a total of ten aircraft were delivered to this
standard, together with 20 of the ASR Stage B (ASV
and *Lindholme*-equipped) version before the definitive
ASR Stage C (RAF designation ASR Mk.1) became
available. This version had increased fuel capacity,
ASV radar and could carry the Mk.IA or Mk.II
Lifeboat, the latter a much improved variant successfully dropped from a Warwick during October 1943.
No.280 Squadron was up to its full strength of 16
Warwick ASR.Is when it became operational from
Thornaby on 21 October 1943, and No.279 was about
to commence re-equipment at the end of the month
when HQ Coastal Command requested that it be
retained on Hudsons and the Warwicks used to form
a new squadron. The Air Ministry agreed and No.281
Squadron, Fighter Command, was disbanded on 22

Testing the rockets which deploy 175 yards of buoyant rope each side of the airborne lifeboat.
(Author's collection)

Warwick I BV411 of No.282 Squadron on patrol carrying its lifeboat. (Time Inc via A.S. Thomas)

November and reformed that same day at Thornaby to work-up on Warwicks.

At the end of the year the Air-Sea Rescue services had saved 1,684 aircrew out of the 5,466 presumed to have 'ditched'—a considerable achievement when the large number undoubtedly killed on impact or trapped in the aircraft is taken into account. Evidence that others appreciated their work is given in a letter from Lt Gen I.C. Eaker, Commanding US VIIIth Air Force to the AOC-in-C Coastal Command on 24 December 1943, which in part read: 'Your superlative Air Sea Rescue service has been one of the prime factors in the high morale of our own combat crews. This organization of yours picked up from the sea nearly 600 of our combat crewmen since we began operations in this theater. This is a remarkable achievement made possible only by the highest

efficiency and the greatest courage and fortitude. It has our unbounded admiration.'

The first operational drop of a Mk.IA Lifeboat was made on 7 January 1944 to the crew of a Mosquito 170 nm south of Lands End. It was completely successful, both survivors boarding it without difficulty from their *K* Type dinghies. During the same month No.269 Squadron was reformed at Davidstow Moor in readiness for transfer to Lagens, Azores, as a general purpose unit engaged in meteorological reconnaissance, anti-submarine and air-sea rescue duties, and in February No.282 Squadron, Fighter Command, was absorbed by No.278 and reformed in Coastal Command as a Warwick unit—the completion of the original programme! No.278 Squadron became operational in No.19 Group on 15 April and achieved its first successful rescue with an airborne lifeboat just

No.251 Squadron took over the ASR task at Reykjavik in August 1944. Warwick I HG184 was one of their aircraft. (RAF Museum)

Lancaster III RF324/RL-K of No.279 Squadron carrying a Lifeboat IIA at Thornaby in 1945. (via C. Bowyer)

12 days later when one was delivered to the crew of a 'ditched' Halifax. No.269 Squadron, which arrived in the Azores early in March, was also soon able to chalk up an operational drop, made on 26 July to the survivors of a Liberator 'ditching'.

Over the years, the number of rescue craft in UK waters had gradually increased, peaking at 182 RAF boats (130 HSL, 25 pinnaces and 27 seaplane tenders); and 78 Royal Navy vessels (50 rescue launches, 14 anti-submarine craft and 14 air rescue boats) in March 1944. Air Defence Great Britain (ex-Fighter Command) became responsible for rescue work in the whole of the English Channel and southern part of the North Sea on 15 April 1944 so that only one authority was involved in the area during *Overlord*, and Warwicks were added to the complement of Nos.276 and 278 Squadrons to cover the 'deep search'

requirement. Responsible for the rest of the North Sea, No.280 Squadron was very active, being instrumental in saving 150 men from the sea, between June and September, many of them VIIIth Air Force bomber crews or the occupants of gliders forced down or accidentally cast adrift during the Arnhem operation. Further north No.281 Squadron concentrated on cover around the northern part of Britain using *Lindholme Gear* almost exclusively until May 1944 when airborne lifeboats were more generally available.

On D-Day there were 136 RAF rescue launches positioned in the assault area, and during the first ten days of *Overlord* 163 aircrew and 60 other personnel were recovered. During the whole month 355 were saved by the crews of these small craft in the face of the weather and enemy action, a task which was no sinecure!

A dramatic view of the release of a Mk.IIA Airborne Lifeboat from a Lancaster III of No.279 Squadron, 23 October 1945. (via C. Bowyer)

Warwick I HG192/HK-G of No.269 Squadron at Lagens in 1946. (K. Hogbin)

The general Coastal Command ASR set-up was not affected by the assumption by No.85 Group, Second Tactical Air Force, of responsibility for ASR on the Continent in August, using the Spitfires of No.276 Squadron, or by the formation in Iceland of No.251 Squadron with the dual tasking of meteorology and ASR. Indeed by the summer of 1944 the effort being put into the rescue services, both air and seaborne, for every major RAF and USAAF operation was enormous, but it was still sheer guts and knowledge on the part of both survivors and rescuers, plus a big slice of luck, which remained the vital ingredients for success. Examples are legion, but outstanding was the rescue of part of the crew of a Leigh Light Wellington of No.172 Squadron, captained by Flt Lt G.E. Whitely, shot down into the Bay of Biscay during an attack on a U-Boat on 26 August. Four of the crew survived the 'ditching', two of them having been assisted into the one small dinghy available by the navigator, Flg Off R.B. Gray, RCAF, while he clung to the side with the fourth crewman. Though severely injured, he steadfastly refused to risk the lives of the others by overloading the dinghy, and during the night he succumbed. The remaining three survivors were spotted the next day by the crew of a Sunderland of No.10 Squadron, RAAF, captained by Flt Lt W.B. Tilley. Joined by another Sunderland and a Wellington, Tilley's aircraft circled the dinghy for an hour before he decided that the survivors could wait no longer for surface forces to arrive. He therefore jettisoned his depth charges and touched down on the water, picked up the survivors, and after bouncing alarmingly from wave-top to wave-top on take off flew them safely to Mount Batten. Following earlier accidents it was forbidden for flying boats to alight on the open sea in rescue attempts—but nothing was said about contravention of orders! Flg Off Gray was awarded a posthumous George Cross for his gallant actions which were undoubtedly instrumental in the survival of two of his comrades.

Another example of survival in the face of many setbacks, and of the difficulties and hazards faced by the ASR squadrons, followed the 'ditching' of a No.489 Squadron Beaufighter on 2 October 1944. The crew, WOs D. Mann and D. Kennedy, managed to scramble aboard the aircraft's *L* Type dinghy, but an unfortunate combination of circumstances, not least the loss of two Warwicks, one due to enemy action, resulted in it being eight days before they were taken aboard a HSL and transferred to hospital.*

The Allied successes on the Continent and the shift of Coastal operations northwards resulted in a major re-organization of ASR in October. Nos.15 and 18 Group ASR assets were strengthened and modified in nature, Walrus amphibians being substituted for some of the Warwicks in Irish Sea areas, while Hurricanes took over 'rapid response' coverage from Flamborough Head to the Orkneys. In Nos.16 and 19 Group areas such in-shore 'quick response' operations were provided by USAAF and ADGB aircraft, the former using a squadron of P-47 Thunderbolts as 'spotters' and amphibious Catalinas as pick-up aircraft. Further afield, the majority of operations were now covered by 'airborne standbys', Warwicks flying a line patrol so that any distress call could be quickly answered, and in November it was suggested that most of the dedicated 'fighter-type' ASR aircraft were no longer required. After some controversy this was agreed, and

*A full account can be found in *The Strike Wings* by R.C. Nesbit (Kimber).

on 15 February 1945 Nos.275 and 277 Squadrons were disbanded and No.278 was transferred to Coastal Command. The intention was to re-equip all amphibious Flights of the six remaining ASR squadrons with Sea Otters but the installation of rescue equipment in these aircraft was delayed, and only a few had been delivered by the end of the war in Europe when the established strength of Coastal Command's ASR component was 74 Warwicks and 38 Walrus/Sea Otter.

The rundown of the Air-Sea Rescue units in Coastal Command at the end of hostilities was quite slow. This was logical because there was no sudden cessation in aerial activity, there being many unit transfers across the North Sea, and a continuous stream of aircraft returning to the United States. No.282 Squadron, the first ASR unit to disband, went on 9 July 1945, followed by Nos.278 and 281 Squadrons in October when No.251 also faded away in Iceland. No.279

Squadron relinquished its Warwicks and Hurricanes during September and reformed as a four-Flight unit working up for transfer to ACSEA with Lancaster ASR Mk.IIIs carrying Mk.IIA lifeboats, the first of which arrived at the end of December. On 15 January 1946 A Flight (five aircraft and six crews) left on transit to Pegu, Burma, and B Flight was to follow six weeks later, but bad weather held up departure for two days, during which the policy was changed. The unit was ordered to disband, the detachment in Burma became No.1348 Flight, and during February the rest of the aircraft were handed over to No.179 Squadron at St Eval. It was the beginning of the end for the dedicated ASR squadrons—for the time being anyway!

A total of 10,663 persons were rescued in ASR operations during the war, 5,721 Allied aircrew, 277 enemy aircrew and 4,665 non-aircrew.

CHAPTER 13

Training and Development 1936-45

Training

WITHIN SIX MONTHS of the birth of Coastal Command two Groups had been formed to take over direct responsibility for the day to day functions of the organization, and it is indicative of the scale of the training requirement that one of them, No.17 Group, was concerned primarily with that task. Formed on 1 December 1936 at Wykeham Hall, Lee-on-Solent, No.17 Group took control of four RAF stations, Calshot, Gosport, Southampton/Eastleigh and Lee, and responsibility for the diverse training units operating on those stations. Southampton was exclusively concerned with shore training of operational Fleet Air Arm (FAA) units when disembarked, Lee-on-Solent with the training of naval observers and telegraphist air gunners on courses at the School of Naval

Co-operation, Gosport with torpedo training and Calshot the Seaplane Training Squadron (which actually used flying boats)—and was also the home of No.201 Squadron, a lodger unit belonging to No.16 Group.

Following the decision in 1937 to transfer all responsibility for the FAA to the Admiralty, preparations were made for handover of all naval training. This left No.17 Group with flying boat and torpedo-bomber training at Calshot and Gosport respectively, and with the much bigger problem of providing instruction for the crews of land-based general reconnaissance aircraft which were entering the Command in some numbers.

During the 1920s and early 30s the only fully trained aircrew were pilots, other crew members being volunteers from skilled ground trades who underwent

Singapores and a Stranraer of the Flying Boat Training Squadron (No.240 Squadron) with a depot ship off Calshot in 1939. (via A.S. Thomas)

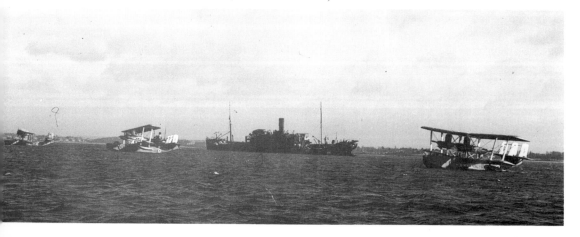

Amongst the most widely used maritime training aircraft during 1940-42 was the Blackburn Botha. L6250/1-F belonged to No.1 Squadron of No.3 School of General Reconnaissance, Squires Gate. (RP/MAP)

a short course in gunnery and bomb aiming. Pilots were responsible for navigation, and when accurate plotting was essential, as for general reconnaissance (GR) work, a second pilot was carried. Early in 1936 the Air Navigation School had been formed at Manston to take over this training, running 10-week courses for all pilots destined for Bomber and Coastal Commands, further training for the latter being given at Calshot during the flying boat conversion.

To cope with the rapid influx of new pilots for equally new Coastal landplane squadrons, the School of General Reconnaissance was established at Thorney

Island in April 1938, and with pilots expected to be in short supply it was agreed 'in principle' that '*Observers* would be responsible for navigation of aircraft in wartime'—the pilot remaining responsible in peacetime! This strange dictat was abandoned in May 1939 when the status of the observer was raised to equal that of a pilot, and it was officially decreed that they should take over navigation in peacetime as well. The change could not be implemented immediately, however, and pilots in the Command continued to be employed as navigators, and to receive training as such. Operational training was carried on within

A course at No.4 (C) OTU, Stranraer, pose in front of the Stranraer flying boat K7295 in 1941. The aircraft still retains its old No.209 Squadron codes (WQ-L). (via A.S. Thomas)

No.16 Group units, though there was precious little armament practice pre-war except by the torpedo-bomber squadrons. Each flying boat squadron spent a week during the summer co-operating with naval units from Portland, and by 1939 fleet exercises were more common, while Anson units practised regularly with submarines from Portland or Portsmouth.

C Flight of the mis-named Seaplane Training Squadron (STS) had been increased in size and re-designated No.240 Squadron in March 1937, the new unit continuing to operate as part of the STS until January 1939 when it was declared operational. The STS was then renamed the Flying Boat Training Squadron (FBTS) though, employed on the same task using a very mixed collection of biplanes. Conversion to operational types, principally the Sunderland, remained a squadron responsibility.

No.17 Group HQ moved to Fort Grange, Gosport, on 24 February 1939 and Lee-on-Solent, Ford, Donibristle and Worthy Down were transferred to the Admiralty on 24 May. This left the Group with the School of General Reconnaissance at Thorney Island

flying Ansons, the FBTS at Calshot with Singapore, Scapa and Stranraer aircraft, and the Torpedo Training School at Gosport with Swordfish.

All operational Commands were faced with an increase in the number of 'raw' aircrew in September 1939, the need for intermediate training prior to joining a squadron being very apparent. Bomber Command nominated a number of squadrons as training units, while Fighter Command immediately expanded their already existing Group Pools, but Coastal Command was overstretched operationally from the first day of the war and could not devote any more squadron effort to training. Strenuous efforts were made to increase the output of the three existing training units, but 'conversion to type' remained a problem only partially solved by 'on the job' training on flying boat units, and the formation of a Pilots' Pool at Silloth where landplane pilots learnt to fly 'operational' aircraft, and advanced training was given to wireless operators and gunners.

The Torpedo Training Unit moved from Gosport to Abbotsinch in March 1940, and on 1 April the

Top left: *Beauforts of No.2 Squadron, No.3 (C) OTU flying from Chivenor during 1941. (J. Blundell)*

Left: *Lerwick I L7257/TA-S of No.4 (C) OTU in April 1941. This aircraft sank at its moorings, 10 November 1941. (RAF Museum)*

Below left: *On navigational exercises No.4 (C) OTU carried a weapon load and were occasionally able to attack a U-Boat—as in this instance off south-west Norway, 24 May 1942. (via B. Robertson)*

Below: *Beaufighter VICs of No.1 Squadron, No.2 (C) OTU, 17 March 1943. (Wg Cdr H. Randall via C. Bowyer)*

Pool at Silloth became No 1 (Coastal) Operational Training Unit equipped with Hudsons, Beauforts and Blenheims. Later in the month the School of General Reconnaissance (S of GR) completed its transfer to Guernsey with 27 Ansons, but the breakthrough by German forces into France resulted in a hurried departure for Hooton Park, Cheshire, in June. On arrival the unit became No.1 S of GR, a second school forming at Squires Gate on the 17th. A week later the FBTS also left the south coast for the relative peace of Stranraer, taking with it just four Singapore IIIs as equipment. Continuing its nomadic existence No.1 S of GR joined No.2 at Squires Gate in August 1940, but went to South Africa in October as part of the Joint Air Training Scheme. The following month No.3 S of GR was formed, the situation finally stabilizing when No.2 S of GR was sent to Canada in December, leaving No.3 as the sole GR School in the United Kingdom.

The introduction of complicated equipment such as radar caused more training problems. Groundcrew training started in a small way in October 1939, and during 1940 an instructional team visited units allocated radar-equipped aircraft. The following year groundcrew and aircrew operator training was centralized at No.3 Radio School (RS), Prestwick, using Bothas, but the groundcrew courses were soon transferred to No.1 RS, Cranwell, and then to No.7 RS in 1942.

With observers fully integrated into Coastal crews it was decided that they should, like pilots, all be GR trained, but the policy could not be fully implemented until late 1941 because there was still a chronic shortage of capacity despite the enlargement of the training units. By the late summer of 1940 No.1 (C) OTU at Silloth was bursting at the seams and the Blenheim fighter/strike component had to be moved, first to Prestwick and then to Catfoss where it became No.2 (C) OTU in October. No.3 (C) OTU formed at Chivenor as the second GR conversion unit on 27 November, the additional capacity allowing a doubling in the length of the course from four to eight weeks; very necessary in view of the increasing variety of roles the GR crew was expected to master. Much of the non-pilot aircrew flying experience was provided by the Botha which, having failed operationally, did good work with No.17 Group and other training units during 1940–42 alongside the Anson.

The FBTS gradually increased in size as more aircraft became available, and when it reformed as No.4 (C) OTU on 16 March 1941 the unit had 13 on establishment, a mixture of Catalinas, Londons, Stranraers, Lerwicks, Sunderlands and Singapores—the need to continue operating biplanes reflecting the paucity of 'operational boats' in the Command. Landplane OTUs also suffered from a lack of aircraft, resulting in their output being unable to keep pace with casualty replacement and postings—and produce enough trained aircrew to allow the formation of the additional squadrons which increased production at home and promised deliveries from America would shortly allow. It was a difficult situation, for any cut in the current course lengths would clearly be counter-productive, and to make matters worse it was found necessary to increase the OTU course to ten weeks during the winter months because of poor weather. A

At Silloth, Wellingtons were much in evidence from March 1943, including this Mk.X HE221/27 of No.6 (C) OTU. (via J.D.R. Rawlings)

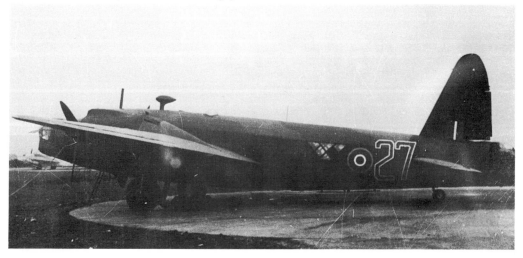

This ASV Mk.II arrayed Wellington VIII at Haverfordwest belongs to No.7 (C) OTU—or possibly No.4 Refresher Flying Unit which took over the OTU's role and aircraft in May 1944. (A.W. Preston)

partial remedy was found by replacing second pilots of twin-engined GR aircraft by an observer, but more effective was the formation of Nos.5 (C) and 6 (C) OTUs during the summer of 1941 for GR/Strike (Beauforts) and GR (Hudson) training respectively, instructors and aircraft having been scraped together by a relentless 'trawl' of units. Hardly had these new units started to increase the flow of new aircrew, however, than an upsurge in the requirement for trained personnel for overseas theatres occurred—a drain which went on into 1944.

The flying boat supply situation eased early in 1942 but crews were still a major problem, and with great misgivings it was decided in February that co-pilots of flying boats and multi-engined landplanes would no longer be required to be qualified on the aircraft before joining their squadron. In effect they became second pilots, able to fly the aircraft in the air under supervision, but not to take-off or land. The sequence of training for pilots of long-range aircraft, was henceforth to be: Advanced Flying Unit (Flying Training Command), GR School, OTU (experience

Hudson V AM562/X was at Turnberry with No.5 (C) OTU until it crashed into the sea off the Maidens, Ayrshire, on 21 January 1945. (RAF Museum)

Sunderland III W6066/CL of No.131 OTU, Killadeas, January 1945. (RAF Museum)

only), Squadron (as 2nd Pilot for six months/300 hrs), OTU (1st Pilot training). Operational crew training continued on the squadrons for it had to be an on-going process if personnel, particularly those flying anti-submarine aircraft, were to remain capable of taking the few chances presented to them. Buoys fitted with radar reflectors were positioned near all main Coastal Command bases, and launches towing simulated U-Boat targets were provided so that crews could carry out dummy attacks using smoke floats by day and markers at night. Strike crews practised on the many bombing and gunnery ranges around the UK coasts.

Five more Coastal OTUs were formed during 1942, No.7 on 1 April at Limavady for Wellington GR/ASV training, No.8 (PR), No.9 on 7 June at Aldergrove for long-range fighter work using Beaufighters, No.131 on 20 July with Catalinas at Killadeas, Northern Ireland and finally No.132 OTU on 24 November at East Fortune. Using personnel and aircraft transferred from No.60 OTU, the latter unit employed Beaufighters and dual Beauforts for long-range fighter and strike training, while No.8 OTU put the PR training organization on a much firmer footing. Formed at Frazerburgh on 18 May by combining the Conversion Flight of No.3 S of GR and the operational training Flight of the PRU, the unit had an initial establishment of 20 Spitfires, two Oxford, one Mosquito and three Masters, 14 of the older Spitfires at Benson being sent north in June to provide the nucleus. In December No.2 Torpedo

Training Unit (TTU) was formed to take care of the enlarged *Torbeau* commitment, and No.1 TTU was reformed during January 1943 from the torpedo training element of No.5 (C) OTU (which had absorbed the original TTU when the OTU moved north to Turnberry in May 1942).

These additions enabled No.17 Group to cope with the ever increasing demand for personnel both from Coastal and for overseas, the Command being responsible for the training of all GR, torpedo, coastal fighter and PR crews. The overseas commitment alone had increased to 120 crews per month by the end of 1942 and another commitment which arose directly from their training was the requirement for them to fly reinforcement aircraft to their theatre of operations. This required additional training, the United Kingdom-Gibraltar leg being particularly hazardous, and it was decided to form Ferry Training Units. No.17 Group became responsible for No.302 FTU (Catalina/Sunderland), No.303 (Wellington), Nos.304 (Beaufighter) and 306 (Beaufort) FTUs, all formed in January 1943 and No.308 FTU (Sunderland) which started operations from Pembroke Dock in March. No.302 concentrated on Catalinas, no less than 18 being on establishment while No.303 had 20 Wellingtons, No.304 had 35 Beaufighters and No.306 FTU 25 Beauforts. The courses lasted 18 days including inoculation, kitting up and a minimum of nine hours flying on the type to be ferried.

Big changes in the overseas situation during 1943, particularly in the Mediterranean, produced violent fluctuations in the demand for crews. Initially this resulted in surplus Beaufort trained personnel, most of whom were retrained on torpedo Wellingtons, only for the requirement to disappear just as they completed the course. The majority were eventually absorbed by the Warwick ASR commitment, while a surplus of Catalina crews caused by delivery delays resulted in some personnel being lent to Transport Command for Atlantic ferry duties. More changes followed the decision to hand over Wellington, Beaufort and Beaufighter ferrying to Transport Command in October 1943, No.17 Group being left with the two flying boat FTUs, Nos.302 and 308 and a PR FTU, activities considered highly specialized.

Other specializations resulted in the formation of new units including the Combined Anti-Submarine Training Centre at Maydown during May 1943, the School of Air/Sea Rescue at Blackpool equipped with Ansons, and on 28 June the Warwick Training Unit at Bircham Newton. Many Liberator crews had received training at Nassau in the Bahamas with a Day Bomber/GR OTU, No.111, and to provide them with UK experience a Conversion Flight was formed at Beaulieu as a detachment of No.6 OTU. By March No.1 OTU was running courses for Halifax and Fortress crews, but with the Hudson commitment at an end, No.1 (C) OTU was disbanded in October and the Halifax/Fortress courses were taken over by No.1674 Heavy Conversion Unit at Aldergrove.

No.17 Group's output peaked in August 1943 when 238 crews completed training using the 1,007 aircraft on charge at this time. During the year, 1,863 crews (totalling 11,482 men) were trained on 14 different types of aircraft in 255,800 hours, about half

the flying achieved by the whole Command! A combination of changed requirements and the formation of more specialist advanced training units overseas reduced the task in 1944, and the 1943 figures proved to be the highest annual total attained by the Group during its existence. Nos.2, 3, 7 and 9 OTUs were closed during 1944, only No.7 continuing in another form as No.4 Refresher Flying Unit (RFU), but courses became even more specialist, the 26 different syllabuses taught in 1943 increasing to 38 by July 1944. The average course length/hours had also increased, rising to 12 weeks during which 87 hours were flown. Anti-submarine flying training was now in two stages, conversion to type taking five/six weeks and 32 hours day/night flying, and the 'operational' phase a further five weeks during which 55 hours was flown, 30 on 'operational' flight exercises, ten on armament training and 15 on radar homings. The crew, averaging nine on long-range GR types of aircraft, also came together in two stages, the Captain (1st pilot) being joined by the Flight Engineer, Flight Mechanic (flying boats only), and air gunners at the start of the course, the Second Pilot, Navigator and Wireless Operators joining at the commencement of the operational stage.

Some of the 'operational' navigational exercises were flown fully armed and this paid off in dramatic form on 24 May 1944 when the crew of a No.4 OTU Sunderland spotted a U-Boat fully surfaced at about five miles range. As the captain, Flt Lt T.F.P. Frizzell DFC, turned onto the target the aircraft was seen by the submarine's lookouts and the gun crew started firing long before the flying boat was in range. Frizzell continued to close, rolling the heavy Sunder-

Catalina IV JX383/BC of No.131 OTU pulled up on the slip at Killadeas, 22 August 1945—its work finished. (FAA Museum)

land from side to side to try to spoil the German gunner's aim. At the last minute the U-Boat suddenly turned but Frizzell's line-up was good and the stick of six DCs straddled the target, one of them hitting the conning tower before rolling into the sea. The blast ripped the U-675 (Type VIIC) apart, and as she sank an internal explosion finished the job. A perfect demonstration for the new crew!

More rationalization of units took place in the autumn/winter. The Fortress element of No.1674 HCU was disbanded in September and No.4 RFU faded away the following month. In February 1945 the Sunderland component of No.131 OTU was transferred to No.4 OTU, the former unit closing down completely in June. No.8 OTU, which had moved from Scotland to Wales in January, transferred to Mount Farm, Oxfordshire, on 21 June to continue training PR crews, albeit on a much reduced scale, while more surprisingly, No.111 OTU was moved to Lossiemouth at the end of July with Wellingtons and Liberators. No.5 (C) OTU disbanded in August and No.6 moved to Kinloss with Warwicks and Wellingtons.

Its job done, No.17 Group was disbanded on 1 September 1945, the remaining training units being placed temporarily in No.18 Group. Their future is discussed in Chapter 14.

Development

Development work with air-dropped torpedoes and other maritime weapons was carried out at Gosport throughout most of the inter-war years with no sense of urgency until *B* Flight became the Torpedo Development Unit (TDU) in November 1938—the time of the Munich Crisis. The Admiralty had started development of new anti-submarine bombs in 1924 but problems with fuses caused long delays, and when the 100-lb and 250-lb versions finally went into production ten years later it was found that the weapon had an unpredictable underwater path. A better shaped nose cap improved the situation, but only the 100-lb weapon was in full production in 1939, despite it being well known that an AS bomb needed to contain much more explosive, and a delayed action fuse that ensured detonation below the surface.

Work on airborne radar had been in progress for a much shorter period, but a crude set mounted in a Heyford managed to detect shipping at sea during 1936, and on 3 September 1937 experimental Air to Surface Vessel (ASV) equipment in an Anson successfully located warships during an exercise in a fogbound English Channel. Trials continued and deliveries of production ASV MK.1 to Gosport started in November 1939. The first submarine detection was

Below: *Beaufort I N1174 of the CCDU undergoing early ASV trials. (Imperial War Museum)*

Top right: *Wellington VIII T2977 fitted with ASV Mk.II and the nose-mounted Helmore Light which lost out to the Leigh Light in CCDU trials. (Bristol Aeroplane Co. via J.D. Oughton)*

Right: *Beaufort IA DW828 of the ATDU Gosport with a trial Mk.XV 18" torpedo fitted with a gyro stabilized MAT Mk.4 tail. (via R. Hayward)*

Below right: *Wellington VIII LB129/G fitted with Leigh Light and ASV Mk.III for trials. (Author's collection)*

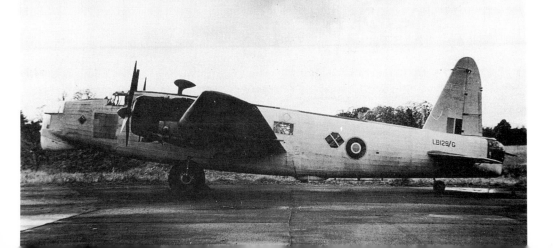

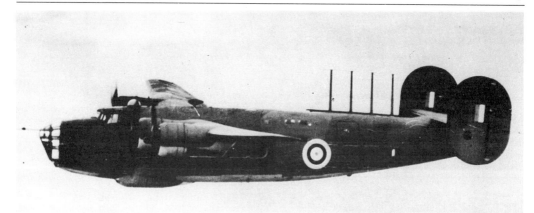

Liberator I AM910 fitted with ASV and a gun pack under the fuselage after modification by Heston Aircraft Ltd. After a short period of trials with the A&AEE it went to No.120 Squadron but crashed on 13 April 1942. (RP/MAP)

made the following month during Hudson trials, which demonstrated a maximum range of five miles from a height of 3,000 ft. But the contact could only be held to four miles before disappearing in sea returns, the latter decreasing at lower altitudes—but so did the maximum range. Efforts to improve ASV performance centred on the Mk.II set, essentially a Mk.I with a more powerful transmitter, more sensitive receiver and an improved aerial array. Ranges up to 20 miles resulted though interpretation remained difficult.

The accidental bombing of a British submarine early in the war highlighted the uselessness of the 100-lb bomb, and in November 1939 the Torpedo & Mining Establishment at HMS *Vernon*, Portsmouth,

was tasked with finding a solution. The result was the 450-lb naval Mk.VII depth charge suitably modified for air launching. Early tests were promising but surprisingly the Air Ministry decided not to proceed with it, and only the fierce insistence of the AOC-in-C Coastal Command forced continuation of the tests and small-scale introduction into service during the summer of 1940.

In March 1940 the TDU and its associated Torpedo Section were renamed the Air Torpedo Development Unit (ATDU) which remained at Gosport as a Ministry of Aircraft Production establishment. Fortunately most of the extensive testing of air-dropped mines was carried out from Weston-super-Mare using a range in the Severn Estuary, for Gosport was

The ASV Mk.II equipped Beaufort II AW304 went to the TDU for trials work. (Bristol)

Beaufighter VI EL223/G was one of the early 'Torbeaus' used by the TDU at Gosport to prove the installation and devise tactics. (Bristol)

attacked by Ju87s on the 16 and 18 August causing some damage to the Unit's facilities and the destruction of two aircraft, several torpedoes and some equipment—a hit on the mine store might have been disastrous!

The first radars were not only temperamental, but to be effective required new operating techniques and trained personnel. The Coastal Command Development Unit (CCDU) was therefore formed at Carew Cheriton during December 1940 to carry out service trials on new radars and to develop tactics for their employment. The first ASV Mk.I trial was flown on a Sunderland 'borrowed' from Pembroke Dock—an arrangement which continued for some time, as did the use of No.217 Squadron aircraft at Carew Cheriton, but the unit also had its own aircraft—a

Hudson, Beaufort and Whitley. The value of the CCDU was quickly recognized and its size and scope expanded, it becoming responsible for the service trials of all new Coastal Command aircraft and equipment. For instance, in January 1941 two Wellingtons were allocated for trials on the use of parachute flare illuminants for night attacks, and dive bomber tests were being made on a Hudson—the latter soon abandoned!

The immunity of the submarine at night exercised experts throughout 1940, but it was an ex-pilot administrative officer, Wg Cdr H de V. Leigh, who was instrumental in solving the problem. His solution, submitted in October 1940, was to install a searchlight in the nose or belly of the aircraft, arranged so that it could be trained in azimuth and elevation. He

'Torbeaus' air bellows-operated dive brakes. (Bristol Aeroplane Co.)

Mosquito VI HJ732/G fitted with a 57-mm (six-pounder) gun in the belly—the trials aircraft for the Mk.XVIII. (Author's collection)

suggested the 90-cm Army ground defence searchlight fitted in a Wellington, the DWI version of which already had a motor generator installed. Coastal Command staff enthusiastically supported Leigh's ideas and he refined his proposals during November, advocating the use of a 24-in (61-cm) 10 Kw naval searchlight in a suitably modified retractable Fraser Nash ventral gun turret of the type originally designed for the Mk.1 Wellington. A lash-up of the light was installed in an aircraft designated the DWI Mk.III (as a cover), and trials during March 1941 proved its practicality. After considerable delay caused mainly by differences of opinion over the type of searchlight to be employed, and opposition from the RAE who favoured a towed flare, the Leigh Light went ahead, development resulting in the motor generator being abandoned and a block of seven 12-volt accumulators being installed, trickle-charged by an engine driven generator, and capable of sustaining the 80-million candle power light for up to half a minute. The Leigh Light was a great success, particularly after the beam width had been increased by a spreader lens, and an under-wing mounted version was later developed for installation on Liberators and Catalinas.

The establishment of the ATDU in January 1941 included Vildebeest, Swordfish, Albacores, Bothas and Beauforts, but it was the Swordfish and Beaufort which did most of the routine torpedo testing for the RAF. All aircraft which might be involved in dropping maritime weapons were required to be tested by the unit, however, usually on completion of A&AEE Boscombe Down release clearances, but sometimes direct from the manufacturers. Thus Bothas, Beauforts, Hampdens and Wellingtons all completed torpedo trials at Gosport, and even an Albemarle and a Manchester were used, the latter to test acoustic mines.

Early Barracudas were used for both torpedo and dive bombing trials, but one of the most important aircraft tested was undoubtedly the torpedo-fighter version of the Beaufighter. The first arrived in May 1942, and its potential had already been proved when an engine failure resulted in a crash on 16 June, killing both pilots. The standard air-launched torpedo used by the RAF was the 18″ Mk.XII, but the Beaufighter was also cleared to drop the 21″ American MK.XIII with box tail. Much of the torpedo work at Gosport revolved around the development of the successful gyro-stabilized Monoplane Air Tail, and the unsuccessful 'Toraplane', an 18″ torpedo with wings and extended monoplane tail which was intended to glide to the target after release some three miles away. Beauforts were used for these experiments and for the development of Mk.XV and Mk.XVII torpedoes.

Development of the depth charge continued, a specially designed 250-lb version, the Mk.VIII, being introduced during the Spring of 1941. It was a radical improvement, though lagging fuse development prevented its full potential being established until 1942 when *Torpex*, a filling 30% more powerful than the earlier *Amatol* explosive was also introduced. By July 1942 further improvements had been made, including a breakaway tail, concave nose spoiler* and the Mk.XIII pistol. The ideal detonation depth of 15–25 ft was finally achieved with the Mk.XI DC which incorporated all the Mk.VIII improvements and went into production in the summer of 1942.

Meanwhile ASV Mk.II was being fitted to increasing numbers of aircraft types, and the CCDU was tasked with carrying out comparative trials, following

*To reduce risk of 'skipping' on contact with the sea and of trapping air bubbles which delayed detonation.

Liberator V FL927/G fitted with Leigh Light, nose-mounted ASV and rocket projectiles for trials. (RAF Museum)

complaints about the effectiveness of the equipment. While unserviceability was the prime cause of trouble, the positioning of the receivers and the standard of operators was also a problem, radar being a part-time occupation of navigators and wireless operators in the early days. The unit also got involved in the development of the Leigh Light, the service trials of which were completed in November 1941, and followed by operational trials of a 'productionized' version in March 1942 when the CCDU provided expertise for No.1417 Flight. At the end of November 1941 the CCDU moved to Ballykelly, trials continuing mainly on ASV Mk.II. On 18 June 1942 the unit was transferred to Tain to make way for operational squadrons at Ballykelly, and concentrated on radar

interrogators following a spate of 'disappearing radar contacts' during 1942 which raised the suspicion that U-Boats had been fitted with ASV detectors. This proved to be the case but fortunately the magnatron valve had been invented enabling development of radars using a shorter wavelength (10-cm) which was undetectable by the German *Metox* receiver. There were production delays, but trials work on the equipment, designated ASV Mk.III, started at the CCDU in January 1943, using LL Wellingtons from Chivenor. ASV Mk.III was soon displaying its superiority, giving ranges of up to 40 miles on convoys and 20 miles on surfaced submarines, while the Plan Position Indicator (PPI) display was judged much easier to use than earlier types. Continual development

Beaufighter X RD327/M—an ASWDU trials aircraft, 1945. (Author's collection)

produced the American 3-cm ASV Mk.V, tested in a Liberator by the CCDU from Dale with good results, but U-Boat detection rate started falling again during the autumn of 1943, and again the CCDU was tasked with determining the reasons. Wellingtons fitted with *Green Bottle* ECM could indeed be homed on to radar transmissions in the ASV Mk.III waveband and it was considered that the new *Naxos* equipment aboard U-Boats was able to perform this function. Methods of confusing the operators were studied, an attenuator code-named Vixen which decreased the radiated power as the target got closer was tested, but was not altogether successful.

Another problem was the inability of many oper-ators to hold a radar contact in the descent. To overcome this the Americans developed a system which fed information from ASV MK.V to the autopilot and bombsight, virtually a blind bombing facility, and the CCDU experimented with a similar installation in a Wellington XIV in which azimuth information from ASV Mk.VIA, which had a 'lock and follow' target facility, was fed to a direction indicator in the cockpit, and also to the Leigh Light operator. Another major development for night operations was the completion of successful trials on radio altimeters—vital when attack heights could be as little as 40 feet above the sea.

Tests on the endurance and handling characteristics

of the Halifax II were made by the CCDU, and of the Mk.III as a torpedo bomber carrying four 18″ or two 21″ and six DCs—probably a cover for compatibility trials of the Mk.24 *Fido* homing torpedo for the aircraft's use against shipping targets would have been suicidal.

The introduction of the rocket projectile as an anti-shipping and submarine weapon in Coastal Command was not initially an unmitigated success. A 60-lb semi-armour piercing (SAP) warhead had been de-signed for the task but it proved effective only if it hit above the water line. Fortunately it was discovered that the standard 25-lb armour-piercing anti-tank weapon was not only easier to aim but also remained intact on hitting the water, and trials in November 1942 on the Pendine Range demonstrated its effective-ness against submerged targets. The 25-lb head was therefore adopted for general use by Coastal Com-mand.

As early as May 1940 Coastal Command had requested development of a passive sonar detector that could be dropped from an aircraft and radio back information. Little progress was made until the Americans took over the idea, and they completed the initial trials on the device in March 1942. It consisted of a 14-lb buoyant canister enclosing an hydrophone and a radio transmitter. When the buoy hit the water the hydrophone was released and hung on its cable

Warwick V PN705/W—the aircraft used by ASWDU for general service trials, 1945. (Author's collection)

about 20 ft below the surface. At the same time the aerial of the transmitter erected so that sounds picked up by the hydrophone could be received in the aircraft. Because the hydrophone was omni-directional a pattern had to be dropped and signal strengths compared to obtain a 'fix' on the submarine sufficiently accurate for a homing torpedo to be dropped within range. Production started late in 1942 but was slow, and although Coastal Command received its first buoys in August 1943 for trials by the CCDU, it was a long time before the equipment entered squadron service.

The development of the six-pounder (57-mm) gun installation in an aircraft followed suggestions made by the Molins Machine Company. A trial installation was made in a Mosquito during 1943, and tests by the A&AEE in June were very successful, the ammunition feed proving the only problem. The Mk.XVIII variant of the aircraft went into limited production for anti-submarine work.

Meanwhile, by August 1944, ASV Mk.VII (Mk.III adapted for 3-cm X Band operation) had undergone trials but was found to be inferior to the American APS-3 tested in a Catalina. Designated ASV Mk.VIII by the British the APS-3 was described as 'outstanding' by the CCDU, and similar praise was heaped on APS-15 (ASV Mk.X) which, installed in a Liberator, arrived at Angle for tests in August 1944. Even the Mk.X was extremely restricted in range on a 'snorting' submarine. However, the introduction of the *Schnorkel* air breathing tube resulting in a 'crash' trial by the CCDU using HMS *United*, an *Ursula*-class

British submarine fitted with a dummy tube. It was proved conclusively that the metric ASV Mk.II was useless against such a small target and that the centrimetric radars were little better if the sea state was anything but calm.

On 14 January 1945 the CCDU moved to Thorney Island and was renamed the Air Sea Warfare Development Unit (ASWDU) on arrival, Sunderlands being based at nearby Calshot. The testing of radar modifications aimed at improving efficiency against *Schnorkel* fitted U-Boats occupied ASWDU for the remainder of the war and for many months afterwards, some trials being made with ASV Mk.VI and X against Buna rubber-covered 'snorts' which were supposed to 'absorb' radar transmissions. In April 703 Squadron of the FAA reformed at Thorney as the naval component of ASWDU and although most of its work was strictly naval their ECM equipment trials were of common interest, and formed the basis of later ASWDU activity.

At the end of the war the main activity at the ATDU concerned Firebrand trials, though the unit was preparing for the Brigand, an aircraft continually delayed in service by technical problems, but used by the unit for *Dealer* homing torpedo trials—a weapon that was subsequently developed post-war as the Mk.30.

Slowly the hectic pace of wartime slackened, but trials continued, many of them concerned more with research than practical applications. The latter are dealt with in Chapters 14 and 15.

CHAPTER 14

An Uncertain Peace 1946-56

THE CAPITULATION OF Germany in May 1945 was followed by a rapid rundown of Coastal Command with the immediate disbandment of Catalina squadrons and the wholesale transfer of Liberator units to Transport Command. The number of Sunderland squadrons, several of which were Commonwealth units whose personnel were immediately recalled home, were also cut severely and the powerful Beaufighter/Mosquito strike force was decimated.

The sudden end of the conflict in the Far East a bare three months later also had its repercussions, and there were many changes of plan in the immediate post-war era; some downright perverse. Not until the end of 1945 did the situation start to stabilize and Coastal Command entered the New Year with a distinctly lop-sided appearance. Of the five remaining Groups, Nos.16, 18, 19 and 247, all had strong meteorological reconnaissance and ASR elements but very unbalanced anti-submarine/strike forces. No.16 Group's only first-line unit was No.254 Squadron at Langham with Beaufighters, while No.18 had none at all. In the Azores No.247 Group still sported No.269 and a detachment of Liberators from No.224 Squadron, but the bulk of the operational assets were with No.19 Group in the south-west where No.201 Squadron had Sunderlands at Pembroke Dock, No.248 Squadron's Mosquito VIs were at Chivenor, while No.179 Squadron's Warwick Vs and the bulk

of No.224 Squadron's Liberators resided at St Eval. Only No.106 Group with its two squadrons at Benson could be called a balanced force, well able to cope with its initial peacetime task of photographic survey.

While it was widely recognized that the size, distribution, and composition of the units left in Coastal Command did not constitute a viable minimum peacetime force, it was well into 1946 before final agreement was reached on the changes required. The particularly awkward stage in the development of intended replacement aircraft did not help the situation, for the Short/Saro Shetland, intended as the successor to the Sunderland, had been rejected even before its first flight, and an interim flying boat, the Seaford, ran into development and performance problems and was cancelled after eight had been completed. Problems also dogged the Brigand, though its much delayed entry into service was still expected, while despite the sudden end of Lend/Lease in August 1945* the Liberator successor, a maritime version of the Lincoln, had still to be ordered.

The Sunderland was, therefore, going to have to 'soldier on' until a new 'boat' could be designed and built, and Liberators would either have to be pur-

*Resulting in all airframes delivered by the USA under the scheme having to be returned, scrapped or purchased, except for a specified number of transport aircraft.

Top right: *Beaufighter X RD438/QM-H of No.254 Squadron flying from Chivenor in late 1945. (via A.S. Thomas)*

Above right: *Mosquito VIs of No.6 (C) OTU lined up at Kinloss in 1946. (R.C. Gray)*

Right: *Mosquito PR.34 RG300/OT-A of No.58 Squadron at St Eval during 1947. (via A.S. Thomas)*

A selection of aircraft types equipping ASWDU and the associated 703 Squadron, FAA, at Thorney Island in May 1947. Warwicks, Beaufighters, Lancasters, Sea Otters and Barracudas are seen with single examples of Halifax, Liberator, Avenger, Mosquito and Proctor. (H.M. Quinton)

chased with extremely scarce dollars or an interim replacement found to fill the gap until the R5/46 Lincoln development (later renamed Shackleton) was in service. The latter course was adopted and a modified Lancaster, an aircraft already replacing the Warwick in the ASR role, was chosen. The aircraft also joined the Command for overseas photographic survey work with No.541 Squadron.

Now well settled in at Thorney Island ASWDU and its naval component, No.703 Squadron, continued their many-faceted activities, though ASV trials, ECM work and the testing of helicopters in the search and

rescue role provided most of the work. Over at Gosport the ATDU was mainly concerned with homing torpedoes, the Brigand replacing the Firebrand and ubiquitous Swordfish as the main test vehicle.

On 8 March 1946 No.16 Group was reduced to Wing status, and sea areas around the British Isles were divided between the remaining two maritime Groups, Nos.18 and 19. Two days later Nos.269 and 279 Squadrons were disbanded, the former at Lagens together with its controlling group, and the latter at Thornaby. This was the beginning of the end for dedicated fixed-wing ASR squadrons and for most of

Sunderland V PP117/4X-W of No.230 Squadron on Havel See, Berlin, during the 'Airlift' in 1948. (A. Donaldson via J. Evans)

the meteorological units, despite No.1402 Flight having been resurrected early in December 1945 to resume *THUM* flights from Langham. All except No.518 Squadron had gone by the end of the following June.

Meanwhile, No.201 Squadron moved to Calshot on 1 April to make way at Pembroke Dock for No.230 which arrived a fortnight later from Seletar, Singapore, thus stabilizing the operational flying boat element of No.19 Group at two squadrons. Surprisingly No.302 FTU survived until April and No.132 OTU until May when the clumsy training organization was streamlined. The Mosquito/Beaufighter strike courses were transferred to No.6 OTU at Kinloss where the first Lancaster courses commenced in July, resulting in the cessation of Liberator training at Lossiemouth and the disbandment of No.111 OTU, and leaving just No.4 OTU at Alness for flying boat training and No.6 at Kinloss for all landplane conversion courses.

By the end of May 1946 the two remaining strike squadrons, Nos.248 and 254, formed a Wing at Thorney Island, and the operational strength of the Command had been further increased by the arrival of No.203 Squadron from the Far East. It was joined at Leuchars by No.160 in June, both units soon re-equipping with Lancasters. Two long-serving units reformed at St Eval, Nos.210 Squadron (by re-numbering No.179Y Squadron [Lancasters]) and No.228 from 224Y Squadron [Liberators]). Nos.179X and 224X then reverted to the standard designation of Nos.179 and 224 Squadrons and all four units were soon engaged on small-scale Fleet exercises, No.210 also carrying out *Epicure* 'met' flights.

The new-found strength did not last long, No.280 Squadron disbanding on 21 June when the ASR task was completely absorbed by the anti-submarine units and more rationalization was to follow. No.8 OTU, now equipped with Spitfire PR Mk.XIX and Mosquito PR Mk.34s, moved to Chalgrove, and a month later, in August, No.106 Group was disbanded and replaced at Benson by the Central Photographic Establishment, the CIU having moved from Medmenham to Nuneham Park earlier in the year. No.230 Squadron joined No.201 at Calshot during September and No.4 OTU journeyed south to Pembroke Dock. At the end of the month No.179 Squadron was disbanded and so was No.228 Squadron, the latter lacking replacements for its Liberators, for all available Lancasters were being used to re-equip No.224 Squadron.

The value of close co-operation between surface forces and Coastal Command aircraft had been fully established by the end of the war and it was maintained by the formation of a Joint Anti-Submarine School at Londonderry, Northern Ireland. Submarines and anti-submarine vessels based on Lough Foyle were joined by ships whose crews were on the course together with aircrew from the FAA and the RAF, aircraft being based at Eglinton or Ballykelly and flying boats at Castle Archdale. Courses commenced in 1946 and quickly became a valued annual commitment for both RAF and Royal Navy personnel—the school a worthy successor of wartime units.

Air Ministry policy requiring long-serving or particularly famous squadron numbers to be retained was extended on 1 October 1946 to include re-numbering. The two PR squadrons at Benson, Nos.540 and 541, became Nos.58 and 82 Squadrons respectively, while at Thorney Island No.248 was re-numbered 36 and No.254 became 42. At Leuchars No.160 became No.120 Squadron, and over at Aldergrove No.518 Squadron was re-numbered No.202, continuing daily

Mosquito PR.34s of the reborn No.540 Squadron at Benson, 1948. The nearest aircraft is PF679/DH-A. (MAP)

Lancaster GR.3 RE207 of No.120 Squadron at Leuchars carrying an Airborne Lifeboat Mk.IIA, 1948/49. (I. Stott)

Bismuth meteorological flights out over the Atlantic and operating a detachment at Gibraltar.*

In January 1947 No.203 Squadron moved to St Eval, and the Command's disposition hammered out during 1946 was complete. The majority of the front line operational strength remained in the south-west to cover the traditional 'approaches' to the British Isles from across the Atlantic or the Bay of Biscay, No.19 Group having two Sunderland squadrons, Nos.201 and 230, at Calshot and three Lancaster squadrons, Nos.203, 210 and 224, at St Eval. Additionally the Group had the Strike Wing at Thorney Island to cover the southern part of the North Sea and the English Channel, while in the north No.18 Group had to make do with No.120 Squadron at Leuchars and the 'Met' squadron at Aldergrove. Each maritime squadron had an establishment of six aircraft and eight crews, forming an Order of Battle which provided the basis of a viable force, though chronic shortages of personnel made it very difficult to fulfil the flying task in the early post-war years when demobilization was at its height. Training and the occasional Fleet exercise, JASS courses, ASR operations and supplementary meteorological flights certainly kept the squadrons stretched. The PR squadrons were also busy, for by mid-1947 No.58 was flying extensively over the United Kingdom for the Ordnance Survey Department and the Ministry of Town & Country Planning, and in July carried out a survey of Portugal operating from Gibraltar. At the same time Spitfire XIXs of No.82 Squadron were completing a survey of Scotland, and the unit's Lancasters were in East Africa completing their lengthy radar-controlled mapping work.

At the end of July Nos.4, 6 and 8 OTUs became

Nos.235, 236 and 237 OCUs respectively. No.236 OCU was planning the arrival of Buckmasters and Brigands, but when it became obvious that the Brigand was subject to further lengthy delay it was decided to scrap the Strike Wing altogether, the Beaufighter/Mosquito element of the OCU being disposed of immediately and Nos.36 and 42 Squadrons were summarily disbanded on 15 October 1947.

Meanwhile overseas detachments, known as 're-inforcement flights', had started in August 1947 when Lancasters of No.210 Squadron went to Ein Shemer in Palestine for a week. They were followed by the other Coastal Lancaster squadrons, the aircraft being used from November to support local reconnaissance units on Operation *Bobcat*, the search for illegal Jewish immigrant ships. Up to four aircraft were detached at a time, a task not made easier by a severe shortage of navigators, partially resolved by using co-pilots, most of whom had received some navigational training at the OCU.

No.224 Squadron had been disbanded in November 1947 but in March of the following year was reformed at Aldergrove with Halifax VI as a 'Met' unit operating mainly on detachment at Gibraltar, replacing No.202 Squadron. The following month No.237 OCU moved to Leuchars and, with survey work in Kenya and Uganda complete, No.82 Squadron's Lancasters moved from Eastleigh to Tabora and Salisbury in readiness for operations over Tanganyika (Tanzania), Nyasaland (Malawi) and Southern Rhodesia (Zimbabwe). Despite the strain on the limited resources of the Command caused by these various

*Started by No.518 Squadron on the demise of 520 Squadron in April 1946 to carry out *Nocturnals*.

Lancaster GR.3 RE200/K7-K of No.236 OCU flying from Kinloss, December 1949. (A.J.L. Craig)

detachments, especially as the British Mandate in Palestine entered its final stage and terrorist attacks on British installations increased, exercises were stepped up in 1948, the largest post-war naval exercise to date, *Dawn*, (13-14 May) involving all available aircraft.

ASWDU moved from Thorney Island to Ballykelly in May 1948 and gradually the variety of aircraft was reduced, the Lancaster being the main trials vehicle for very extended testing of flare illuminants, photo flashes and sonics equipment. A Beaufighter carried out tests on the ASV Mk.XIII intended for the Shackleton and an Anson was employed on early *Autolycus* work.

At Coastal Command HQ work continued on plans for updating the Lancaster, the introduction of the Shackleton and revision of both Operational Requirement (OR) 320 and 321 for landplane and flying boat projects were being progressed in response to new developments. More immediate, however, was the impact of Operation *Plainfare* (the *Berlin Airlift*) which had started on 28 June as a joint British/American transport aircraft operation. Coastal Command became involved because flying boats were the only aircraft with internal anti-corrosion treatment allowing bulk salt to be transported. Nine of Nos.201 and 230 Squadron's flying boats were at Castle Archdale for a JASS course, but this was immediately abandoned, the aircraft returned to Calshot and the next day, 3 July, started moving to the Blohm und Voss shipyard at Finkenwerder, Hamburg, together with 235 OCU aircraft. The first sortie to Havel See, a lake within Berlin, was made on the 5th by Flg Off Holt of No.230 Squadron, but operations were slow and intermittent until a 30,000 gallon tanker barge became available. By the 13th the daily sortie rate had risen to 16, and despite the departure of the OCU

Lancaster PR.1 TW905/G of No.82 Squadron at Heany, Southern Rhodesia in 1950 during the unit's extensive aerial survey of Africa—but still under the control of Coastal Command. (M. Retallack)

Halifax Met.VI ST804/B-K of No.224 Squadron pauses briefly at St Mawgan on its way to No.48MU for scrapping, November 1951. Note the 'met' instruments on the side of the nose. (Author's collection)

detachment on 22 July, it continued to rise as turn-round times were reduced. Each aircraft took in four tons of supplies, mainly salt and potatoes, and brought out manufactured goods and refugees. From August, Sunderland flying hours had to be limited to 360 per month, but this order was rescinded in October when an all-out effort produced 214 sorties involving 518 hours. The flights were no sinecure for the Elbe was full of uncharted wreckage and sandbanks, and the Havel See was often deliberately obstructed by logs and other debris floated in from

East Germany. From November onwards the weather was also a problem and, with an increasing risk of becoming icebound, the flying boat operation, which had included two civilian *Hythe* 'boats', was stopped on 14 December. Over 1,000 sorties had been made, carrying 4,500 tons of supplies and evacuating 1,113 refugees, mainly children.

Planned servicing was introduced in Coastal Command, this involving the rearrangement of minor/ major inspections so that items were checked in a logical sequence and tradesmen did not constantly get

Shackleton MR.1 WB821/T-L of No.220 Squadron low over the palm trees of Ceylon during a Far East detachment, February 1952. (No.220 Sqn records)

in each other's way. In theory a Sunderland major which had taken 28 days/4,000 man hours to complete should now take five days/2,300 manhours, but in practice, though substantial savings were made they were not of this order and the system was disliked because of its impersonal nature.

After a gap of two years Gibraltar again had a permanent unit when No.224 Squadron moved its HQ to North Front in October 1948, and on 18 January 1949 No.201 Squadron moved back to Pembroke Dock, a base significantly nearer the unit's main operating area in the eastern Atlantic than Calshot. It was followed a month later by No.230 Squadron, but more significant was the first flight of the Shackleton on 9 March, bringing the Command a large step nearer the introduction into service of the RAF's first post-war maritime reconnaissance landplane. There was an urgency about this, for the *Cold War* was escalating and Britain would obviously have a major role to play in maritime defence under the terms of the North Atlantic Security Treaty which was about to be signed.* The Atlantic was naturally the main concern, but involvement in other areas did not cease with the end of the Palestine mandate. Six aircraft of No.210 Squadron went to Singapore in November for Exercise *Centipede* and were away for six weeks—the first of many detachments to the Far East.

The PR element was transferred to Bomber Command on 1 March 1950, though it took time for all the units to be absorbed and the change-over was not complete when the North Koreans sprang their surprise attack on South Korea on 25 June. The call by the United Nations for members to help repel the invasion complicated the *Cold War* situation and increased the pressure for expansion of the whole of

the RAF. In July the modernization of the Sunderland was seriously considered, as was a large order for Varsities to use on inshore anti-submarine work. More immediate was the re-equipment of No.202 Squadron with specially modified Hastings during October 1950, and proposals for the establishment of small SAR helicopter detachments around the country.

It was a time of great upheaval, and when the Chinese, with Russian support, joined in the Korean War a global conflict seemed almost inevitable. The only immediate effect on Coastal Command, however, was an increase in the requirement for Sunderland crews for the Far East, resulting in the strengthening of No.235 OCU. The goodwill tour of Pakistan by three Lancasters of No.120 Squadron during November appeared purely coincidental, though their fleet exercise with the Pakistani and British naval forces did serve as a pattern for annual Command visits to the Far East which was maintained for many years.

In December, No.120 Squadron moved to Kinloss where No.236 OCU was preparing for the introduction of Shackleton training at a time when the Royal Navy's long-standing bid for the take-over of all maritime forces reached a new peak. It was centred around a proposal to scrap the Shackleton and replace it by ship-borne Gannets for mid-ocean anti-submarine work supported by small land-based aircraft to cover inshore waters—a plan fundamentally floored when properly costed. The flying boat lobby was also vociferous at this time, the flexibility of the craft and its ability to operate as a self-contained unit from any sheltered bay being pushed hard. This ignored the 'boats' susceptibility to sea conditions, inherent drag

*On 4 April 1949.

Hastings Met.I TG511 of No.202 Squadron, Aldergrove—an aircraft which was later coverted to T.Mk.5 standard for the Bomber Command Bombing School. (Author's collection)

and weight penalties and, not least, the rapidly increasing number of long runways available world-wide. The argument was really settled, however, by the setting up of the North Atlantic Treaty Organization (NATO) during 1950 in response to the perceived Russian threat, for it resulted in an increase in the British commitment in the Eastern Atlantic and an immediate requirement for more aircraft. Such a requirement could only be met by types currently in production, so additional orders for a developed version of the Shackleton were placed, and special arrangements made for up to 150 P2V Neptunes to be supplied* under the Mutual Defence Aid Pact (MDAP).

In January 1951 six Lancasters of No.203 Squadron went to Negombo to take part in Ceylon's Independence Celebrations, also fitting in a *Fleetex* with the Indian Navy, but thoughts were now firmly on the Shackleton which was about to enter service. It had been decided that No.224 Squadron would be the first with Shackletons, relinquishing its 'met recce' role on receipt of the aircraft, and despite the newness of the Hastings the AOC-in-C was also pressing for No.202 Squadron to be similarly re-equipped for use in a dual Met/AS role. In the event the re-equipment plan was changed, No.120 Squadron receiving the first Shackletons at the end of March, and No.202 retained its Hastings!

In April 1951 NATO became operational and the AOC-in-C Coastal Command was appointed Allied Air Commander-in-Chief, Eastern Atlantic. At the same time Coastal Command's mid-1953 deployment plan was promulgated as:

8 LR/MR Shackleton Sqns SW Approaches 4 NW Approaches 3 Gibraltar 1	8 UE (Total 64)
4 F/B Sunderland Sqns SW Approaches 2 NW Approaches 2	5 UE (Total 20)
4 MR Neptune Sqns NE Approaches 1 Eastern Approaches 3	8 UE (Total 32)
1 Met Hastings Sqn Aldergrove	5 UE (Total 5)
1 Helicopter Sqn Dispersed	16 UE (Total 16)

Supporting this force would be 20 Lancasters at a School of Maritime Reconnaissance (SMR), the

ASWDU, two OCUs, JASS Flight, Marine Craft Units (MCUs) and a Marine Craft Training School. At the outbreak of war No.16 Group would be reactivated at Chatham to control the three Neptune squadrons allocated for Eastern Approaches, and Dutch and Belgian units, No.17 (Trg) Group would reform at Benson and No.19 Group move to Liverpool.

The first practical moves had already been made, St Mawgan reopening in the Spring of 1951 when ASWDU moved in. The SMR formed at St Mawgan in June and took over the initial maritime training of aircrew in a three month/100 flying hour course, allowing the OCUs to concentrate on conversion to type and advanced tactics.

In July 1951 a Sunderland of No.201 Squadron took a British scientific expedition to Seal Lake, North Greenland, only 700 nm from the North Pole. It was an exploratory visit, and a month later the team was picked up again, though not without problems, a weather delay being nearly disastrous for food had almost run out by the time the Sunderland got through four days late.

By the end of August No.120 had triumphantly completed the Shackleton's intensive flying trials, 2,867 hours having been flown with surprisingly little trouble. The pace of re-equipment accelerated, No.224 Squadron and a reformed No.220 being up to strength by the end of the year when Shackleton training at No.236 OCU was in full swing, the last Lancaster course being completed in October.

Personnel who had gone to the United States in September 1951 for Neptune training returned to St Eval with two aircraft on 13 January 1952, No.217 Squadron being reformed the following day to operate them. A fortnight earlier No.269 Squadron had been reformed at Gibraltar as an offshoot of No.224 Squadron, and with most of the anti-submarine equipment now installed the Shackleton was considered 'operational'. This was celebrated by the despatch of six aircraft of No.220 Squadron on Operation *Scull* early in February—the Shackleton's first visit to Ceylon for an Indian Ocean *Fleetex*. It was a year of expansion and redeployment. No.269 moved from Gibraltar to Ballykelly in March, in April No.120 went to Aldergrove to make room at Kinloss for No.217 Squadron, and later in the year three new Shackleton squadrons, Nos.42, 206 and 240 were formed.

Meanwhile, Sycamore helicopters had joined AS-WDU for anti-submarine trials and preliminary SAR work, the last Halifax in squadron service had left Gibraltar, and the Coastal Command version of the Short Seamew in-shore patrol aircraft had been

*Some of them for MEAF.

Shackleton MR.2s of No.220 Squadron during formation practice prior to the RAF Review at Odiham, July 1953. (Author's collection)

ordered. The Air Council approved 'in principle' four SAR Flights of four Whirlwind helicopters in May, and the Saro P104 submission to Specification R112D (ex R.2/48) was judged superior to those of Shorts and Vickers Supermarine. Indeed, its estimated performance was so good that it put the flying boat back in serious contention, and the Operations Staff at HQ Coastal Command reversed their previous opinion about the flying boat's viability, having concluded that the Shackleton would never be capable of covering the *Atlantic Gap*, and being equally suspicious of

the Britannia development proposed by Bristol's.

During the summer five No.230 Squadron Sunderlands had airlifted the complete British North Greenland Expedition and their supplies from Young Sound where they had been off-loaded from the Norwegian sealer *Tottan*, to Britannia Lake. *Castanets*, held in June, was something of a trial run, for in September came the first major NATO maritime exercise *Mainbrace*. Again most Coastal Command units were deployed away from their peacetime bases, No.201 Squadron going to Sullom Voe, Nos.42 and

Representatives of the front-line of Coastal Command in the mid-1950s. Sunderland V of No.230 Squadron leading a Shackleton MR.1 and Neptune MR.1 of No.236 OCU over the Moray Firth, 1954. (Author's collection)

On parade. A very smart Neptune MR.1 WX521/B-L of No.203 Squadron, 1953. (J.D.R. Rawlings)

220 Squadrons to Kinloss, while No.210, due to move permanently from St Eval to Topcliffe with No.203 Squadron, went to Ballykelly for the exercise. Located in the Norwegian Sea the exercise was ruined by appalling weather, but it did allow No.217 Squadron to show off the paces of the Neptune despite still lacking much of the aircraft's operational equipment.

Initial trials on the Shackleton with ASWDU concerned the performance of ASV Mk.13, but by November 1952 tactical trials were well advanced, to be followed by seemingly interminable tests on various RCM/ECM equipment and *Autolycus*. A Shackleton MR.2 replaced the last Lancaster in February 1953 for trials on the *Glow worm* illuminating rocket system, and another MK.2 arrived in September for MAD trials. Neither installation proved very successful and

both were finally abandoned. Fortunately the other mainstays of the unit, *Orange Harvest* ECM, homing torpedoes and various sonics trials were all progressed to operational status, and successful tactics for their employment were devised by the unit.

With the end of 1952 came the realization that time was running out for the placing of new orders if the projected front-line strength of the Command was to be maintained after the end of 1956. Despite the euphoria over the Saro P104 it was only possible to justify two squadrons of flying boats in Coastal Command to cover the *gap* and perhaps a handful in the Far East. The number required was insufficient to support prototype and production contracts, so when Avro's came up with figures which showed that their revised Shackleton could restore the range while still

Sycamore HC.12 WV783/F-X of ASWDU during trials with the unit, 1955. (MAP)

Whirlwind HAR.2 XJ437 of No.228 Squadron about to demonstrate its SAR abilities at an air display. (via A.S. Thomas)

having an adequate take-off performance, both the Air Ministry and Coastal Command air staffs rather reluctantly backed the bid, and the pressure for a replacement aircraft temporarily faded. OR 320, in draft since 1947, was rewritten around the new variant, and in January 1953 the Air Ministry formally requested the Ministry of Supply to order sufficient Shackletons Mk.3, to provision the 180 aircraft required to maintain the front-line strength up to March 1958.

The first Shackleton MR.2s were delivered to squadrons in January 1953, being used to supplement rather than replace the earlier variant, resulting in each unit being established with five Mk.1 and three Mk.2 aircraft. In February, No.210 Squadron Neptunes started appearing at Topcliffe followed by No.203 Squadron in March and the Lancaster was out of front-line Coastal Command service, though still operating with the SMR and in the Mediterranean. A bid for extra Shackletons to re-equip the SMR was ignored, the Varsity being suggested by the Air Ministry but deemed unsuitable, as was a version of the Marathon; and the Lancasters carried on!

A secondary result of the departure of the Lancaster from squadron service was the ending of a daily airborne lifeboat standby, for the replacement 'boat' intended for the Shackleton was not ready. In the event it never entered Coastal Command service, the 24-hour a day SAR standby maintained by Nos.18 and 19 Groups henceforth using the ubiquitous *Lindholme Gear* as standard rescue equipment.

For the Royal Review of the Royal Air Force at Odiham in July the Command put up 18 Shackletons,

five Neptunes and three Sunderlands for the formation flypast, and Lancasters, Shackletons and Neptunes were also displayed on the ground. The Shackleton formation crews (two groups of nine) received special praise from the flypast organizer, Air Marshal The Earl of Bandon, for their station keeping, while the Neptunes on the ground were singled out for commendation in a letter from Air Chief Marshal Sir Dermot Boyle, AOC-in-C Fighter Command to the AOC-in-C Coastal Command which in part read: 'What I would really like to congratulate you on is the smartness and efficiency of your detachments at Odiham, especially the Neptunes. They were quite first class and called forth very favourable comment from those administering Odiham. I only wish I could say the same to all Commands.'

The Neptune force was brought up to full strength with the formation of No.36 Squadron at Topcliffe at the beginning of July despite problems with serviceability, caused by lack of spares. Both Nos.203 and 210 Squadrons were by this time officially 'operational', though none of the weapons systems could be used because of 'teething' troubles, and only half the aircraft had sonics receivers.

Fairisle detachments,* were in full swing, No.230 Squadron's visit in August coinciding with a severe earthquake which devastated the Greek Ionian Islands, and from 14 August to 2 September the Sunderlands were used to fly essential stores, medical supplies and personnel into the disaster area. Much further north,

*Anti-submarine training with Malta-based RN submarines which involved all Coastal Command squadrons in the 1950s.

Less successful was a demonstration for the Press off Selsey Bill on 30 August 1955 when Whirlwind HAR.2 XJ436 of No.22 Squadron suffered an engine failure in the hover. The attendant ASR launch personnel were given a chance to display their life-saving techniques—the crew being rescued unhurt. (MAP)

No.201 Squadron was also in action moving stores from Young Sound to Britannia Lake for the North Greenland Expedition, 69 tons being transported during a week's operations.

The Sunderlands returned to base just in time for *Mariner*, the major NATO sea/air exercise of 1953. It involved nine nations and lasted 19 days, No.220 Squadron going to Quonset Point, Rhode Island, while a US Navy patrol squadron operated from Scotland under the control of the AOC-in-C Coastal Command exercising in his NATO capacity. The AOC No.18 Group functioned as Air Commander Northern Sub Area, AOC No.19 Group as Air Commander Central Sub Area and AOC RAF Element Chatham as Commander Nore, while the AOC Gibraltar also took part as a NATO Sub Commander. *Mariner* proved a great success, for while there were some difficulties in

the control of such a multi-national force it proved that they could work together and that the communications, so vital in any armed conflict, were steadily improving.

Mariner also brought to a head the hoary old subject of the control of Coastal Command. Our allies, most importantly the Americans, could not understand why British maritime air forces did not automatically belong to the Royal Navy—an attitude which the latter did nothing to discourage! The title of the Command was also a problem, causing bewilderment at home and abroad. However, attempts to change it to Maritime Command or Maritime air Command made at irregular intervals were all vetoed by members of the Air Council or AOC-in-Cs of Coastal Command, some Air Marshal's being very nostalgic about the name. They saw no reason to alter

In an unusual light grey colour scheme, WX529/V of No.210 Squadron in 1956. The aircraft has the modified nose and MAD tail boom introduced during an in-service update. (MAP)

Air Marshal Sir Brian Reynolds, AOC-in-C Coastal Command addressing personnel of the School of Maritime Reconnaissance just prior to the departure of the last Lancaster MR.3 in service, 15 October 1956. (No.236 OCU records)

it, though it was patently a misnomer and continued to be the cause of dissension—as did the subject of control!

The eighth Shackleton squadron, No.204, was formed on 1 January 1954 to bring the Ballykelly Wing up to strength, followed six months later by No.228 Squadron at St Eval. This completed the current deployment plan except for the provision of in-shore anti-submarine aircraft and SAR helicopters. Fighter Command had already formed No.275 Squadron with Sycamores for the latter role, but Coastal was still carrying out trials and favoured a more capable machine, the Bristol 173.

The Neptune squadrons continued to be hamstrung by spares problems during the first half of 1954, and Shackleton units were also experiencing increased unserviceability. In an attempt to improve the latter, and also reduce the risk of mishandling by aircrew, it was decided to abandon the mix of variants and equip Shackleton squadrons with either Mk.1 or Mk.2 aircraft. This involved considerable swopping around of aircraft during July/August, with the result that Nos.120, 206, 220, 240 and 269 Squadrons had Mk.1 aircraft, while Nos.42, 204, 224 and 228 were completely equipped with Mk.2. It had been hoped to re-equip more of the squadrons with the Mk.2 variant but the refusal of the Americans to provide sufficient Neptunes for the two MEAF units, and limit the total delivery to 52 aircraft forced a diversion of new Shackletons which slowed down the Coastal re-equipment programme.

No.230 Squadron spent a busy week in August successfully extracting the British North Greenland Expedition from Britannia Lake, and *Morning Mist*,

a fleet shadowing exercise off the Norwegian coast, involved the whole Command during September/October. The other major activities of 1954 were the regular visits to the JASS at Londonderry and the *Fairisle* detachments to Malta—a comparatively quiet year.

As part of the defence review following the end of the Korean War the Admiralty announced the cancellation of their order for the Seamew. Coastal Command still envisaged operating 16 of the aircraft in Flights of four parented by an LR/MR squadron, though doubts were being expressed about the Seamew concept, and about the Mk.3 Shackleton. It had become obvious that the increased range predictions were not achievable, nullifying the reason for ordering this variant. Argument raged throughout the early months of 1955, but in the end it had to be accepted that the choice lay between the Mk.3 or nothing and ranks were closed, assisted by the prospect of yet another attempt at a take-over by the Royal Navy following Admiral Earl Louis Mountbatten's appointment as First Sea Lord.

Meanwhile No.22 Squadron had been formed at Thorney Island on 15 February for search and rescue duties. Initially a few Sycamores were used, but soon Whirlwind HAR.2 helicopters became available and the unit operational, *B* Flight being established at Martlesham Heath in June and *C* Flight at Valley in September. It was the start of a regional distribution which is still maintained.

The tactical trials of the Mk.30 homing torpedo were completed in March 1955, and though it took time to get the rather delicate mechanism to work properly under operational conditions the depth charge was at last on its way out as the primary anti-submarine weapon. Work was also going ahead on *Pentane*, an active homing torpedo which finally fell victim to delay and was cancelled in 1958, a sorry story continued when the update of the Mk.30 was dropped in favour of the American Mk.43, despite trials demonstrating that the latter's success rate was only 25% of that of the Mk.30.

The Neptune 'fleet' was the subject of considerable improvement during 1955. The revised nose section became generally available and some aircraft were fitted with Magnetic Anomaly Detector (MAD) equipment, while weapon clearances had at last been completed. Dutch Neptunes commenced deployments to Topcliffe, and the whole Command took part in *Centre Board*, an exercise which started over the Bay of Biscay under the control of an American carrier group and moved north into areas off the United Kingdom.

Trials on *Orange Harvest* ECM equipment, *Blue Silk* doppler and ASV Mk.21 were now in full swing, and so it was perhaps surprising that a new deployment plan still envisaged the retention of ten Sunderlands until March 1960 in view of the flying boats' inability to carry homing weapons and with no plans to upgrade its avionics. It was now intended to operate the Seamews in two Flights of eight aircraft based at St Mawgan and Ballykelly—despite impending defence cuts aimed at reducing the current operational strength of 130 aircraft to 82 by mid-1957, and to only four MR squadrons (32 aircraft) by June 1958. The Groups would then be disbanded and the squadrons controlled from Northwood.

In August 1955 No.240 Squadron set off on Operation *Cooks Tour*, a photo survey of Christmas and other islands in mid-Pacific required by the team planning Britain's 'hydrogen' bomb trials, and No.42 Squadron made the initial tests of the Shackleton as a 'trooper'. Preliminary planning was also undertaken by No.42 on yet another role, that of *Colonial Policing*. Operation *Suntan* saw four specially prepared Shackletons of No.228 Squadron crossing the Atlantic to South America in October on a goodwill tour which lasted $3\frac{1}{2}$ weeks. Led by AVM G.W. Tuttle CB, OBE, DFC, AFC, the AOC No.19 Group, it was a great success and became the model for other 'show the flag' tours over the next ten years.

Theoretical trooping became practice in January 1956 when renewed terrorist activity in Cyprus resulted in Operation *Encompass*, the transfer of 1,200 men of the Parachute Regiment from the UK to the island. At the peak, 28 Shackletons and 16 Hastings were involved in the lift which was triumphantly completed in 13 days—and justified those uncomfortable trials. During the same month No.42 Squadron

was confirmed in the *Col Pol* role and informed that it would be taking over the task from Bomber Command, while crews of No.269 Squadron found themselves training for meteorological reconnaissance work prior to departure in February for Australia on Operation *Mosaic*.

The last major overseas detachment by Coastal Sunderlands was made by four aircraft during March/April when in the face of many trials and tribulations the crews flew to Singapore for an exercise in which they co-operated with the resident No.205/209 Squadron. Back at home Exercise *Dawn Breeze* occupied the rest of the Command, proving to be the largest of a considerable number completed during the year.

Further delay in the introduction into service of the Shackleton Mk.3 was admitted in March 1956 and, with forward planning reliant on earlier 'firm' dates, the AOC-in-C voiced his concern in the strongest terms, stating that in his opinion it was now impossible to maintain Shackleton front-line strength in 1957, following the replacement of SMR Lancasters by Mk.1 aircraft which could not be delayed any longer. There was no immediate response from the Air Ministry, and when it did come it was less than helpful, merely reiterating that by the end of March 1957 the Sunderlands were to be withdrawn and the Neptune force 'rolled up'. There was no mention of the earlier proposal to reduce the Command to just four front-line squadrons by mid-1958, but the suggestion of a cut in the number of Shackleton squadrons to seven (from nine)—a total of 56 aircraft. In response the AOC-in-C Coastal Command advocated retention of nine squadrons, each reduced to 6 UE aircraft, and again suggested that the 'Met' unit be re-equipped with Shackletons so that it could operate in a dual Met/AS role. This would result in a slightly increased front-line of:

9 LR/MR Shackleton Sqns   54 aircraft
1 Met/MR Shackleton Sqn   5   "
1 SAR Helicopter Sqn   8   "

and a second-line strength of 16 Shackleton MR.1/T.4 for training and three Shackletons for trials at ASWDU. The Seamew had been cancelled by this stage, and a proposed in-shore helicopter replacement abandoned.

The effective front-line strength was, of course, reduced by the long-term secondary roles which the Shackleton was accumulating, another of which started in June with the first phase of *Grapple*, the nuclear bomb tests from Christmas Island. During this first detachment by No.206 Squadron the crews were responsible for ferrying essential stores for the preparation force building the runway and other infrastructure on the island—but there was more to follow!

The expected rundown of the Neptune force started on 31 August 1956 when No.203 Squadron was disbanded, and as the process continued the anti-E-Boat role was handed over to No.228 Squadron. However, the Shackleton was not a great success in this role and it was soon virtually abandoned.

The worsening political situation in the Middle East following the seizure of the Suez Canal by the Eygptians resulted in the trooping role coming to the fore again in August. After much vacillation, the Franco-British intervention, *Musketeer*, went ahead and Operation *Hornblower* was reactivated in October; Shackletons flying out Bomber Command groundcrew to Malta and Cyprus—and with the Suez fiasco over, flying them home again. In the meantime Neptune training had ceased, and with the flying boat element also on the wane the SMR and No.236 OCU were amalgamated at Kinloss on 1 October, the unit renamed the Maritime Operational Training Unit (MOTU) and established with 16 Shackletons—the aircraft which would see Coastal Command through its final twelve years!

CHAPTER 15

Shackletons Supreme– 1957-69

FOR COASTAL COMMAND the first months of 1957 were traumatic. The remaining three Neptune squadrons disbanded, and at Pembroke Dock both long-serving Sunderland units were rather summarily dismissed and the last UK flying boat station closed down. Shackletons reigned supreme, Nos.220 and 228 Squadrons having moved to St Mawgan in preparation for Mk.3s, which could not be operated at full load from St Eval, the latter airfield being left almost deserted when four aircraft of No.42 Squadron left for *Col Pol* duties at Aden.

The effective strength of the Command was reduced still further by conversion of Mk.1s into T.Mk.4 trainers, only partially offset by the disbandment of the JASS Flight which released three much needed aircraft for squadron use. Despite such problems 'goodwill' tours were still considered priority tasks, and four MR.2s of No.224 Squadron left Gibraltar

for South America on 15 March for Operation *Southern Cross*—almost a repeat of No.228 Squadron's trip in 1955.

The initial CA release of the Shackleton MR.3 on 24 April 1957 was received with universal relief even though it was very restricted. It had been envisaged that No.228 Squadron would be the first unit to receive the new aircraft, but the Air Ministry decision not to modernize the Mk.1 and the state of No.220's aircraft forced a change, and the latter unit started re-equipping in August. Introduction of the Mk.3 was slow and troublesome, however, engine fading and hydraulic problems proving very difficult to solve, and the Mk.1s remained until March 1958.

None of this made the AOC-in-C's struggle to keep his front-line up to strength any easier, his difficulties being compounded by the continuance of the *Colonial Policing* role longer than had been expected, and the

Shackleton MR.2 WL751 of No.224 Squadron en route from Gibraltar to Dakar at the start of a South American tour, March 1957. (No.224 Sqn records)

Whirlwind HAR.2 XJ760/K of A Flight No.22 Squadron performs at a Chivenor air display circa 1957. (W. J. Taylor)

involvement of the equivalent of a whole squadron on Hebrides missile range clearance patrols. However, a light could be seen at the end of the tunnel as delivery of T.Mk.4 aircraft for MOTU started, and authorization for the reduction in establishment to six aircraft per squadron finally came in January 1958.

Nos.206 and 228 Squadrons swopped bases on 14 January 1958, it having been decided that the former would be the next Mk.3 unit, while at St Mawgan No.1360 Flight formed with Whirlwind 4s. Within a month it had been redesignated No.217 Squadron, and was on the way to Christmas Island for rescue/liaison duties in connection with *Grapple* operations.

Trooping during June on *Pedestal*, a support operation for King Hussein of Jordan, stretched the Command to the limit, but it was periods of grounding which frustrated attempts to start Shackleton Mk.3 intensive flying trials which really tested the patience of all concerned. They finally got under way in June 1958, the aim being to complete 1,000 hours in nine weeks.

In January 1957 fatigue calculations had shown that the safe life of the Shackleton was only 3,600 flying hours, but this was not considered a problem at the time because no aircraft had achieved anything like that amount of flying, and rectification work was programmed into the Phase I modifications which were pending. In July 1958, however, revised figures were issued for the Mk.1 and 2 aircraft, reducing the safe life prior to major spar modifications to 2,500 hours, with an absolute limit of 2,700 hours, and this, together with the problems associated with the Mk.3, resulted in strong rumours suggesting that the Air Ministry was ready to abandon Coastal Command and relinquish 'Maritime Air' to the Royal Navy. So serious did the position become that the Under-Secretary of State for Air, Mr Ian Orr-Ewing, had to stand up in Parliament and state that such rumours were completely unfounded. This was the effective end of such lobbying by the Royal Navy, for few Admirals really wanted to take over a land-based force, and it was generally realized that the anti-submarine version of the Gannet was not up to the deep sea reconnaissance role, and neither was its helicopter replacement.

Rather more quietly, the Air Ministry informed the AOC-in-C Coastal in August that the latest plan required the front-line strength of the Command to be reduced to 36 aircraft (six squadrons)—though a date was not stated! With the intensive flying trials complete, No.120 Squadron commenced re-equipping with the Shackleton Mk.3 in September, and on 1 October No.220 became No.201 Squadron, the first of a fresh round of renumbering maintaining the existence of the more famous of the original RNAS units taken over by the RAF on 1 April 1918. No.240 Squadron became No.203 on 1 November, and a month later started to receive Mk.3s, the change-over at Ballykelly being completed when No.269, recently re-equipped with Mk.2s, became No.210 Squadron. None of these changes affected the size of the Command, and neither did the transfer of *E* Flight of No.275 Squadron, Fighter Command, to No.22 Squadron, because it promptly became *A* Flight at Chivenor, and the Flight at St Mawgan was disbanded.

No.224 Squadron took over the *Col Pol* commit-

Above left: *A very smart Shackleton MR.3 WR989/B of No.120 Squadron during the early 1960s. (Author's collection)*

Left: *Shackleton MR.2 WL 739/P of No.204 Squadron, June 1960. (MAP)*

Below left: *Hastings Met.1 TG623 of No.202 Squadron visiting Ballykelly in May 1962. (Author's collection)*

Above: *Shackleton MR.2 'B' of No.42 Squadron leading Hunter FGA.9s of the Aden Strike Wing while on detachment to Khormaksar for Radfan operations. (Author's collection)*

ment at the beginning of 1959, just as the modification programme reached a peak, and the Command's front line operation strength stabilized at 24 aircraft in March 1959—a low point which resulted in the disbandment of No.228 Squadron and the closure of St Eval, Coastal Command's most famous airfield.

Immediately after *Dawn Breeze IV* in April, No.120 Squadron returned to Kinloss and prepared three aircraft for *Calypso Stream*, a goodwill tour of the Caribbean extended because of unrest in British Honduras (now Belize). No.204 Squadron started relinquishing its Mk.1s as more Mk.2s became available, and with redeployment complete the Command appeared to be entering a more stable period, an illusion sadly shattered on 19 June by the order to ground all Shackletons which had exceeded 2,150 flying hours following the discovery of more fatigue

problems. The instruction affected nearly all Mk.1, Mk.2 and T.Mk.4 aircraft and, to keep pilots in flying practice, units were supplied with Varsities, while some MOTU 'applied' training was continued using squadron Mk.3s. A 'crash' programme aimed at producing a spar life of 5,000 flying hours was undertaken, and during August aircraft started to return to service, the whole fleet being back in operation by early October.

Meanwhile, the SAR helicopter strength of the Command was suddenly increased on 1 September when No.228 Squadron was reformed at Leconfield by renumbering No.275 on transfer from Fighter Command. The gain was partially offset by the disbandment of No.217 Squadron on completion of its Christmas Island tasks, but it was a definite boost to the Command's strength in this field.

The year ended with No.42 Squadron completing

Calypso Stream II—a detachment popular on both sides of the Atlantic—but activity during the early part of 1960 was at a very low ebb as the Command struggled to recover from the mid-1959 traumas. An earthquake at Agadir, Morocco, on 1 March meant a sudden burst of activity for No.224 Squadron, though, the unit flying supplies in, and a few people out. At home the 1960 version of *Dawn Breeze* occupied the whole Command, followed for No.210 Squadron by *Sea Lion*, a SEATO exercise flown from Singapore.

By April 1960 the Phase I update was complete, and aircraft were already going to industry for the Phase II programme which largely concerned the installation of new avionics. Weapons were also being updated at this time, with the American Mk.44 torpedo joining the Mk.30 as an operational option.

Behind the scenes the long-running saga aimed at finding a suitable replacement for the Shackleton reached a new stage in July with the issuing of OR 350—a mere five years after the OR Branch's projection of March 1960 as a realistic date for a new aircraft's introduction into service! The delay was not entirely the Ministry's fault, however, for soon after the original drafting of the requirements it had become known that the Americans and most of the NATO allies were looking at much the same date for the phasing out of the Neptune, and there was a real

Above left: *Shackleton MR.3 XF704/L of No.201 Squadron at St Mawgan in September 1965. Three months later, on 8 December 1965, it crashed into the Moray Firth. (Author's collection)*

Left: *Shackleton T.4 WB822/T of MOTU over Cornwall, September 1967. This aircraft was unique in spending the whole of a long working life in the training role, first as an MR.1 and after conversion, as a T.4. (Author's collection)*

Below left: *Whirlwind HAR.10 XJ729 of 'A' Flight No. 22 Squadron, Chivenor. (Author's collection)*

Below: *With bomb doors open and ASV Mk.21 radar in the 'attack' position, Shackleton MR.3 Phase III (Viper) WR979/D of the Kinloss Wing demonstrates at an air display during the late 1960s. (Author's collection)*

chance of standardizing on one aircraft. The NATO Armaments Committee started their deliberations, but worked slowly, and it was March 1957 before they appointed a panel of experts to draft the requirements, by which time the Americans had lost patience and produced their own specification for the aircraft which became the Orion. The Air Ministry, however, remained committed, and a specification, closely tailored to European requirements, appeared in March 1958.

From the competing designs the Breguet 1150* emerged triumphant, but the RAF was not happy about operating a twin-engined aircraft out into the Atlantic, and when Avro, the British company in the consortium, expressed strong reservations about the honeycomb sandwich construction of the aircraft, the British pulled out and redrafted the specification to more closely suit Coastal Command's needs. The result was OR 350 which called for an aircraft with a high transit speed combined with the ability to loiter at low speed and level in the patrol area—a difficult combination, and it was obvious that the Shackleton would have to stay in service much longer than previously envisaged, at least until 1968.

In 1960 NATO returned to the autumn for their major maritime exercise, aptly named *Fallex*. Over 400 aircraft and 146 ships took part in a complicated exercise which started off Norway and finished off the north coast of Spain. It was the largest NATO exercise to date, the air component working well under the overall control of the AOC-in-C Coastal Command in his NATO capacity, and the whole exercise was judged a great success.

Earlier in the year *Calypso Stream III* saw No.204 Squadron in the Caribbean, and in October two aircraft from No.206 Squadron went to the Argentine, followed in November by three of No.203 Squadron's Mk.3s to South Africa for a joint naval exercise. Deliveries of Phase II modified aircraft started in January 1961, but No.204 Squadron still had Phase Is when they went to Ceylon in February for *Jetex* 61—the annual fleet exercise in the Indian Ocean.

Not quite so eagerly approached, but hard fought none-the-less, was the annual Aird Whyte Competition. In 1961 it was completely changed, becoming a more realistic test of anti-submarine tactics than hitherto, and a means of choosing the crew who would compete with Australian, Canadian and New Zealand maritime personnel for the newly presented Fincastle Trophy.

Renewed tension in the Middle East in June, this time over Kuwait, resulted in No.42 Squadron going on *Col Pol* standby, and Nos.203 and 204 Squadrons being used for transporting V-Force equipment to Malta. On this occasion the Iraqis backed down in the

face of the prompt response by British forces, and it was the devastation of Belize City by a hurricane on 31 October which resulted in more action, six Shackletons being sent out to Jamaica to transport troops and supplies into the beleaguered colony. After ten days of intensive flying Operation *Skyhelp* was scaled down, but it was Christmas Eve before the last two No.42 Squadron aircraft returned to St Mawgan.

Shackletons were back in the Caribbean in February 1962, this time to fly supplies into British Guiana where rioting had closed the Georgetown docks. No.204 Squadron had been briefed to expect a week's detachment, but it was five weeks before they returned to Ballykelly. *Dawn Breeze* 62 was held off Portugal during March, but the major NATO maritime event was *Strong Gale* in May, unique in that live torpedoes (with dummy heads!) were dropped against a specially padded submarine.

The balancing act between the needs of the front line and the Phase II update programme worked remarkably well, but it was recognized that the most difficult period would be in mid-1962 when operational Mk.3s would be very scarce. The decision, therefore, was taken to start re-equipping No.203 Squadron with Mk.2s, chosen because Ballykelly's other squadrons already operated this variant, the change-over being completed in July.

No.210 Squadron went out to the Far East for the 1962 SEATO exercise *Blue Water* flown from Butterworth, and the same unit was involved in *Internal Security*† training at Khormaksar during June. However, the most interesting event was Operation *Tiara*, the shadowing of the largest Russian fleet exercise held in the Eastern Atlantic to date, while in the SAR world the most significant change for years occurred in August when No.22 Squadron re-equipped with turbine-powered Whirlwind 10s, and for the first time was able to operate with a full fuel load right through the summer months.

The Cuban missile crisis erupted in October 1962 when President John Kennedy called the Russians' bluff and threatened military action if the missiles on Cuban soil were not removed immediately. It was the most serious East/West confrontation for ten years, and all Coastal Command operational squadrons were put on six hours readiness. Surveillance sorties were increased, and things were very tense for several days before the Russians backed down. The Soviet Bloc countries had also been 'flexing their maritime muscles' for some time, their fishing fleets operating around the British Isles in ever increasing numbers, and during 1962 a number of experimental sorties

---

*Later named the Atlantique.
†The new name for *Col Pol.*

were flown from Ballykelly aimed at plotting their movements. At the beginning of 1963, egged on by newspapers, the British public began taking an interest, and it was decided to mount regular surveillance by Shackletons as part of Operation *Chacewater*. It soon became obvious that British fishermen did have a genuine grievance, but more ominous from a military viewpoint were the trawlers which did little or no fishing but loitered in areas covering arrival and departure routes for Allied nuclear-powered submarines based at Faslane on Holy Loch. Known as AGIs, these trawlers were intelligence gatherers, and many weary flying hours were expended on the unexciting task of monitoring their activities during the remaining Coastal years!

The British Aircraft Corporation and Hawker Siddeley both submitted a number of proposals in response to OR 350—as did Lockheed with versions of the Orion. Of these the Avro 776, a design similar in appearance to the Trident, was judged the most interesting, but there were doubts about its single-engined performance, and in June 1963 the Ministry of Defence (MoD) requirements were modified and reissued as Air Staff Target (AST) 357. Requests for feasibility studies were made in August, and replies came quickly and in very varied form. Rather belatedly, however, the OR Branch of the MoD realized that the time-scale* could not be met by designs not based on existing aircraft, which eliminated the more radical proposals. During the autumn the VC-10 and the Trident were assessed, and when the Ministry let it be known that they would probably choose a four-engined aircraft, the Comet was added to the list,

Hawker Siddeley working overtime to revamp their MR proposal for an aircraft first mooted in 1961!

In August No.201 Squadron sent a detachment to Nassau to deter further incursions into Bahamian territorial waters by Cuban forces seeking political refugees, the aircraft remaining for eight weeks during which they flew surveillance, anti-smuggling patrols and relief supplies into Mayaguana Island following its devastation by a hurricane. During October 1963 came the annual round of autumn exercises, and in December No.210 Squadron sent aircraft out to Cyprus for 'recce' duties following another flare-up in the civil war between Greek and Turkish Cypriots, the Command finding itself sending out a series of replacement detachments which continued until August 1964. Another detachment of the 'security' type involved No.224 Squadron which sent two aircraft to Aden in April 1964 to assist No.37 with operations in the Radfan and, closer to home, crews of Nos.120, 201, 204 and 206 Squadrons started flying on Operation *Adjutant*, an attempt to assess Russian submarine movements through a 'choke' area north of the British Isles. Over 2,000 hours had been flown by mid-August when the experiment was concluded.

No.202 Squadron completed 18 years of unremitting effort on 31 July 1964 when the last *Bismuth* was completed, over 40,000 hours having been flown on meteorological reconnaissance flights, and many more on transport work, without a fatal accident despite operating in all weathers, five days a week.† It was

---

*A 1968 start for Shackleton replacement was still envisaged.
†Not Wednesday or Sunday.

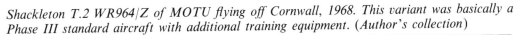

Shackleton T.2 WR964/Z of MOTU flying off Cornwall, 1968. This variant was basically a Phase III standard aircraft with additional training equipment. (Author's collection)

unique in being the only RAF unit routinely cleared to fly over Eire while on operational duty! The famous 'number' was not lost, however, for on 1 September No.228 was redesignated 202 at Leconfield, the unit retaining its detachments at Acklington, Coltishall, Leuchars and Ouston.

The NATO exercise *Teamwork*, held in September 1964, involved all the anti-submarine units in the Command, including for the first time the *shadow* squadron, No.220, formed by MOTU from its staff and senior students. Most units remained at their home bases, but No.224 Squadron flew up to Bodo (Northern Norway) from Gibraltar, and half of No.203 Squadron went to Kinloss.

Meanwhile, in the Far East difficulties with the Indonesians were increasing, and it was decided to strengthen British forces in the area, a six-Shackleton detachment from Coastal Command being among the additional aircraft provided. No.210 Squadron was the first to go on the three-month stint, though the aircraft stayed longer, only returning to the UK when due for major servicing, or when the relief crews operated a different variant of Shackleton.

Immediately after Phase II modifications were completed, aircraft started to be put through the Phase III programme which entailed major reskinning and spar modification, as well as a completely new interior. First deliveries of Phase III aircraft to squadrons were made in February 1965, the same month as the first Viper-fitted Mk.3 flew, a very necessary modification aimed at improving the take-off performance of the aircraft. Two months later, Specification MR254 was issued for the Shackleton replacement, tightly written around the HS 801, a Comet development which had emerged as the aircraft which best met the Ministry's requirements.

For some time it had been evident that the main Russian naval threat to Atlantic shipping was from the Soviet Northern Fleet, and early in 1965 it was decided to concentrate more of the Command's assets in No.18 Group. Consequently No.201 Squadron moved from St Mawgan to Kinloss in March, followed by No.206 in July, occupying accommodation vacated by the MOTU which was re-located at St Mawgan where No.42 Squadron, now No.19 Group's sole operational unit, started re-equipment with Phase III modified Mk.3s.

Kinloss-based Shackletons took over the *Affluent* detachments at Singapore in October, continuing *Hawk Moth* patrols in the seemingly endless undeclared war with Indonesia, while back in the UK Exercise *Calpurnia* was held in the north-western approaches during November/December 1965 to consolidate the new Command deployment. This was 'bread and butter' stuff, however, and more memor-

able was the 'round the world' flight by two aircraft of No.120 Squadron early in 1966 and *Mediterranean Theatre Training* at Gibraltar by No.201 Squadron.

The first Viper-fitted Shackleton reached squadron service in May 1966, and with the Mk.3 Phase III programme nearing completion similar upgrading of the Mk.2s was in full swing. No.203 Squadron started reverting to Mk.3 aircraft, and for the first time since it entered service this variant equipped five squadrons! No.42 sent three of theirs to Capetown at the end of July for what turned out to be the last *Capex*—a victim of the steadily worsening South African political situation.

Much to the AOC-in-C's relief 'confrontation' with the Indonesians ended in August 1966, but with the British Government continuing their policy of reducing the strength of garrisons overseas without significantly scaling down commitments, home-based Commands, including Coastal, found themselves having to plan for more, not less, 'out of area' contingencies. Reinforcement training was, therefore, stepped up to ensure that crews had experience of overseas operations, including more Gibraltar detachments following the sudden disbandment of No.224 Squadron in October.

Centralized servicing was reintroduced as another economy measure, an event which coincided with the arrival of the first Phase III Mk.2 in front-line service. This version quickly proved to be much superior to earlier variants, and also formed the basis for a new sub-variant, the T.Mk.2, ten of which were produced for MOTU to replace outdated T.Mk.4s.

Since March 1966 NEAF Shackleton squadrons had operated a detachment at Majunga (Malagasy) to assist British naval forces attempting to stop the rebellious Smith regime from obtaining oil supplies through the Mozambique port of Beira. Commitments in the Mediterranean and the Aden Protectorate suffered, so in February 1967 Coastal Command took over the patrols,* sending four aircraft from No.42 Squadron. They remained until April, by which time it was obvious that Majunga was unsuitable for the heavy Mk.3, so the task was passed to the Ballykelly Mk.2 squadrons.

Meanwhile, centralization had been extended to the aircraft, now pooled on a Wing basis, and planning for the introduction of the HS 801, soon to be named the Nimrod, was gaining momentum. The detachments proved a severe test for centralization, the situation not helped by the ill-conceived announcement that Britain would withdraw from Aden by the end of 1967, which resulted in escalating attacks on the British and fierce fighting between rival groups jock-

*Code-named *Mizar*.

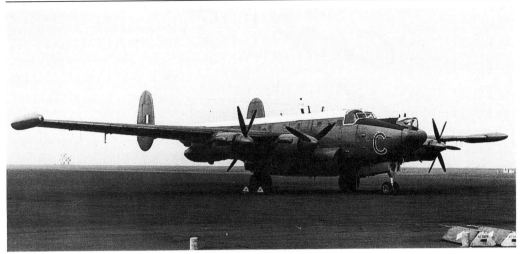

Shackleton MR.3 Phase III (Viper) WR984/C of No.42 Squadron at St Mawgan in November 1967. (Author's collection)

eying for power. The trouble spread to the Persian Gulf, and in August 1967 a Maritime Detachment (*Mardet*) had to be formed under the control of Kinloss and sent to Sharjah to help combat arms smuggling into the Gulf States, and also covered the final withdrawal from the erstwhile colony of Aden. Fortunately, the operation went smoothly, but this detachment and the *Mizar* patrols from Majunga proved a heavy strain, little helped by No.203 Squadron being held in the Mediterranean area at the conclusion of Exercise *Eagle Eye* to help No.38 with patrols around Cyprus following fresh heightening of tension between the ethnic communities.

Little mention has been made of the air/sea rescue services, who maintained their daily vigil year in, year out. During 1967 the Command's helicopters, Shackletons and marine craft, took part in the rescue of 26 servicemen and 176 civilians. This was a typical annual 'score' for an organization which was set up specifically to rescue military airmen, but never turned away calls for help from any quarter, and invariably saved more civilians than servicemen—many in danger through their own ignorance, foolhardiness or just plain stupidity.

In January 1968 the first of the training Mk.2s reached MOTU, though it was to be July before the last Mk.4 departed and the unit could reap the full benefit of an aircraft fitted with the same equipment as that in use on operational squadrons. The overall plan envisaged the Command retaining its seven Shackleton squadrons until the Nimrod entered service, but a steady increase in Russian naval activity in the Mediterranean, started soon after Malta-based

No.38 Squadron had disbanded, forced the redeployment of a maritime reconnaissance unit to the area. Four aircraft of No.42 Squadron 'held the fort' for

The flypast over St Mawgan to mark the disbandment of Coastal Command on 27 November 1969. Nine Shackletons and a Nimrod overfly a Whirlwind HAR.10 helicopter. (No.236 OCU records)

three months prior to February 1969 when No.203 Squadron left Coastal Command on permanent transfer to NEAF.

The impression may have been given that detachments and overseas reinforcements had taken over completely, but that was not the case, for despite the reducing strength of the Command all NATO commitments continued to be honoured, an all-out effort being made during *Strong Gale*, the major exercise of 1969. The Shackleton's long maritime reign was approaching its end, however, for on 2 October 1969 MOTU took delivery of the first Nimrod to enter RAF service. It was the start of a new era, rather appropriately confirmed by the absorption of Coastal Com-

mand by Strike Command some six weeks later.

As Air Marshal Sir John Lapsley took the salute at the disbandment parade on 27 November, two SAR Whirlwinds, nine Shackletons and a single Nimrod overflew St Mawgan—Coastal Command was no more. The following day No.18 (Maritime) Group took over the assets at Northwood, and the existing Nos.18 and 19 Groups at Pitreavie Castle, Fife, and Mount Batten, Devon, became respectively HQ Northern and HQ Southern Maritime Air Region.

During its 33-year existence RAF Coastal Command carried out an amazing variety of tasks during bad times and good. It had truly lived up to the motto on its badge—*Constant Endeavour*.

APPENDIX I

Command Formations

Coastal Command

FORMED 14 JULY 1936 by re-naming Coastal Area with headquarters at Lee-on-Solent. On formation the Command comprised a number of shore stations and also squadrons and flights aboard Royal Navy ships. Control of the Fleet Air Arm was relinquished in July 1937. On 7 August 1939 Coastal Command HQ moved to Northwood, Middlesex, where the Eastbury Park Hotel and surrounding grounds had been acquired. A combined Royal Navy/RAF operations room was established. Disbanded 28 November 1969 when absorbed by Strike Command. Northwood then became HQ No.18 (Maritime) Group.

Air Officers Commanding-in-Chief

Name	Date of Appointment
Air Marshal Sir Arthur M. Longmore KCB, DSO	14 July 1936
Air Marshal P.B. Joubert de la Ferte CB, CMG, DSO	24 August 1936

Air Chief Marshal Sir Frederick Bowhill KCB, CMG, DSO *at his desk at Northwood. Irreverently known as 'Ginger' his recognition feature were his fierce eyebrows. (British Official)*

Above: *Air Chief Marshal Sir Philip Joubert KCB, CMG, DSO and his Group Commanders during a conference at Northwood, March 1942. From left to right: AVM B.E. Baker CB, DSO, MC, AFC (16 Group designate), AC A.H. Primrose CB, DFC (AHQ Iceland), AVM J.M. Robb CB, DSO, DFC, AFC (15 Group), AVM A. Durston AFC (18 Group), AC S.P. Simpson CBE, MC (AHQ Gibraltar), the AOC-in-C, AVM G.R. Bromet CBE, DSO (19 Group), AC I.T. Lloyd CBE (16 Group) and AC H.G. Smart CBE, DFC, AFC (17 Group). (British Official)*

Below left: *Air Marshal Sir John Slessor KCB, DSO, MC. (British Official)*

Below right: *Air Commandant HRH The Duchess of Gloucester with Sir W. Sholto Douglas (when an Air Marshal at HQ Fighter Command). (Imperial War Museum)*

Name	*Date of Appointment*
Air Marshal Sir Frederick W. Bowhill KCB, CMG, DSO (ACM 1.11.39)	16 August 1937
Air Marshal Sir Philip B. Joubert de la Ferte KCB, CMG, DSO (ACM 1.7.41)	14 June 1941
Air Vice Marshal (acting AM) J.C. Slessor CB, DSO, MC (AM 1.6.43) KCB 1943	5 February 1943
Air Chief Marshal Sir W. Sholto Douglas KCB, MC, DFC	20 January 1944
Air Vice Marshal (acting AM) Sir Leonard H. Slatter, KBE, CB, DSC, DFC (AM 1.7.47)	30 June 1945
Air Vice Marshal J.W. Baker CB, MC, DFC (AM 1.1.49) KCB 1949	1 November 1948
Air Vice Marshal (acting AM) C.R. Steele CB, DFC (AM 1.7.50) KCB 1951	1 January 1950
Air Vice Marshal A.C. Stevens CB (AM 1.7.51) KBE 1952	8 June 1951
Air Marshal Sir John N. Boothman KBE, CB, DFC, AFC (ACM 1.10.54) KCB 1954	15 November 1953
Air Marshal Sir Bryan V. Reynolds KCB, CBE	5 April 1956
Air Vice Marshal (acting AM) Sir C. Edward Chilton KBE, CB (AM 1.7.59)	1 June 1959
Air Marshal Sir Anthony D. Selway KCB, DFC	10 August 1962
Air Vice Marshal (acting AM) P.D. Holder CB, DSO, DFC, M.Sc., Ph.D. (AM 1.7.65) KBE 1965	23 January 1965
Air Vice Marshal (acting AM) J.H. Lapsley CB, OBE, DFC, AFC (AM 1.7.69) KBE 1969	2 September 1968

Groups

No.15
Originally formed at Mudros in October 1918. Reformed as No.15 (Reconnaissance) Group 15 March 1939 at Lee-on-Solent. Transferred to Mount Wise Barracks, Plymouth, 6 June 1939. HQ to Egg Buckland Keep 16 August 1940. To Derby House, Liverpool early in 1941, assuming operational control 14 February 1941. Disbanded 1 August 1945 when absorbed by RAF Northern Ireland.

No.16
Formed as No.16 (Reconnaissance) Group at Wykeham Hall, Lee-on-Solent on 1 December 1936. To Chatham 1 November 1938 and formed an Area Combined HQ. Disbanded 8 March 1946 becoming HQ (Unit) 16 Wing.

No.17
Formed as No 17 (Training) Group at Wykeham Hall, Lee-on-Solent on 1 December 1936, moving to Fort Grange, Gosport on 24 February 1939. On 5 February 1942 moved to Mackenzie's Hotel, 58 Melville Street, Edinburgh, where the HQ remained until disbanded 1 September 1945 when all stations and units transferred to No.18 Group.

No.18
Originally formed at Harborough October 1918 but disbanded 18 October 1919. Reformed as No.18 (Reconnaissance) Group 1 September 1938 at Lee-on-Solent. Moved to Scotland 1 November 1938, establishing an operations room at Donibristle and Administrative HQ at Pitreavie Castle, Dunfermline. In February 1940 an Area Combined HQ formed at Pitreavie Castle and moved into an underground operations room in grounds. On disbandment of Coastal Command 28 November 1969 reformed as No.18 (Maritime) Group, Strike Command with HQ at Northwood, the unit at Pitreavie Castle being renamed HQ Northern Maritime Air Region.

No.19
Formed at Mount Wise, Plymouth, during January 1941 and assumed operational control of south-west approaches 5 February from an operations block in Egg Buckland Keep, an old fort on the northern outskirts of Plymouth. On 10 January 1942 the operations staff moved into a new underground Area Combined Operations HQ below Mount Wise together with naval staff of C-in-C Plymouth. HQ No.19 Group moved to Mount Batten 1 May 1948, the operations room remaining below Mount Wise. Disbanded 28 November 1969 to become Southern Maritime Air Region.

No.106 (PR)
Formed 14 April 1944 at Benson from No.106 Wing and took over the photographic reconnaissance assets of HQ Coastal Command. Disbanded 15 August 1946 and reorganized as the Central Photographic Establishment.

No.200 (Coastal)
Formed at Gibraltar 25 September 1939 with the HQ in the Bristol Hotel. Operated as part of RAF Mediterranean Area in control of No.202 Squadron. Transferred to Coastal Command 12 August 1940 and assumed command of all flying boats and maritime landplanes based on Gibraltar. Disbanded 21 December 1941 and reformed as AHQ Gibraltar.

No.247
Formed October 1943 in the Azores to operate Lagens airfield, Terceira, and the maritime units based in these Portuguese islands. Disbanded 1 March 1946.

Air Headquarters

Gibraltar
Formed on 21 December 1941 from the disbanded No.200 (Coastal) Group, the AHQ operating from premises in Cathedral Square, and reporting direct to Coastal Command HQ. An Area Combined HQ was formed with the Royal Navy at the Tower in the Dockyard, and commenced operations early in 1942. The airfield at North Front was transferred from FAA to RAF control 1 May 1942, and at the same time the flying boat station became RAF New Camp. In November 1942 all units at Gibraltar were transferred to North West African Coastal Forces for Operation *Torch*, the AHQ coming under the command of the Moroccan Sea Frontier Force (US Casablanca) although Coastal Command was still responsible for the supply of aircraft and crews. Returned to Coastal Command 8 October 1943. The ACHQ closed 29 May 1945, RAF personnel moving into AHQ Gibraltar at Engineer House. The AHQ was disbanded in October 1966.

Iceland
Work started on a base in Iceland in August 1940 when No.30 Wing arrived to administer landplane forces under the command of No.18 Group. AHQ Iceland formed 19 March 1941 to control Nos.30 and 100 Wing, the latter arriving aboard the SS *Manela* later in the month to administer flying boat units using Reyjavik harbour. Area Combined HQ formed June 1941 at Mentaskolinn, Reyjavik, the ACHQ being joined by the administrative section by 10 July. Later both moved into Atlantic Camp. No.100 Wing ceased operations from Iceland July 1944. Disbanded July 1945.

West Africa
Formed September 1941 at White House, Fourah Bay with SS *Manela* as depot ship. Controlled No.95 Squadron and attached units. Coastal Command relinquished control on 22 October 1941 to West African Command.

APPENDIX II

Order of Battle
3 September 1939

No.15 (GR) Group **Air Commodore R.G. Parry** DSO
  No.204 Squadron   Sunderland   Mount Batten
  No.210 Squadron   Sunderland   Pembroke Dock (2 a/c detached Woodhaven)
  No.217 Squadron   Anson   Warmwell
  No.228 Squadron   Sunderland   Pembroke Dock
  No.502 Squadron   Anson   Aldergrove

No.16 (GR) Group **Air Commodore R.L.G. Marix** DSO
  No.22 Squadron   Vildebeest   Thorney Island
  No.42 Squadron   Vildebeest   Bircham Newton
  No.48 Squadron   Anson   Thorney Island (detachments at Detling and Guernsey)
  No.206 Squadron   Anson   Bircham Newton
  No.500 Squadron   Anson   Detling

No.17 (T) Group **Air Commodore T.B. Howe** CBE, AFC
  Torpedo Training School   Gosport
  School of General Reconnaissance   Thorney Island
  Seaplane Training Squadron   Calshot

No.18 (GR) Group **Air Vice Marshal C.D. Breese** CB, AFC
  No.201 Squadron   London   Sullom Voe, Shetland
  No.209 Squadron   Stranraer   Invergordon
  No.220 Squadron   Anson   Thornaby
  No.224 Squadron   Hudson   Leuchars
  No.233 Squadron   Anson/Hudson   Leuchars
  No.240 Squadron   London   Invergordon
  No.269 Squadron   Anson   Montrose
  No.608 Squadron   Anson   Thornaby
  No.612 Squadron   Anson   Dyce

APPENDIX III

Order of Battle
1 November 1940

No.15 (GR) Group — **Air Commodore R.G. Parry** DSO

No.48 Squadron	Anson	Hooton Park
No.209 Squadron	Lerwick	Pembroke Dock
No.217 Squadron	Anson/Beaufort	St Eval
No.236 Squadron	Blenheim IVF	St Eval
No.321 Squadron	Anson	Carew Cheriton
No.502 Squadron	Botha/Whitley	Aldergrove
No.10 Sqn, RAAF	Sunderland	Pembroke Dock

No.16 (GR) Group — **Air Vice Marshal J.H.S. Tyssen** CB, DSO

No.22 Squadron	Beaufort	North Coates
No.53 Squadron	Blenheim IV	Detling
No.59 Squadron	Blenheim IV	Thorney Island
No.206 Squadron	Hudson	Bircham Newton
No.220 Squadron	Hudson	Thornaby
No.235 Squadron	Blenheim IVF	Bircham Newton
No.500 Squadron	Anson	Detling
No.608 Squadron	Anson/Botha	Thornaby

No.17 (T) Group — **Air Commodore T.E.B. Howe** CBE, AFC
Numerous training units

No.18 (GR) Group — **Air Vice Marshal C.D. Breese** CB, AFC

No.42 Squadron	Beaufort	Wick
No.98 Squadron	Battle	Kaldadarnes
No.201 Squadron	Sunderland	Sullom Voe
No.204 Squadron	Sunderland	Sullom Voe
No.210 Squadron	Sunderland	Oban
No.224 Squadron	Hudson	Leuchars
No.233 Squadron	Hudson	Leuchars
No.240 Squadron	Stranraer	Stranraer
No.248 Squadron	Blenheim IVF	Dyce
No.254 Squadron	Blenheim IVF	Dyce
No.320 Squadron	Anson/Hudson	Leuchars
No.612 Squadron	Anson	Dyce

No.200 (Coastal) Group — **Group Captain A.D. Rogers** CBE, AFC

No.202 Squadron	London/Swordfish	Gibraltar

APPENDIX IV

Order of Battle
12 February 1942

No 15 (GR) Group	**Air Vice Marshal J.M.Robb** CB, DSO, DFC, AFC	
No.53 Squadron	Hudson	Limavady
No.120 Squadron	Liberator	Nutts Corner
No.143 Squadron	Blenheim IV	Aldergrove
No.201 Squadron	Sunderland	Lough Erne
No.206 Squadron	Hudson	Aldergrove
No.210 Squadron	Catalina	Oban
No.220 Squadron	Fortress	Nutts Corner
No.228 Squadron	Sunderland	Stranraer
No.240 Squadron	Catalina	Lough Erne
No.1402 (Met) Flt	Spitfire/Gladiator	Aldergrove
No.1405 (Met) Flt	Blenheim/Hudson	Aldergrove

No.16 (GR) Group	**Air Commodore I.T.Lloyd** CBE	
No.22 Squadron	Beaufort	Thorney Island
No.59 Squadron	Hudson	North Coates
No.217 Squadron	Beaufort	Thorney Island
No.233 Squadron	Hudson	Thorney Island
No.248 Squadron	Beaufighter	Bircham Newton
No.279 Squadron	Hudson (ASR)	Bircham Newton
No.280 Squadron	Anson (ASR)	Detling
No.407 Squadron	Hudson	North Coates
No.415 Squadron	Hampden/Beaufort	Thorney Island
No.500 Squadron	Hudson	Bircham Newton
No.502 Squadron	Whitley	Bircham Newton
No.1401 (Met) Flt	Blenheim	Bircham Newton
Photographic Reconnaissance Unit	Spitfire	Benson

No.17 (T) Group	**Air Commodore H. G. Smart** CBE, DFC, AFC
Numerous training units	

No.18 (GR) Group	**Air Vice Marshal A. Durston** CB, AFC	
No.42 Squadron	Beaufort	Leuchars
No.48 Squadron	Hudson	Wick
No.235 Squadron	Beaufighter	Dyce
No.320 Squadron	Hudson	Leuchars

No.404 Squadron	Blenheim IV	Sumburgh
No.413 Squadron	Catalina	Sullom Voe
No.489 Squadron	Blenheim IV	Leuchars
No.608 Squadron	Hudson	Wick
No.1406 (Met) Flt	Blenheim	Wick
No.1408 (Met) Flt	Hudson	Wick

No.19 (GR) Group   **Air Commodore G.R. Bromet** CBE, DSO

No.22 Squadron	Beaufort	St Eval (rear party)
No.86 Squadron	Beaufort	St Eval
No.209 Squadron	Catalina	Pembroke Dock
No.217 Squadron	Beaufort	St Eval (Det)
No.224 Squadron	Hudson	St Eval
No.254 Squadron	Blenheim IVF	Carew Cheriton
No.502 Squadron	Whitley	St Eval (Det)
No.10 Sqn, RAAF	Sunderland	Mount Batten
No.1404 (Met) Flt	Hudson	St Eval
No.1417 Flt	Wellington	Chivenor
Photographic Reconnaissance Unit	Spitfire	St Eval

AHQ Gibraltar   **Air Commodore S.P. Simpson** CBE, MC

| No.202 Squadron | Catalina/Sunderland |

AHQ Iceland   **Air Commodore W.H. Primrose** CBE, DFC

No.269 Squadron	Hudson	Kaldadarnes
No.330 Squadron	Northrop N3P-B	Reykjavik
No.612 Squadron	Whitley	Reykjavik
No.1407 (Met) Flt	Hudson	Reykjavik
VP-73(USN)	PBY-5 Catalina	Reykjavik

Order of Battle
15 February 1943

No.15 Group	**Air Vice Marshal T.A. Langford-Sainsbury** OBE, DFC, AFC	
No.120 Squadron	Liberator	Aldergrove (det Keflavik)
No.201 Squadron	Sunderland	Lough Erne
No.206 Squadron	Fortress	Benbecula
No.220 Squadron	Fortress	Aldergrove
No.228 Squadron	Sunderland	Lough Erne/Castle Archdale
No.246 Squadron	Sunderland	Bowmore
No.422 Squadron	Sunderland	Oban
No.423 Squadron	Sunderland	Lough Erne/Castle Archdale
No.1402 Flight	Spitfire/Gladiator/Hudson	Aldergrove
No.16 Group	**Air Vice Marshal B.E. Baker** CB, DSO, MC, AFC	
No.53 Squadron	Hudson	Docking
No.86 Squadron	Liberator	Thorney Island
No.143 Squadron	Beaufighter	North Coates
No.236 Squadron	Beaufighter	North Coates
No.254 Squadron	Beaufighter	North Coates
No.320 Squadron	Hudson	Bircham Newton
No.407 Squadron	Hudson	Docking
No.521 Squadron	Spitfire/Hudson/Mosquito/Gladiator	Bircham Newton
No.540 Squadron	Mosquito	Benson
No.541 Squadron	Spitfire	Benson
No.542 Squadron	Spitfire	Benson
No.543 Squadron	Spitfire	Benson
No.544 Squadron	Spitfire/Wellington/Maryland	Benson
833 Squadron FAA	Swordfish	Thorney Island
836 Squadron FAA	Swordfish	Thorney Island
No.17 Group	**Air Commodore H.G. Smart** CBE, DFC, AFC	
Numerous training units		
No.18 Group	**Air Vice Marshal A.B. Ellwood** CB, DSC	
No.144 Squadron	Beaufighter	Leuchars
No.190 Squadron	Catalina	Sullom Voe

No.235 Squadron	Beaufighter	Leuchars
No.455 Squadron	Hampden	Leuchars
No.489 Squadron	Hampden	Wick
No.540 Sqn (Det)	Mosquito	Leuchars
No.547 Squadron	Wellington	Tain
No.612 Squadron	Whitley	Wick
No.1406 (Met) Flt	Spitfire/Hudson	Wick
No.1408 (Met) Flt	Hampden	Wick
No.1477 Flight	Catalina	Woodhaven

No.19 Group   **Air Vice Marshal G.R. Bromet** CB, CBE, DSO

No.58 Squadron	Whitley/Halifax	Holmsley South
No.59 Squadron	Fortress	Chivenor
No.119 Squadron	Sunderland	Pembroke Dock
No.172 Squadron	Wellington	Chivenor
No.179 Sqn (Det)	Wellington	
No.210 Squadron	Catalina	Pembroke Dock
No.224 Squadron	Liberator	Beaulieu
No.248 Squadron	Beaufighter	Predannack
No.304 Squadron	Wellington	Dale
No.311 Squadron	Wellington	Talbenny
No.404 Squadron	Beaufighter	Chivenor
No.405 Squadron	Halifax	Beaulieu
No.461 Squadron	Sunderland	Hamworthy
No.502 Squadron	Whitley	St Eval
No.543 Sqn (Det)	Spitfire	St Eval
No.1404 (Met) Flt	Hudson/Ventura	St Eval
No.10 OTU	Whitley	St Eval
No.10 Sqn, RAAF	Sunderland	Mount Batten
No.1 AS Sqn, USAAF	B-24 Liberator	St Eval
No.2 AS Sqn, USAAF	B-24 Liberator	St Eval

AHQ Iceland   **Air Commodore K.B. Lloyd** AFC

No.120 Sqn (Det)	Liberator	Reykjavik
No.269 Squadron	Hudson	Reykjavik
No.330 Sqn (Det)	Northrop N3P-B	Reykjavik
No.1407 (Met) Flt	Hudson	Reykjavik
VP-84, USN	Catalina	Reykjavik

AHQ Gibraltar   **Air Commodore S.P.Simpson** CBE, MC

No.48 Squadron	Hudson	North Front
No.179 Squadron	Wellington	North Front
No.202 Squadron	Catalina	Gibraltar Harbour
No.210 Sqn (Det)	Catalina	Gibraltar Harbour
No.233 Squadron	Hudson	North Front
No.544 Sqn (Det)	Spitfire	North Front

APPENDIX VI

Order of Battle 6 June 1944

No.15 Group	Air Vice Marshal Sir Leonard Slatter KBE, CB, DSC, DFC	
No.59 Squadron	Liberator	Ballykelly
No.120 Squadron	Liberator	Ballykelly
No.281 Squadron	Warwick (ASR)	Tiree
No.422 Squadron	Sunderland	Castle Archdale
No.423 Squadron	Sunderland	Castle Archdale
No.518 Squadron	Halifax (Met)	Tiree
No.1402 Met Flight	Spitfire/Gladiator	Aldergrove
No.16 Group	**Air Vice Marshal F.L. Hopps** CB, CBE, AFC	
No.143 Squadron	Beaufighter	Manston
No.236 Squadron	Beaufighter	North Coates
No.254 Squadron	Beaufighter	North Coates
No.279 Squadron	Hudson (ASR)	Bircham Newton
No.280 Squadron	Warwick (ASR)	Strubby (det Thornaby)
No.415 Squadron	Wellington	Bircham Newton
No.455 Squadron	Beaufighter	Langham
No.489 Squadron	Beaufighter	Langham
No.521 Squadron	Ventura/Gladiator (Met)	Docking
819 Squadron, FAA	Swordfish	Manston
848 Squadron, FAA	Avenger	Manston
854 Squadron, FAA	Avenger	Hawkinge
855 Squadron, FAA	Avenger	Hawkinge
No.1401 Met Flight	Spitfire	Manston
No.17 Group	**Air Vice Marshal H.G. Smart** CBE, DFC, AFC	
Numerous training units		
No.18 Group	**Air Vice Marshal S.P. Simpson** CB, CBE, MC	
No.86 Squadron	Liberator	Tain
No.210 Squadron	Catalina	Sullom Voe
No.281 Squadron	Warwick (ASR)	Gt Orton/Wick/Sumburgh
No.330 Squadron	Sunderland	Sullom Voe
No.333 Squadron	Mosquito/ Catalina	Sumburgh/Leuchars Woodhaven
No.521 Squadron	Ventura/Spitfire (Met)	Skitten
No.1693 Flight	Anson	Wick

No.19 Group	**Air Vice Marshal B.E. Baker** CB, DSO, MC, AFC	
No.53 Squadron	Liberator	St Eval
No.58 Squadron	Halifax	St Davids
No.144 Squadron	Beaufighter	Davidstow Moor
No.172 Squadron	Wellington	Chivenor
No.179 Squadron	Wellington	Predannack
No.201 Squadron	Sunderland	Pembroke Dock
No.206 Squadron	Liberator	St Eval
No.224 Squadron	Liberator	St Eval
No.228 Squadron	Sunderland	Pembroke Dock
No.235 Squadron	Beaufighter	Portreath
No.248 Squadron	Mosquito	Portreath
No.282 Squadron	Warwick (ASR)	Davidstow Moor
No.304 Squadron	Wellington	Chivenor
No.311 Squadron	Liberator	Predannack
No.404 Squadron	Beaufighter	Davidstow Moor
No.407 Squadron	Wellington	Chivenor
No.461 Squadron	Sunderland	Pembroke Dock
No.502 Squadron	Halifax	St Davids
No.517 Squadron	Halifax (Met)	Brawdy
No.524 Squadron	Wellington	Davidstow Moor
No.547 Squadron	Liberator	St Eval
No.612 Squadron	Wellington	Chivenor
No.10 Squadron, RAAF	Sunderland	Mount Batten
816 Squadron, FAA	Swordfish	Perranporth
838 Squadron, FAA	Swordfish	Harrowbeer
849 Squadron, FAA	Avenger	Perranporth
850 Squadron, FAA	Avenger	Perranporth
VPB-103, USN	PB4Y-1	Dunkeswell
VPB-105, USN	PB4Y-1	Dunkeswell
VPB-110, USN	PB4Y-1	Dunkeswell
VPB-114, USN (det)	PB4Y-1	Dunkeswell
No.106 Group	**Air Commodore J.N. Boothman** CB, DFC, AFC	
No.540 Squadron	Mosquito	Benson
No.541 Squadron	Spitfire	Benson (det St Eval)
No.542 Squadron	Spitfire	Benson
No.544 Squadron	Mosquito	Benson
No.247 Group	**Air Vice Marshal G.R. Bromet** CB, CBE, DSO	
No.220 Squadron	Fortress	Lagens, Azores
No.269 Squadron	Hudson/Walrus	Lagens
	Spitfire	
AHQ Gibraltar	**Air Vice Marshal W. Elliott** CB, CBE, DFC	
No.202 Squadron	Catalina	New Camp
No.520 Squadron	Halifax/Gladiator (Met)	North Front
AHQ Iceland	**Air Commodore C.G. Wigglesworth** AFC	
No.162 Squadron, RCAF	Canso	Skerja Fjord, Reykjavik
No.1407 Met Flight	Hudson	Reykjavik

APPENDIX VII

Coastal Command Squadrons 1936-69

Number	From*	To*	Aircraft Type	From	To
14	24/10/44	1/6/45	Wellington XIV	10/44	6/45
22	14/7/36	1/2/42	Vildebeest I/IV	7/36	2/40
			Beaufort I	11/39	2/42
	15/2/55	28/11/69	Sycamore 12	3/55	1/56
			Whirlwind 2	6/55	8/62
			Whirlwind 10	8/62	11/69
36	1/10/46	15/10/47	Mosquito VI	10/46	10/47
	1/7/53	28/2/57	Neptune 1	7/53	2/57
42	14/12/36	18/6/42	Vildebeest III	12/36	12/37
			Vildebeest IV	3/37	4/40
			Beaufort I	4/40	4/42
			Beaufort II	3/42	6/42
	1/10/46	15/10/47	Beaufighter X	10/46	10/47
	28/6/52	28/11/69	Shackleton 1	6/52	7/54
			Shackleton 2	1/53	6/66
			Shackleton 3	11/65	11/69
48	14/7/36	21/2/44	Anson I	7/36	12/41
			Beaufort I	6/40	11/40
			Hudson III/V	9/41	12/42
			Hudson VI	11/42	2/44
52	20/2/44	31/3/44	Baltimore V	2/44	3/44
53	3/7/40	25/6/45	Blenheim IV	7/40	8/41
			Hudson V	7/41	2/43
			Whitley VII	2/43	4/43
			Liberator V	5/43	2/45
			Liberator VI	5/44	4/45
			Liberator VIII	1/45	6/45
58	5/4/42	25/5/45	Whitley V	4/42	12/42
			Whitley VII	6/42	12/42

*Dates refer to Coastal Command service only.

Number	From*	To*	Aircraft Type	From	To
			Halifax II	12/42	3/45
			Halifax III	3/45	5/45
	1/10/46	1/50	Mosquito 34	10/46	1/50
			Anson 19	10/46	1/50
59	3/7/40	10/6/45	Blenheim IV	7/40	8/41
			Hudson III	7/41	12/41
			Hudson V	12/41	8/42
			Hudson VI	7/42	8/42
			Liberator III	8/42	12/42
			Fortress II	12/42	4/43
			Liberator V	4/43	3/45
			Liberator VIII	3/45	6/45
82	1/10/46	/50	Lancaster 1	10/46	/50
86	6/12/40	10/6/45	Blenheim IV	12/40	6/41
			Beaufort I	6/41	2/42
			Beaufort II	12/41	8/42
			Liberator III	10/42	10/44
			Liberator V	4/43	9/43
			Liberator V	7/44	3/45
			Liberator VIII	1/45	6/45
95	15/1/41	22/10/41	Sunderland I	1/41	10/41
119	13/3/41	17/4/43	Short G Boat	3/41	10/41
			Short C Boat	4/41	8/41
			Catalina I	6/41	7/41
			Catalina III	5/42	10/42
			Sunderland III	9/42	4/43
	19/7/44	25/5/45	Albacore I	7/44	2/45
			Swordfish III	1/45	5/45
120	1/6/41	4/6/45	Liberator I	6/41	10/43
			Liberator II	11/41	10/42
			Liberator III	7/42	1/44
			Liberator V	12/43	1/45
			Liberator III	12/44	6/45
	1/10/46	28/11/69	Liberator VIII	10/46	6/47
			Lancaster III	11/46	4/51
			Shackleton 1	3/51	10/56
			Shackleton 2	3/53	8/54
			Shackleton 2	10/52	11/58
			Shackleton 3	9/58	11/69
143	15/6/41	25/5/45	Beaufighter I	6/41	11/41
			Blenheim IV	12/41	9/42
			Beaufighter I	8/42	9/42
			Beaufighter II	9/42	3/43
			Beaufighter XI	3/43	5/44
			Beaufighter X	9/43	10/44
			Mosquito II	9/44	10/44
			Mosquito VI	10/44	5/45

Number	From*	To*	Aircraft Type	From	To
144	21/4/42	25/6/43	Hampden I	4/42	3/43
			Beaufighter VI	1/43	5/43
			Beaufighter X	5/43	6/43
	5/8/43	25/5/45	Beaufighter X	8/43	5/45
160	7/5/42	30/5/42	Liberator II	5/42	5/42
	23/6/46	30/9/46	Liberator VIII	6/46	9/46
			Lancaster III	8/46	9/46
172	4/4/42	4/6/45	Wellington VIII	4/42	3/43
			Wellington XII	12/42	10/43
			Wellington XIV	8/43	6/45
179	1/9/42	30/9/46	Wellington VIII	9/42	9/43
			Wellington XIV	8/43	11/44
			Warwick V	11/44	5/46
			Lancaster III	2/46	9/46
190	17/2/43	31/12/43	Catalina I	2/43	12/43
			Catalina IV	10/43	12/43
200	25/5/41	22/10/41	Hudson IV	6/41	10/41
201	14/7/36	28/2/57	Southampton II	7/36	12/36
			London I	7/36	6/38
			London II	1/38	4/40
			Sunderland I	4/40	1/42
			Sunderland II	5/41	3/44
			Sunderland III	1/42	6/45
			Sunderland V	2/45	2/57
	1/10/58	28/11/69	Shackleton 3	10/58	11/69
202	10/9/39	4/6/45	London II	9/39	6/41
			Swordfish	10/40	6/41
			Catalina I	4/41	1/45
			Sunderland I/II	12/41	9/42
			Sunderland III	3/42	9/42
			Catalina IV	10/44	6/45
	1/10/46	28/8/64	Halifax VI	10/46	5/51
			Hastings I	10/50	8/64
203	19/5/46	1/9/56	Liberator VIII	5/46	10/46
			Lancaster III	7/46	3/53
			Neptune I	3/53	8/56
	1/11/58	28/11/69	Shackleton I	11/58	2/59
			Shackleton 3	11/58	7/62
			Shackleton 3	6/66	11/69
			Shackleton 2	4/62	12/66
204	14/7/36	28/8/41	Scapa	7/36	1/37
			London I/II	10/36	7/39
			Sunderland I	6/39	8/41
			Sunderland II	6/41	8/41

Number	From*	To*	Aircraft Type	From	To
	1/1/54	28/11/69	Shackleton 2	1/54	5/58
			Shackleton 2	5/59	11/69
			Shackleton 1	5/58	2/60
206	14/7/36	10/6/45	Anson I	7/36	6/40
			Hudson I	3/40	8/42
			Hudson II/III/IV	4/41	8/42
			Hudson V	10/41	8/42
			Fortress II	7/42	3/44
			Liberator VI	3/44	4/45
			Liberator VIII	3/45	6/45
	27/9/52	28/11/69	Shackleton 1	9/52	5/58
			Shackleton 2	2/53	6/54
			Shackleton 3	1/58	11/69
209	14/7/36	30/3/42	Singapore III	7/36	3/39
			Stranraer	12/38	4/40
			Lerwick I	12/39	5/41
			Catalina I	4/41	3/42
210	14/7/36	4/6/45	Rangoon	7/36	9/36
			Singapore III	8/36	11/38
			Sunderland I	6/38	4/41
			Catalina I	4/41	3/44
			Catalina II	7/42	3/43
			Catalina IV	1/44	6/45
	1/6/46	31/1/57	Lancaster III	6/46	12/52
			Neptune 1	2/53	1/57
	1/5/58	28/11/69	Shackleton 2	5/58	11/69
217	15/3/37	7/3/42	Anson I	3/37	12/40
			Beaufort I	9/40	11/41
			Beaufort II	11/41	3/42
	14/1/52	31/3/57	Neptune 1	1/52	3/57
	1/2/58	13/11/59	Whirlwind 4	2/58	11/59
220	17/8/36	25/6/45	Anson I	8/36	12/39
			Hudson I/III/VI	9/39	6/42
			Fortress I	12/41	8/42
			Fortress II	7/42	12/44
			Fortress III	7/44	4/45
			Liberator VI	12/44	6/45
	24/9/51	1/10/58	Shackleton 1	9/51	2/58
			Shackleton 2	3/53	7/54
			Shackleton 2	3/57	10/57
			Shackleton 3	8/57	10/58
221	21/11/40	8/1/42	Wellington I	11/40	12/41
			Wellington VIII	1/42	1/42
224	1/2/37	10/11/47	Anson I	2/37	7/39
			Hudson I	5/39	5/41
			Hudson III	3/41	2/42
			Hudson V	5/41	9/42

Number	From*	To*	Aircraft Type	From	To
			Liberator III	7/42	4/43
			Liberator II	11/42	4/43
			Liberator V	1/43	12/44
			Liberator VI	12/44	3/45
			Liberator VIII	2/45	11/46
			Lancaster III	10/46	11/47
	1/3/48	31/10/66	Halifax 6	3/48	3/52
			Shackleton 1	7/51	8/54
			Shackleton 2	3/53	10/66
228	15/12/36	5/6/39	Scapa	2/37	8/38
			London I	2/37	9/38
			Singapore III	4/37	9/37
			Stranraer	4/37	4/39
			Sunderland I	11/38	6/39
	10/9/39	10/6/40	Sunderland I	9/39	6/40
	28/8/41	26/9/41	Sunderland I	8/41	9/41
	9/10/41	4/6/45	Sunderland I/II	11/41	3/43
			Sunderland III	3/42	4/45
			Sunderland V	2/45	6/45
	1/6/46	30/9/46	Liberator VIII	6/46	9/46
	1/7/54	6/3/59	Shackleton 2	7/54	3/59
	1/9/59	28/8/64	Sycamore 14	9/59	6/60
			Whirlwind 2/4	9/59	12/62
			Whirlwind 10	9/62	8/64
230	14/7/36	10/10/36	Singapore III	7/36	10/36
	15/4/46	28/2/57	Sunderland 5	4/46	2/57
233	18/5/37	5/3/44	Anson I	5/37	12/39
			Hudson I	8/39	6/41
			Blenheim IV	10/39	1/40
			Hudson III	1/41	3/44
			Hudson V	6/41	8/42
235	27/2/40	10/7/45	Blenheim I	2/40	5/40
			Blenheim IV	2/40	12/41
			Beaufighter I	12/41	9/42
			Beaufighter VI	7/42	11/43
			Beaufighter X	10/43	5/44
			Beaufighter XI	4/44	6/44
			Mosquito VI	6/44	7/45
236	29/2/40	25/5/45	Blenheim I	2/40	7/40
			Blenheim IV	7/40	2/42
			Beaufighter I	10/41	2/43
			Beaufighter VI	9/42	7/43
			Beaufighter X	7/43	5/45
240	30/3/37	29/5/42	Scapa	3/37	1/39
			Singapore III	11/38	7/39
			Lerwick I	7/39	9/39
			London II	7/39	7/40
			Stranraer	6/40	4/41

Number	From*	To*	Aircraft Type	From	To
			Catalina I	3/41	5/42
			Catalina II	3/42	5/42
	1/5/52	1/11/58	Shackleton 1	5/52	11/58
			Shackleton 2	3/53	8/54
246	5/8/42	30/4/43	Sunderland III	10/42	4/43
248	24/2/40	1/10/46	Blenheim I	2/40	5/40
			Blenheim IV	3/40	7/41
			Beaufighter I	7/41	6/42
			Beaufighter VI	5/42	7/43
			Beaufighter X	6/43	12/43
			Mosquito VI	12/43	10/46
			Mosquito XVIII	1/44	1/45
251	1/8/44	30/10/45	Ventura I	8/44	10/44
			Hudson III	8/44	8/45
			Anson I	8/44	10/45
			Fortress II	3/45	10/45
			Warwick I	8/45	10/45
252	21/11/40	15/6/41	Blenheim I/IV	12/40	4/41
			Beaufighter I	12/40	6/41
254	28/1/40	1/10/46	Blenheim I	1/40	4/40
			Blenheim IV	1/40	8/42
			Beaufighter VI	7/42	9/43
			Beaufighter X	8/43	10/46
			Mosquito XVIII	3/45	5/45
269	7/12/36	10/3/46	Anson I	12/36	6/40
			Hudson I	4/40	5/41
			Hudson III	5/41	12/43
			Hudson III	2/44	8/45
			Walrus	2/44	3/46
			Spitfire V	2/44	3/46
			Warwick I	9/44	3/46
272	19/11/40	28/5/41	Blenheim IV	11/40	4/41
			Beaufighter I	4/41	5/41
278	15/2/45	14/10/45	Walrus	2/45	10/45
			Sea Otter	5/45	10/45
279	16/11/41	10/3/46	Hudson III/V/VI	11/41	12/44
			Warwick I	11/44	9/45
			Hurricane II	2/45	9/45
			Sea Otter	7/45	9/45
			Lancaster III	9/45	3/46
280	10/12/41	21/6/46	Anson I	1/42	10/43
			Warwick I	10/43	6/46
281	22/11/43	24/10/45	Warwick I	12/43	10/45
			Sea Otter	3/45	10/45

Number	From*	To*	Aircraft Type	From	To
282	1/2/44	19/7/45	Warwick I	2/44	7/45
			Walrus	3/45	7/45
			Sea Otter	3/45	7/45
304	7/5/42	14/6/45	Wellington I	5/42	4/43
			Wellington X	4/43	6/43
			Wellington XIII	6/43	9/43
			Wellington XIV	9/43	6/45
311	30/4/42	25/6/45	Wellington I	4/42	6/43
			Liberator V	6/43	3/45
			Liberator VI	3/45	6/45
320	1/6/40	15/3/43	Fokker T VIII	6/40	11/40
			Anson I	6/40	10/41
			Hudson I	10/40	9/42
			Hudson II	3/41	9/41
			Hudson III	7/41	9/42
			Hudson V	1/42	5/42
			Hudson VI	8/42	3/43
321	1/6/40	18/1/41	Anson I	6/40	1/41
330	25/4/41	30/5/45	Northrop N3P-B	5/41	6/43
			Catalina III	7/42	1/43
			Sunderland III	2/43	4/45
			Sunderland II	3/43	3/44
			Sunderland V	4/45	5/45
333	10/5/43	30/5/45	Catalina I	5/43	1/45
			Mosquito II	5/43	10/43
			Mosquito VI	9/43	5/45
			Catalina IV	3/44	5/45
334	26/5/45	30/5/45	Mosquito VI	5/45	5/45
404	1/5/41	25/5/45	Blenheim IV	4/41	1/43
			Beaufighter II	9/42	4/43
			Beaufighter XI	3/43	11/43
			Beaufighter X	9/43	3/45
			Mosquito VI	3/45	5/45
407	8/5/41	4/6/45	Blenheim IV	5/41	7/41
			Hudson III	6/41	5/42
			Hudson V	6/41	4/43
			Wellington XI	1/43	4/43
			Wellington XII	3/43	2/44
			Wellington XIV	6/43	6/45
413	30/6/41	4/3/42	Catalina I	7/41	3/42
415	20/8/41	26/7/44	Beaufort I	9/41	2/42
			Hampden I	1/42	9/43
			Wellington XIII	9/43	7/44
			Albacore I	10/43	7/44

Number	From*	To*	Aircraft Type	From	To
422	2/4/42	5/6/45	Lerwick I	7/42	9/42
			Catalina I	8/42	11/42
			Sunderland III	11/42	6/45
423	18/5/42	5/6/45	Sunderland II	7/42	4/43
			Sunderland III	9/42	5/45
455	26/4/42	25/5/45	Hampden I	4/42	12/43
			Beaufighter X	12/43	5/45
458	29/1/45	8/6/45	Wellington XIV	2/45	6/45
461	25/4/42	20/6/45	Sunderland II	4/42	5/43
			Sunderland III	8/42	6/45
			Sunderland V	2/45	6/45
489	12/8/41	1/8/45	Beaufort I	8/41	1/42
			Blenheim IV	1/42	3/42
			Hampden I	3/42	10/43
			Beaufighter X	10/43	5/45
			Mosquito VI	6/45	8/45
500	7/11/38	19/11/42	Hind	11/38	3/39
			Anson	3/39	4/41
			Blenheim IV	4/41	11/41
			Hudson V	11/41	11/42
502	11/38	25/5/45	Hind	11/38	4/39
			Anson I	1/39	10/40
			Botha I	8/40	11/40
			Whitley V	9/40	2/42
			Whitley VII	2/42	2/43
			Halifax II	2/43	3/45
			Halifax III	2/45	5/45
517	7/8/43	21/6/46	Hudson III	8/43	9/43
			Hampden I	8/43	12/43
			Halifax V	11/43	6/45
			Halifax III	3/45	6/46
518	6/7/43	1/10/46	Halifax V	7/43	6/45
			Halifax III	3/45	5/46
			Hurricane II	9/45	10/46
			Spitfire VII	9/45	10/46
			Halifax VI	3/46	10/46
519	7/8/43	31/5/46	Hampden I	8/43	10/43
			Spitfire VI	8/43	11/44
			Hudson III	9/43	10/43
			Hudson III	8/44	3/45
			Ventura V	9/43	10/44
			Fortress II	10/44	9/45
			Spitfire VII	11/44	12/45
			Halifax III	8/45	5/46

Number	From*	To*	Aircraft Type	From	To
520	20/9/43	25/4/46	Hudson III	9/43	3/44
			Hudson III	1/45	1/46
			Gladiator II	9/43	8/44
			Halifax V	2/44	5/45
			Spitfire V	2/44	5/45
			Hurricane II	6/44	4/46
			Halifax III	5/45	4/46
			Warwick I	7/45	4/46
			Hudson VI	10/45	1/46
521	22/7/42	22/3/43	Blenheim IV	7/42	3/43
			Gladiator II	7/42	3/43
			Spitfire V	7/42	3/43
			Mosquito IV	7/42	3/43
			Hudson III	7/42	3/43
	1/9/43	31/3/46	Hudson III	9/43	12/43
			Hampden I	9/43	12/43
			Gladiator II	9/43	3/45
			Spitfire IX	9/43	11/45
			Ventura V	10/43	12/44
			Hurricane II	9/44	3/45
			Fortress II	12/44	2/46
			Fortress III	12/45	2/46
			Halifax III	12/45	3/46
524	20/10/43	29/1/44	Mariner I	10/43	12/43
	7/4/44	25/6/45	Wellington XIII	4/44	1/45
			Wellington XIV	12/44	5/45
540	19/10/42	30/9/46	Spitfire IV	10/42	12/42
			Mosquito I	10/42	5/43
			Mosquito IV	10/42	8/43
			Mosquito VIII	12/42	8/43
			Mosquito IX	7/43	3/45
			Mosquito XVI	5/44	12/45
			Mosquito VI	11/44	6/45
			Mosquito 32	11/44	8/45
			Mosquito 34	11/45	9/46
	1/12/47	/50	Mosquito 34	12/47	/50
541	19/10/42	1/10/46	Spitfire D	10/42	1/43
			Spitfire IV	10/42	9/44
			Spitfire IX	11/42	12/42
			Spitfire XI	12/42	3/46
			Spitfire X	5/44	4/45
			Spitfire XIX	6/44	10/46
			Mustang III	7/44	6/45
			Meteor III	10/45	4/46
			Lancaster I	2/46	10/46
	1/11/47	/50	Spitfire XIX	11/47	/50
542	19/10/42	27/8/45	Spitfire IV	10/42	7/43
			Spitfire XI	3/43	8/45
			Spitfire X	5/44	8/45
			Spitfire XIX	6/44	8/45

Number	From*	To*	Aircraft Type	From	To
543	19/10/42	18/10/43	Spitfire IV	10/42	10/43
			Spitfire XI	4/43	10/43
544	19/10/42	13/10/45	Anson I	10/42	3/43
			Maryland I	10/42	3/43
			Wellington IV	10/42	3/43
			Spitfire IV	10/42	10/43
			Mosquito IV	3/43	10/43
			Spitfire XI	8/43	10/43
			Mosquito IX	8/43	2/45
			Mosquito XVI	4/44	8/45
			Mosquito 32	10/44	10/45
			Mosquito 34	4/45	10/45
547	21/10/42	4/6/45	Wellington VIII	10/42	5/43
			Wellington XI	5/43	11/43
			Wellington XIII	10/43	11/43
			Liberator V	11/43	10/44
			Liberator VI	8/44	5/45
			Liberator VIII	3/45	6/45
608	20/3/39	18/12/42	Anson I	3/39	5/41
			Botha I	6/40	11/40
			Blenheim I	2/41	8/41
			Blenheim IV	3/41	9/41
			Hudson V	7/41	12/42
			Hudson III	8/41	8/42
612	11/38	9/7/45	Hector	11/38	11/39
			Anson I	6/39	1/41
			Whitley V	11/40	1/42
			Whitley VII	9/41	6/43
			Wellington VIII	11/42	3/43
			Wellington XIII	3/43	3/44
			Wellington XIV	6/43	7/45
618	1/4/43	30/10/44	Mosquito IV	4/43	10/43
			Beaufighter II	4/43	6/43
			Mosquito XVIII	10/43	1/44
			Mosquito VI	7/44	10/44
			Mosquito XVI	9/44	10/44

Data–Operational Coastal Command Aircraft

Type	Cruising Speed (mph)	Endurance (hrs)	Weapon Load (lbs)	Armament
Anson	103	$4\frac{1}{2}$	200	2 × 303″
Beaufighter 1/VI	180	5		4 × 20mm 6 × 303″
Beaufighter X (T/B)	180	$4\frac{1}{2}$	1 × Torp	4 × 20mm
Beaufighter X (R/P)	180	$4\frac{1}{4}$	8 × RP	4 × 20mm
Beaufighter X (F/B)	180	4	2000	4 × 20mm
Beaufort	150	6	1500 or 1 × Torp	4 × 303″
Botha	160	$5\frac{1}{2}$	1500 or 1 × Torp	3 × 303″
Catalina 1	100	$17\frac{1}{2}$	2000	6 × 303″
Catalina IV	106	$15\frac{1}{2}$	1500	2 × 5″
Fortress II	140	$10\frac{3}{4}$	1750	9 × 5″
Halifax II	135	$10\frac{1}{2}$	2250	9 × 303″
Halifax III	145	10	5500	9 × 303″
Hampden (T/B)	120	$7\frac{1}{4}$	1 × Torp	6 × 303″
Hudson I	125	6	1000	7 × 303″
Hudson VI	140	$6\frac{3}{4}$	1000	7 × 303″
Lancaster III	165	13	6000	6 × 303″
Lerwick I	150	9	2000	7 × 303″
Liberator I	150	16	2000	6 × 303″ 4 × 20mm
Liberator II/III	145	$11\frac{1}{2}$	3000	6 × 5″
Liberator V	150	$15\frac{1}{2}$	1500	6 × 5″
Liberator VI/VIII	138	$10\frac{1}{2}$	3500	6 × 5″
London	86	$5\frac{1}{4}$	2000	3 × 303″
Mosquito VI (F/B)	210	$3\frac{1}{4}$	1000	4 × 20mm 4 × 303″
Mosquito VI (R/P)	210	5	8 × RP	4 × 20mm 4 × 303″
Neptune	170	16	6000	2 × 20mm 4 × 5″

Type	Cruising Speed (mph)	Endurance (hrs)	Weapon Load (lbs)	Armament
Shackleton 1/2	160	$14\frac{3}{4}$	6000	$2 \times 20mm$
Shackleton 3	160	16	6000	$2 \times 20mm$
Stranraer	92	$7\frac{1}{4}$	1000	$3 \times 303''$
Sunderland I/II/III	115	$12\frac{1}{2}$	2000	$7 \times 303''$
Sunderland V	110	$13\frac{1}{2}$	2000	$7 \times 303''$
Warwick V	164	11	2000	$3 \times 5''$
				$4 \times 303''$
Vildebeest	82	$4\frac{1}{4}$	1000 or	$2 \times 303''$
			$1 \times$ Torp	
Wellington VIII	125	$10\frac{1}{2}$	1500	$6 \times 303''$
Wellington XII	140	$8\frac{1}{4}$	2400	$7 \times 303''$
Wellington XIII	140	8	3200	$7 \times 303''$
Wellington XIV	140	10	1500	$7 \times 303''$
Whitley V/VII	110	9	1500	$5 \times 303''$

Data–Main Axis Operational Submarine Types–1939-45

Type	Displacement (tons)	Torpedo Tubes	Surface Speed (knots)	Underwater Speed (knots)	Range (nm)
German					
IA	860	6	$17\frac{3}{4}$	$8\frac{1}{4}$	6700
VII	769	5	17	7	6500
IX	1150	6	18	7	11000
XIV	1688	-	$14\frac{1}{2}$	$6\frac{1}{4}$	9300
XXI	1620	6	$15\frac{1}{2}$	16	11000
XXIII	232	2	$9\frac{3}{4}$	$12\frac{1}{2}$	1350
Italian					
Enrico Tazzoli	1332	8	17	$8\frac{3}{4}$	13500
Sirena	787	6	14	$8\frac{1}{2}$	
German 'Midgets'					
XXVII *Seehund*	15	2	$7\frac{3}{4}$	6	300
Biber	$6\frac{1}{4}$	2	$6\frac{1}{2}$	$5\frac{1}{4}$	130
Molch	11	2	$4\frac{1}{2}$	5.0	50

Note: Type XIV was a tanker/supply submarine. Four torpedoes were carried as cargo.

Glossary and Abbreviations

A&AEE	Aeroplane & Armament Experimental Establishment
AFC	Air Force Cross
AHQ	Air Headquarters
Allah	Pre-planned 'Met' sortie over Atlantic
AOC	Air Officer Commanding
AS	Anti-submarine
Asdic	Ship-borne sonar detection equipment
ASR	Air-Sea Rescue
ASV	Air to Surface Vessel (radar)
ASWDU	Air Sea Warfare Development Unit
ATDU	Air Torpedo Development Unit
Autolycus	Airborne ship/submarine detection equipment
AVM	Air Vice Marshal
BEF	British Expeditionary Force (to France)
Bismuth	Pre-planned 'Met' sortie over Atlantic
Bowser	PR Spitfire with increased fuel capacity (jargon)
BPC	British Purchasing Commission (in USA)
CAS	Chief of Air Staff
CB	Companion of the Order of the Bath
CBE	Commander of the Order of the British Empire
CCDU	Coastal Command Development Unit
C-in-C	Commander-in-Chief
CIU	Central Interpretation Unit
CMG	Companion of the Order of St Michael & St George
CO	Commanding Officer
DC	Depth Charge
Det	Detachment
DFC	Distinguished Flying Cross
DGAS	Director General of Aircraft Safety
Dicer	Low-level PR flight
Ditch	Emergency descent into the sea
DSC	Distinguished Service Cross
DSO	Distinguished Service Order
DWI	Directional Wireless Installation
E	East
ECM	Electronic Counter Measures
Epicure	Pre-planned 'Met' sortie over Atlantic
FAA	Fleet Air Arm
FBTS	Flying Boat Training Squadron
Fido	Codename for acoustic homing torpedo (also known as Mk. 24 Mine)
Flak	Anti-aircraft gunfire (specifically German)
Flg Off	Flying Officer
Flt Lt	Flight Lieutenant
F/Sgt	Flight Sergeant
FTU	Ferry Training Unit
GP	General Purpose
GR	General Reconnaissance
GRU	General Reconnaissance Unit
GU	Convoy designator—Gibraltar to USA
HE	High Explosive
HG	Convoy designator—Gibraltar to Britain
High Tea	Codename for sono-buoy equipment
HQ	Headquarters

HSL	High-speed launch	ON	Convoy designator—Britain to Halifax, NS
HX	Convoy designator—Halifax, NS to Britain	ONS	Convoy designator—Britain to Halifax, NS(slow)
IFF	Identification Friend or Foe	OS	Convoy designator—Britain to West Africa
Instep	Offensive fighter patrol over SW approaches	OT	Convoy designator—USA to Tangier
IR	Immediate reserve (of aircraft for a unit)	OTU	Operational Training Unit
JASS	Joint Anti-submarine School	*Pampa*	'Met' ascent
Jim Crow	Reconnaissance by fighter aircraft (over English Channel)	PDU	Photographic Development Unit
		PIU	Photographic Interpretation Unit
		PLE	Prudent limit of endurance
KBE	Knight Commander of the Order of the British Empire	Plt Off	Pilot Officer
KCB	Knight Commander of the Order of the Bath	PQ	Convoy designator—Britain to Russia
		PR	Photographic Reconnaissance
		PRATA	'Met' ascent
LL	Leigh Light	PRU	Photographic Reconnaissance Unit
Lt	Lieutenant		
Lt Cdr	Lieutenant Commander	QP	Convoy designator—Russia to Britain
MAC	Merchant Aircraft Carrier		
MAD	Magnetic Anomaly Detector	RAAF	Royal Australian Air Force
Madcat	Catalina fitted with MAD equipment (jargon)	RAF	Royal Air Force
		RCAF	Royal Canadian Air Force
Magnum	Pre-planned 'Met' sortie over Atlantic	RCM	Radio Counter Measures
		Recipe	Pre-planned 'Met' sortie over Atlantic
MC	Military Cross		
MEAF	Middle East Air Force	RFU	Refresher Flying Unit
Mercer	Pre-planned 'Met' sortie over Atlantic	*Rhombus*	Pre-planned 'Met' sortie over North Sea
Met	Meteorological	RN	Royal Navy
Metox	Radar emission detector (German)	RNAS	Royal Naval Air Service
Milch Cow	U-Boat operating as refueller for blockade running ships or other U-Boats (jargon)	RNVR	Royal Naval Volunteer Reserve
		RNZAF	Royal New Zealand Air Force
		RP	Rocket projectile
MKS	Convoy designator—Gibraltar to Britain (slow)	RS	Radio School
MOTU	Maritime Operational Training Unit	SAP	Semi-armour piercing (bombs/rockets)
MTB	Motor Torpedo Boat		
		SAR	Search and Rescue
N	North	SC	Convoy designator—Britain to USA
NATO	North Atlantic Treaty Organisation	Sgt	Sergeant
Naxos	Radar emission detector (German)	*Sharon*	Pre-planned 'Met' sortie over Atlantic
NNW	North-north-west		
Nocturnal	Pre-planned 'Met' sortie over Atlantic	SIS	Secret Intelligence Service (British)
		SL	Convoy designator—West Africa to Britain
NW	North-west		
		SLS	Convoy designator—West Africa to Britain (slow)
OBE	Order of the British Empire		
OCU	Operational Conversion Unit	SMR	School of Maritime Reconnaissance
OG	Convoy designator—Britain to Gibraltar	*Snort*	U-Boat air breathing tube (jargon)
		SoC	Struck off Charge

S of GR	School of General Reconnaissance	UG	Convoy designator—USA to Gibraltar
Sperrbrecker	Heavily-armed mine detector flak ship (German)	*Ultra*	British decrypts of German *Enigma* encodes
Sqn	Squadron		
Sqn Ldr	Squadron Leader	USAAF	United States Army Air Force
STS	Seaplane Training Squadron	USN	United States Navy
(T)	(Training)	VHF/DF	Very High Frequency/Direction Finding equipment
TDU	Torpedo Training Unit		
Tenente di		VLR	Very Long Range
Vascelles	Lieutenant Commander (Italian)	VP	Patrol Squadron of USN
THUM	'Met' ascent	VPB	Patrol Bomber Squadron of USN
TIM	Time Impact Mine		
TO	Convoy designator—Tangier to USA	W	West
		W. Anz	Receiver for detecting radar emissions (German)
Torbeau	Torpedo-carrying Beaufighter (jargon)		
		Wg Cdr	Wing Commander
UE	Unit Equipment (of aircraft)	*Wimpy*	Wellington aircraft (jargon)

Index